THE I TATTI
RENAISSANCE LIBRARY

*James Hankins, General Editor*

# BRANDOLINI

# REPUBLICS AND KINGDOMS

# COMPARED

ITRL 40

# AURELIO LIPPO BRANDOLINI

✦ ✦ ✦

# REPUBLICS AND KINGDOMS COMPARED

EDITED AND TRANSLATED BY

## JAMES HANKINS

THE I TATTI RENAISSANCE LIBRARY
HARVARD UNIVERSITY PRESS
CAMBRIDGE, MASSACHUSETTS
LONDON, ENGLAND
2009

Series design by Dean Bornstein

*Library of Congress Cataloging-in-Publication Data*

Brandolini, Aurelio Lippo, d. 1497 or 8.
[De comparatione reipublicae et regni. English & Latin]
Republics and kingdoms compared / edited and translated by James Hankins.
p.   cm. — (I Tatti Renaissance library ; ITRL 40)
Includes bibliographical references and index.
ISBN 978-0-674-03398-6 (cloth : alk. paper)
1. Political science — Early works to 1800.   I. Hankins, James.   II. Title.
JC121.B73  2009
320.3 — dc22          2008048495

# Contents

꩜

## Book III · 160

· CONTENTS ·

# Introduction

꒰꒱꒰꒱

Aurelio Lippo Brandolini's *Republics and Kingdoms Compared* is the most fascinating work of humanist political theory written before Machiavelli. It is also among the least known. The work was never printed during the Renaissance and survives only in two manuscript copies: the dedication copy to Lorenzo de' Medici, written circa 1492/94, and a presentation copy written for Lorenzo's son, Cardinal Giovanni (later Pope Leo X), sometime in the first decade of the sixteenth century. In his preface Brandolini asks Lorenzo to see that the work is published if he approves of it, but since the *Comparison* (as the work will be called hereafter) had no diffusion to speak of, one may reasonably suppose that Lorenzo did not care to see such an anti-republican work circulated under his aegis. The work could only have been an embarrassment to Lorenzo, the unofficial ruler of Florence, a city that still maintained the façade of its old republican institutions, behind which lurked the Medici principate. Modern scholarship has only been slightly more interested in the dialogue. The work has been edited twice, once in a rare Hungarian imprint of 1890 and once in an unpublished Italian *tesi di laurea*.[1] Apart from some antiquarian studies in Hungarian, there is, in English, only a single article and an unpublished M.Phil. thesis devoted to the work. It receives passing mention in a handful of other works.[2] But it is a work that deserves to be much better known.

Its author, Aurelio Lippo Brandolini (1454?–1497), was hardly in the first rank of Italian humanists. Considering, however, that he suffered from a congenital ocular disease that made him nearly blind (the word *lippus* indicates a severe inflammation of the eyes), the success he had was remarkable.[3] Born in Florence to a family of middling status, he became an economic exile along with his

family while still a boy. The family moved to Naples and Brandolini was educated there in the *studia humanitatis*. It is perhaps significant that this move took place in 1466, a year when Florence was rocked by an anti-Medicean coup. He taught rhetoric at a school in Capua, and eventually gained a certain fame as a poet and extemporaneous *rimatore* under the patronage of King Ferdinand I of Naples. Around 1480 he moved to the Rome of Sixtus IV, where he taught at the university and wrote a commentary on Vergil's *Georgics* that shows the influence of the great Roman scholar Pomponio Leto. In 1489 he left Rome for Hungary, where he was called to teach rhetoric. Hungary had been undergoing a revival of interest in classical and modern Latin literature under the patronage of its enlightened king, Mattias Corvinus, and his cultivated wife, Beatrice, who was the daughter of Aurelio's former patron, Ferdinand I of Naples.[4] Brandolini had enjoyed Mattias's favor for only a few months when the king died (6 April 1490). In that short time, however, he had dedicated one work to Mattias, *The Human Condition and Tolerating Illness* (*De humanae vitae conditione et toleranda corporis aegritudine*), and started another, the *Comparison*, which he also intended to dedicate to the king.[5] After Mattias's death, Aurelio moved back to Florence, where he attempted to win the patronage of Lorenzo de' Medici, with what success is uncertain. In the school year 1490–91 he taught Latin poetry at the University of Florence. Eventually he came under the influence of the Augustinian preacher fra Mariano da Gennazzano—a Medici adherent and a critic of Savonarola—and joined the Augustinian order (1491). He devoted his last years to preaching in various cities of Italy, and died of the plague back in his Florentine monastery in October of 1497.

In both of the works Brandolini dedicated to Mattias Corvinus, the king himself appears as an interlocutor, and it is significant, though hardly surprising, that Mattias is the spokesman for the winning side in both. Unlike in the case of many Renaissance dia-

logues, in the *Comparison* Mattias's scathing critique of Florentine republican institutions leaves little doubt whose side Brandolini is on. Mattias's unequal opponent in the dialogue is Domenico Giugni, a Florentine knight and merchant following the royal court, about whom little is known. The dialogue itself describes him as shrewd but untrained in letters. The third interlocutor, Mattias's illegitimate son János (1473–1504), is present only as a witness to the debate conducted by the other two speakers. The debate is ostensibly undertaken to educate Prince János in order that he might one day take up his appointed role as successor to King Mattias (a role in which the historical János, however, failed spectacularly).

The action of the dialogue extends over the last three days of Carnival before Lent, and each day is devoted to a different point of comparison between kingdoms and republics: their claims to promote liberty (Book I), justice (Book II), and good, effective government (Book III). The subject comes up because János asks a question about which form of government is better, and states that his classical studies have led him to suppose that republics are better than kingdoms. His father Mattias spends the rest of the dialogue disabusing his son and heir of this notion. This indeed is the first remarkable thing about Brandolini's dialogue, the simple fact that it contains a detailed analysis and comparison of the two forms of rule at all. As the great historian Nicolai Rubinstein once remarked, such direct comparisons are not at all common in Renaissance political literature.[6] Such comparisons as we do find, like the one in the fourth book of Baldassar Castiglione's *Cortegiano*, tend to be more rhetorical than analytical. Each side is allowed to speak for its point of view in the Ciceronian manner, criticism of the opposite point of view is muted, and the reader is left to draw his own conclusions. In the most popular humanist handbooks of republican and royal government, the twin treatises of Francesco Patrizi of Siena, *Republican Education* (*De rei publicae institutione*) and

*On Kingdoms and the Education of the King* (*De regno et regis institutione*), the two constitutions are treated in entirely separate works, similarities are emphasized, and explicit comparisons avoided. The same is true of Bartolomeo Platina's pair of treatises *On the Prince* and *On the Best Citizen* (*De principe* and *De optimo cive*) and of course of Machiavelli's *Prince* and *Discourses*. In general it can be said that humanists of the early Renaissance avoided ideological confrontations over constitutional forms, preferring to direct their reforming energies at improving the virtues of the ruling class. Their reforms were generally about governors, not governments.

In the case of Brandolini's work, however, the ideological differences are sharply emphasized, and indeed one aim of the dialogue is to demolish the historical and philosophical arguments in favor of republican government commonly invoked by civic humanists since the beginning of the Quattrocento. Hence the work constitutes a sharp critique of Florentine civic humanism by someone familiar with how the Florentine government worked, both in theory and in practice. The work also aims to show that the fundamental humanist goals of a return to ancient virtue, ancient literary and artistic excellence, and Roman military glory are better achieved under monarchical governments than under republican ones. In historical terms the dialogue represents a return to the cultural politics of Petrarch and a rejection of the neoclassical republican ideology invented in the late fourteenth century by the Florentine chancellor Coluccio Salutati and elaborated in the fifteenth by civic humanists such as Leonardo Bruni, Poggio Bracciolini, and Matteo Palmieri, among others.

The aims of the work are subserved by its unusual literary form. It is indeed a second remarkable thing about Brandolini's *Comparison* that it explicitly argues *Socratico more*, in the Socratic manner, instead of employing the Ciceronian dialogue form standardly used by humanists from the time of Petrarch onwards.

Brandolini's work in fact may well be the only example of the use of Socratic dialogue by an Italian Renaissance humanist. This entails a shift away from the usual humanist rhetoric of praise and blame and away from the urbane Ciceronian skepticism that marks so much humanist discourse. Ciceronian dialogue allows its interlocutors to develop their positions at length and permits only isolated moments of criticism or cross-examination. It is lineally descended from the sophistic discourses pilloried as *macrologia* by Plato in the *Gorgias*. It is also nearly related to the magisterial dialogue as found in Augustine and many medieval authors, where a student may ask questions and ask for apparent contradictions to be clarified, but does not challenge the master's authority or develop a rival position. Socratic dialogue on the other hand aims to expose received opinions to probing cross-examination and criticism, following a question-and-answer format. The result is the refutation of those opinions, and Socrates' interlocutors are reduced to *aporia*, a state where one experiences emptiness of belief and therefore openness to new beliefs.[7] Socrates' interlocutors achieve self-knowledge, or at least are knocked out of their uncritical assumptions, by having the logical inconsistencies in their beliefs exposed to view, a type of refutation called the *elenchus*.

This is approximately what happens in the *Comparison*, though Brandolini, who was after all a professional teacher of rhetoric, cannot resist putting numerous flights of eloquence into King Mattias's mouth. Yet there are also numerous extended passages of Socratic question-and-answer, where Domenico is asked for and gives a definition, only to be driven from it under close questioning. The discussion of republican liberty, for instance, begins with Domenico's naïve definition of liberty, that it means the power to do what you wish. When Mattias points out that this would make the free man one who can commit crimes with impunity, Domenico is forced to draw the usual distinction between liberty and license, so liberty only applies to desires acceptable in everyday

life. When Mattias points out that kingdoms generally allow greater personal liberty than republics, for example in consumption — dress, banquets, funerals, building — Domenico again has to recast his definition of liberty as something akin to modern "positive" liberty. He now says that what makes Florentines free is that they impose laws on themselves. Matthias then forces Domenico to admit that there is no difference between having laws imposed on you by a king and imposing them on each other — in neither case is one truly autonomous. Republican self-rule is really at best the chance to have a limited voice, on rare occasions, in decisions affecting yourself, but not the freedom to say "I will do this but not that." True freedom is to be ruled by virtue, and the Florentine method of choosing rulers by lot prevents that. Florentines are ruled by the luck of the draw: by fortune, not virtue. Lacking as he does a concept of representation, Domenico is unable to articulate a more modern argument for the intrinsic value of autonomy or for the dignity of self-rule, and is thus compelled to give up his claim that republics are more free. The first book ends with János declaring that he now has decided that he prefers the *libertas regni* to that of the republic.

As this summary suggests, Corvinus takes on the role of Socrates in the dialogue, and his own preferred constitution, the kingdom as exemplified by Hungary, is rarely itself subjected to serious criticism by Domenico. So the goal of the dialogue is not, as in the Ciceronian dialogue, to air all the leading positions with a view to edification, then choose the one that is most probable according to the criteria of Academic skepticism. Brandolini's goal is rather to find the truth and to produce a firm, reasoned conviction that a kingdom ruled by a virtuous monarch is a better constitutional form than a republic or commune of the Florentine sort, where magistrates are chosen by lot from an approved list of citizens. "Views that are argued on both sides in the Socratic manner," says Mattias, "by questioning and response become more efficacious

and clearer by using the barbs of argumentation, and are fixed more sharply and easily in the mind by having all doubt taken away" (1.26). The method is effective and by the end Domenico admits that his mind has been completely changed, and despite his republican upbringing he has now been convinced by rational argument to become a monarchist; indeed, if he can find a good king such as Mattias has described, he will leave his dearest homeland and move to that kingdom. So total a rout of one interlocutor by another is extremely rare in humanist dialogue.

The form of Brandolini's *Comparison* is by no means its only rare and original feature. Among other points of interest, the dialogue demotes Domenico's reliance on Aristotle's *Politics*, by far the most important ancient authority in Renaissance political reflection, preferring instead Plato's *Laws* and *Statesman*.[8] Brandolini's is thus among the first works of political philosophy since antiquity where these late works of Plato are present as a major influence. This is perhaps not all that surprising given that they had become widely available only six years before, in 1484, when Ficino's Latin translation was printed in Florence.[9] More speculatively, Brandolini may be the first modern European political philosopher to show a knowledge of Book 6 of Polybius, a key text in early modern republican thought.[10] Brandolini's dialogue contains as well a forceful critique of the mercenary system from the point of view of a Renaissance king, a critique that was by no means common in Italian humanism before Machiavelli; and it raises the question, which also recalls Machiavelli, whether the spread of Christianity is to be blamed for the fall of the Roman empire. This is a view Mattias firmly rejects, but it is interesting, in light of Machiavelli's later discussion, that Domenico states it to be a common belief in his time.

In Book II there is, moreover, an almost unprecedented discussion of the morality of international commerce, in which King Mattias attacks Florentine mercantilist policies and defends free

trade. He defends free trade, needless to say, not on the modern grounds that it leads to greater prosperity for all, but on the grounds that free trade is more just. Free trade is sanctioned by the *ius gentium* and promotes the *communio humani generis*, the unity of the human race, whereas Florentine mercantile policy serves only Florence and the greed of her merchants and artisans. Mattias himself as king allows other nations equal access to Hungarian markets, for small import fees, and free passage through his lands. *Censeo tamen commertia inter homines maxime libera esse oportere*, says Mattias: "I believe that commercial relations between men should be as free as possible."

This does not mean that Mattias is enthusiastic about mercantile activity in general. In fact he prohibits his own subjects from engaging in trade on the grounds that it corrupts morals. Citing Plato's *Laws*, Mattias maintains that merchants introduce corrupt foreign ways and debase speech with foreign language. They make a people want luxuries when they should be training themselves in an austere way of life. A kingdom which does not need luxuries will never want for necessities. In short, the whole discourse of hostility to commerce and the need to preserve severity of morals against the corrupting effects of wealth, the discourse that J. G. A. Pocock famously attributed to the early modern republican tradition, is in Brandolini's text seen as natural to kingdoms, while republics are seen as naturally inclined to commerce and the corrupting influence of greed and international trade. This suggests that some recent revision of Pocock's thesis, emphasizing the full compatibility of Renaissance republican ideology with Italian commercial society, may be on the mark.[11]

It is in fact the very compatibility of commercial society and republican government that Mattias sees as the fatal weakness of a city like Florence and republican regimes generally. It is avidity for wealth, for example, that makes Florentine claims to republican equality a sham. Florentines boast that they have equal access as

citizens to political power, equality under the law, and an equality of social intercourse backed by sumptuary laws that prevents anyone from expressing his superiority by means of dress, building styles, and public displays of wealth in banquets, weddings, and funerals. Mattias subjects each of these claims to withering criticism. All Florentine boasts about their egalitarian mores, in the king's view, are fully discredited by the extreme economic inequality characteristic of Florentine society. Their outward shows of equality in dress and style of life only mask real inequalities of wealth. Lycurgus, the great Spartan legislator, did not allow such inequalities, says Mattias, citing Plutarch. He wanted equality of possessions to avoid crimes and lawsuits and other such marks of corrupt societies. Most problems in human society come from wealth or the search for wealth.

> But if republics were so founded from the beginning to equalize possessions among the citizenry, and no one were allowed to have more than another, neither, surely, would any thefts, lawsuits and discords at all arise in cities, and citizens would not expend so much effort on trade, voyages, agriculture and the rest of the arts of gain out of an insane lust for profit. They wouldn't plot so much against the lives of their relatives and friends for the sake of an inheritance; they wouldn't, finally, put themselves and their lives so frequently at risk and face death so many times in the most obvious ways possible (2.39).

The republican claim that equality under the law is a substitute for economic equality is likewise a sham. The legal safeguards for private property about which republicans boast only guarantee the permanence of inequality. The state is so lacking in charity that it gives no help to the poor, even when they are good citizens, but relies on the safety net provided by families and friends. The law protects the rich and powerful, who can break it when they wish

with impunity, but it persecutes the poor, who have no ties of family or clientage to protect them from its rigors. Nor do republican institutions give equal access to power, since the poor are excluded from office when in arrears on their taxes, i.e., most of the time. This in effect makes them the slaves of the rich. The subject cities of the Florentine *contado* are likewise exploited and stripped bare by greedy Florentines who act like lords and not equals when appointed by the Florentine Signoria to provincial governorships. Provincials have no access to power under the Florentine republic.

In the best kingdom, from which commercial greed and its corruptions have been banished, all such problems are avoided. Overwhelming wealth is concentrated in the hands of a king, and his other subjects are left with approximately equal possessions. The king is not a minister or instrument of the laws, "but has charge of them and dominates them" (2.15).

Being by definition virtuous, he has no lust for profit or power, and can thus administer the law without fear or favor. He is not bound rigidly by the letter of the law, as a magistrate must be, but can adapt it to circumstances and persons in the interest of equity. In the best kingdom the provinces are governed by the king's ministers, and representatives of the several towns have a voice on the king's council. They are chosen by the king and not by lot, which ensures that they are men of virtue. All this prevents exploitation of the periphery at the expense of the center and promotes unity and harmony. The king's counsellors are not restrained by fear from speaking their minds in council, unlike republican councils, where magistrates use pressure to compel assent and councilors are so fearful of malignant reprisals that they are forced to conceal their views in secret ballots. A king's counsellors give *sententiae* not *suffragia*, considered opinions, not votes. They speak truth because they know a virtuous prince will welcome truth and reward them for their honesty. They give better counsel because they are statesmen knowledgeable about civil affairs, not merchants on holiday

from the wool-shop or the counting-house. Distinctions of dress and style of life are preserved in kingdoms because they are rewards of honor that encourage virtue, not merely evidence of wealth and successful greed as they would be in republics. With the influence of commerce and unequal wealth excluded from government and society, justice and harmony is restored and the natural tendency of mankind to seek glory can be focused once more, as in Roman times, on military virtue. The kingdom will expand its borders, the Turkish barbarians will be defeated, and peace and unity will be once more established in the civilized, Christian world.

We are obviously dealing here with an idealized royal constitution, and the comparison between the reality of the Florentine republic and the idealization of Corvinus's kingdom could hardly be considered fair. In fact the argument in favor of monarchy is conducted with magnificent unfairness throughout. But the exposure of the ideological assumptions underlying kingships and republics that is enabled by the comparison is nonetheless revealing. As has recently been argued,[12] the idea of a republican tradition in early modern European history needs to be complicated by seeing within it two rival models of virtuous government. There is a neo-Roman tradition, based principally on Cicero and Livy, that argues for the priority of the right to private property in the design of a polity, privileges military virtue and expansionism, and embraces the idea of glory and sacrifice for the commonwealth. This is the Renaissance republicanism celebrated by Quentin Skinner, J. G. A. Pocock, and the so-called "Cambridge School."[13] But alongside this neo-Roman tradition is a "Greek tradition," indebted more to Plato and Aristotle than to Cicero and Livy, that privileges the public good and the goal of collective happiness over private entitlements and Spartan austerity over Roman imperialism and its attendant corruption. It allows for no imprescriptable property rights but holds that the state should equalize property

in the interests of stability and unity; it prefers contemplative *otium* to active *negotium*, longevity to expansion, Machiavelli's "republic for preservation" to his "republic for expansion." In this account, the revival (or rather invention) of a "Greek tradition" begins with More's *Utopia* of 1516, but a reading of Brandolini's *Comparison* shows that elements of the "Greek tradition" can be traced back into fifteenth-century Italy, and may have their roots in the much-neglected political writings of "signorial" humanists. To be sure, King Mattias endorses imperialism and glory as signs of a virtuous polity, which would put him in the "neo-Roman" tradition, but on the key issues of equalizing property and avoiding the corrupting effects of wealth he is much more of a Greek than a Roman.

Interestingly, one of the few claims made for the commercial republic that gives Mattias pause is the claim that wealth and republican government are responsible for the remarkable flowering of the arts and literature that everyone agrees to be the unique glory of contemporary Florence. This leads to another uncommon discussion about the conditions for cultural flourishing. The discussion is meant to challenge the entrenched Florentine belief, going back to Leonardo Bruni, that the late medieval revival of republican government had been a necessary precondition for the Renaissance revival of antiquity, centered in Florence. Mattias easily—too easily—dismisses the claim that the thirst for wealth is a necessary condition of cultural flourishing, since (he says) even in an austere kingdom with equality of possessions there would still be a division of labor, and hence arts of some kind. But the claim that Florence owes its cultural brilliance to its republican institutions and education is one that Mattias feels compelled to refute in detail.

Domenico's claim is built on several considerations. He states, first of all, that the social equality of the Florentines makes them eager to distinguish themselves, and hence the arts flourish

through competition. Equality here acts as a positive motivator rather than a compensatory one, "For so long as no one wishes to be inferior to others, everyone competes to reach the summit of achievement. Hence the finest minds are nurtured among us and numerous outstanding persons in every art and discipline are found in our city" (2.45).

Domenico seems to assume a virtuous circle where the effort to equal one's peers makes everyone better and thus raises the standard overall. Florence's social equality is a product of its republican constitution, which is thus seen as favorable to liberal education, insofar as the latter can act as a source of great personal distinction.

Mattias attacks this explanation for Florentine cultural preëminence both on the level of fact and on that of theory and argument. First, he denies that Florence's celebrated cultural achievements have anything to do with its republican institutions. If that were the case, one would expect all republics to excel all kingdoms in all departments of culture; but this is not so. Venice, Lucca, and Siena do not produce anything like the number of great artists and writers that Florence does, and the flourishing of the liberal arts, as measured by the size and reputation of universities, is found as much in kingdoms as in republics. Mattias's strategy here is to step away from the comparison between Florence and Hungary and generalize his argument to all republics and all kingdoms. From this perspective it can be seen that the arts and liberal disciplines flourish no more in republics than in kingdoms. The Naples of Ferdinand I has talented people in all the disciplines, as does the Rome of the popes and the university of Pavia sponsored by the dukes of Milan. Paris, "though you call it a barbarian city," has between twenty and thirty thousand students in all the best disciplines, who come there from all over Europe. When it comes to painting and sculpture, however, Mattias has to admit that Florence is unmatched by any city in Europe. But here again, other re-

publics do not display an equal tendency to produce great artists. Thus the only possible explanation for Florence's excellence in the arts is nature, not culture: the climate or atmosphere of Tuscany is what produces her great artists — certainly not her education. The Florentines have weak bodies, since they don't engage in military exercise, and the weakness of their bodies leads to a hypertrophy of their minds. Florence's vaunted social equality in the end is a negative influence, since the lack of recognition and reward accorded to her great geniuses is responsible for the tendency of talented Florentines to emigrate elsewhere. Artists and writers are without honor in their own country, and this artistic brain-drain is laid at the door of the Florentine republic's pseudo-equality.

By the end of the *Comparison* Domenico is so ground down by continual defeat in argument that his only remaining question is why there should be any republics at all. This leads to an interesting exposition by Mattias, possibly without parallel in humanist political thought, of the reasons for the historical rarity of the republican constitution. Through most of history, Matthias correctly states, most governments have been monarchical. This is true of the Hebrews, the Egyptians, the Assyrians, Medes, and Persians; it is true of the government of Alexander and his successors, of the Turks and the Byzantines. Even in modern Europe it is the dominant constitution, as we see in England, France, Spain and the Empire. Such republican regimes as have existed in history have been transitory and unstable; the Athenians and Spartans soon abandoned their *respublicae* for monarchy, and when the Carthaginians embraced republican government they were quickly beaten by the Romans. So the most successful of the ancient republics, the Roman republic, which modern republicans look to as their model, is something of an outlier in the grand sweep of history. But even the Romans were dependent on dictators to keep order in the worst periods of their republic, and eventually they

too saw the wisdom of one-man rule. And though the modern Romans have changed the name of *princeps* and now have a *pontifex maximus* in place of their emperor, they keep to the form of the principate even today. The Venetians retain a kind of appearance and image of a king in their doge. Even the Florentines have an "effigy" of a king in their formal head of state, the Standard-Bearer of Justice. It's no wonder then that Christ chose to come to earth in the time of Augustus and to found his church, putting it under Peter as the sole head of his disciples. He was merely imitating the governance of heaven itself, which is of course monarchical.

The reason why republics have usually been temporary affairs, explains Mattias, is because they are inherently unstable. Following, apparently, the analysis in Book 6 of Polybius, Mattias describes the stages of corruption through which governments pass. When kings are corrupted and become tyrants, if a good king can't be found, the nobility try to take his place; when they in turn are corrupted the people step in and try to establish a popular government run according to principles of justice and virtue. But they eventually fail, and the worst form of government, democracy, the *plebeius principatus*, takes its place. The correct solution to this spiral of degeneration is not to try to return to the virtuous but unstable republican constitution. Rather, one should seek a good king who can restore virtue, order, and peace. Most men in most times and places have realized this, which is why most governments have been monarchies. Republics are in this perspective just a stage in the degeneration of human government, but in time nature will revert to the norm. This contrasts strongly with Aristotle's view that the existence of popular governments is a natural fact reflecting differences of climate and the quality of human material available at a given place and time. Mattias cites many examples in nature to show that governance by a single principal is natural and normal. So the end of the state, which is harmony and union, is best achieved by kings. The goal of politics and of educa-

tors alike should thus be to produce the virtuous prince. Accordingly, a kind of miniature "mirror of kings," describing the kingly virtues, concludes the work.

There can be no doubt that in the *Republics and Kingdoms Compared* Brandolini stands revealed as someone deeply alienated and hostile to the political traditions of his native city — perhaps a natural state of mind for someone who began life as an economic refugee from that city and who spent his adult life seeking patronage from princes. It is instructive to compare the grounds of his critique of Florentine political institutions with an equally alienated son of Florence, Machiavelli. Machiavelli, whose experience of Florentine politics was shaped by the disastrous experiences of the 1490s and the early years of the sixteenth century, became disgusted with Florentine government because of its weakness and vacillation, its military failures, and the absence of loyalty to the state. He hardly comments on Florentine commercial life and sees her military weakness as the result of her reliance on *condottieri* rather than native levies. Most of Florence's ills are ultimately due to ill-designed institutions and a corrupt culture and religion, which Machiavelli compares unfavorably with those of the Roman republic. Brandolini's critique is quite different; it is in some respects much more traditional and moralistic. He sees the main source of Florence's ills in its lust for money, which leads to inequality and injustice, to an inflammation of the passions and the impotence of reason, to a fatal disinterest in military glory and power. Its pluralistic division of power leads inevitably to a chaotic decision-making process and constant dissension and disunity. He sees Florentine politics and history through a Platonic and Sallustian filter, and notes with approval her drift to one-man power in the person of Lorenzo de' Medici. Yet for all his traditionalism, Brandolini deploys far more analytical rigor and a far broader historical vision than most humanistic writing on politics, and stands, furthermore, on the threshold of a period when Eu-

rope would become ever more divided ideologically into republican and monarchical camps. It is these qualities which make him by far the most interesting humanistic writer on politics before Machiavelli.

I should like to thank Francesco Bausi and Nicoletta Marcelli for helping me obtain research materials in Italy, and the staffs of the Biblioteca Riccardiana and the Biblioteca Medicea Laurenziana in Florence for access to the manuscripts of the *Comparison*. Arthur Field kindly collated the last few folios of the Laurenziana MS for me, and Ariane Schwartz checked my collation of the Riccardiana MS. I am grateful most of all to Martin Davies, who read the whole translation, solved a number of problems, and offered many stylistic improvements. This book is dedicated to the memory of my former teacher, Eugene F. Rice, Jr., a great scholar whose life exemplified the best republican virtues.

J. H.

Cambridge, Massachusetts

September 2008

## NOTES

1. See the Note on the Text and the Bibliography for the manuscripts and editions.

2. See Bibliography.

3. For the details of Brandolini's life, see Mayer, Rotondò, Mitchell and Biagini's introduction to her text of the *Comparison* (see Bibliography for full references).

4. A guide to the enormous literature on Mattias Corvinus may be found in *Matthias Corvinus the King*.

5. The work can be dated on internal grounds to 1490 or 1491, since in Book III (3.63) Brandolini says that the Emperor Frederick III has ruled as emperor (crowned 1452) for 39 years, and that Corvinus has ruled for 26 (presumably calculated from Mattias's crowning in 1454).

6. Rubinstein, 35.

7. This stage is reached at 3.83.

8. The arguments for and against kingship in Aristotle's *Politics* 3.14–18, the so-called "Treatise on Kingship," are of central importance in the discussion. Brandolini implicitly rejects Aristotle's constitutional "relativism," which holds that the royal constitution is appropriate to some societies where there is one clan or family in particular of surpassing merit, to insist on the "exclusivist" view that monarchy is always better than republican government. On the rise of constitutional exclusivism see Hankins, "Exclusivist Republicanism and the Non-Monarchical Republic," forthcoming in *Political Theory*.

9. See James Hankins, *Plato in the Italian Renaissance* (Leiden and London: E. J. Brill, 1990), for details about the publication history of Ficino's translations of the *Laws* and the *Statesman*.

10. See 3.86, 3.91 and notes. The first reference to Book VI of Polybius in the Renaissance is said by Arnaldo Momigliano to be in the *De honesta disciplina* of Pietro Crinito (1504); see his article, "Polybius' Reappearance in Western Europe," in *Polybe: Neuf exposés suivis de discussions*, ed. Emilio Gabba (Vandoeuvres–Geneva, 1974), 360.

11. J. G. A. Pocock, "Civic Humanism and Its Role in Anglo-American Political Thought," in his *Virtue, Commerce and History* (Cambridge: Cambridge University Press, 1985), 37–50; for a recent critique see Mark Jurdjevic, "Virtue, Commerce and the Enduring Florentine Republican Moment: Reintegrating Italy into the Atlantic Republican Debate," *Journal of the History of Ideas* 62.4 (2001): 721–43.

12. Eric Nelson, *The Greek Tradition in Republican Thought* (Cambridge: Cambridge University Press, 2004).

13. See Anthony Grafton, "The History of Ideas: Precept and Practice, 1950–2000 and Beyond," *Journal of the History of Ideas* 67.1 (2006): 1–32.

# REPUBLICS AND KINGDOMS
## COMPARED

# Proemium[1]

1   Cum animalia omnia sui generis societatem appetunt, tum homo imprimis, qui et rationis est particeps et ad vivendum per se mancus atque infirmus. Altero enim fit ut innumerabiles societatis fructus voluptatesque cognoscat, altero ut aliena semper ope auxilioque indigeat. Ac cetera quidem animalia aequo inter se iure agunt neque vel suo vel alieno generi aut praeesse aut subesse satis curant, quippe quae neque imperandi neque parendi discrimen intellegant; homo autem ingenio ac ratione insignis, qui parendi atque imperandi differentiam probe norit, seque ab[2] Deo ad imperandum ipsius exemplo genitum esse putet, non ceteris modo animalibus, sed suo quoque generi praeesse ac dominari cupit. Atque haec quidem cupiditas, ut societas illa communioque servetur, necessario est homini a natura data. Nam cetera quidem animalia, cum ratione careant neque multis ad vivendum rebus indigeant, et ea quibus indigent, pastum et latibula, sine aliena ope a natura exposita passim inveniant, propterea quod coetus vim utilitatemque non sentiunt, principe inter se et rectore non egent; homo autem, cuius et vita magni momenti est et imbecillitas maior, multo plura ad traducendam vitam desiderat, neque ea sibi solus facile potest comparare. Coetum itaque et societatem colat necesse est: ea porro sine lege, sine ordine, sine moderatore servari non potest; quem quidem et unum et optimum et prudentissimum esse necesse est, a quo omnis vivendi ratio petatur,[3] omnis ordo, omnis lex rebus praescribatur, omnia denique societatis iura serventur.

2     His igitur de causis, unus communi consensu princeps initio constitutus est qui ceteris imperaret, ceteros in pace ac societate

# Preface

While all animals seek the society of their own kind, man in particular does so as he partakes of reason and on his own is too crippled and weak to undertake the tasks of living. Reason enables him to recognize the innumerable fruits and pleasures of social life; his weakness means he always needs the resources and help of others. The rest of the animals act on a basis of equal right among themselves and take few pains to dominate or defer to either their own kind or other kinds, as they have no sense of what it is to lead or obey. But man — remarkable for his mind and reasoning power, who has a fine awareness of the difference between obeying and commanding and who believes himself created by God to rule after His example — man desires to have preëminence and lordship not only over other animals, but also over his own kind. Indeed, nature gives this desire to man of necessity so that that social and community life may be preserved. The other animals lack reason and need little to survive, and what they do need, food and shelter, they find everywhere provided for them by nature without the help of others. Hence they do not feel the urge or the utility of uniting together and do not require a leader or ruler among themselves. Man's life, however, is of great value and he is much weaker, so he wants many more things to get through life, and is not easily able to get those things for himself on his own. Thus he necessarily cultivates a communal and social life. Furthermore, these things cannot be preserved without law, order and a ruler, and the ruler must necessarily be one person who is the best and the wisest. From him one should solicit a complete pattern of life; by him all order and law in public affairs should be prescribed; in short, it is by him that all the legal principles of society should be preserved.

For these reasons, a single prince was in the beginning established by common consent who might rule the rest and hold them

contineret; eum homines, propterea quod ab eo regerentur, regem
appellavere. Ita hoc in terris nomen atque imperium exortum est.
Quoniam autem parere animus bene informatus non vult nisi optime et iustissime et ex sua utilitate imperanti, qui vero ita se gereret non facile reperiebatur, crescente in dies imperandi cupiditate,
cum iam nemo vellet parere et imperare omnes simul non possent,
multorum principatus in quo omnes vicissim imperare possent inventus est.

3      Ita duo imperii genera exorta sunt, ac superius quidem illud
regnum, haec respublica nuncupata est; atque horum quidem
principatuum uter potior habendus esset, magna inter veteres
philosophos quaestio semper fuit. Plato quidem et Aristoteles,
philosophorum sine controversia principes, unius optimi viri principatum[4] praetulerunt, et est profecto, ut opinor, praeferendus, si
modo is omni ex parte perfectus atque absolutus inveniatur; iidem
tamen, quoniam reperiri qualem optabant posse inter homines
diffidebant, rempublicam in suis libris, non regnum instituerunt.

4      Utriusque autem principatus comparationem attigerunt quidem
multi, sed neque veterum neque nostrorum quisquam, quod ego
quidem sciam, est hactenus satis exacte absoluteque executus. Ego,
cum essem ex optima et florentissima republica oriundus et apud
Matthiam, praestantissimum Pannoniorum regem, a quo ex urbe
Roma accitus fueram,[5] hieme proxima commorarer, velletque animus, qui nihil agere non potest, aliquo se opere exercere, rem
neque illi principi iniucundam neque meis civibus ingratam me
facturum existimavi, si de utriusque principatus comparatione
perscriberem rationesque omnes quibus uterque se defendere
consuevit, in medium afferrem et utriusque mores atque instituta
explicarem. Socratico itaque more disputationem institui ut ratio-

together in peace and social life. Men called this person a 'king' [*regem*] because they were ruled [*regerentur*] by him. That is how this name and this dominion arose on earth. But since a well-formed intellect does not want to obey a ruler unless it is being ruled in the best and justest way and in its own interest, and since a ruler who conducts himself this way is not easy to find, the desire to rule increased day by day, for no one wanted to obey and it was impossible for all to command simultaneously. Thus there was discovered the government of the many, in which everyone is able to command in his turn.

Thus two genera of dominion arose, and the earlier[1] was named 3 *kingdom*, the other *republic*; and it was a matter of considerable debate among the ancient philosophers which form of government was preferable. Plato and Aristotle, indisputably the two foremost philosophers, preferred the government of the single best man, and it is, I believe, preferable, so long as that one person is completely and unqualifiedly so; yet since these two philosophers doubted they could find the sort of man they wanted, in their books they established republics, not kingdoms.[2]

Many theorists have touched upon a comparison of the two 4 governments, but none of the ancients nor any of our [modern] authors, as far as I know, have dealt with the subject hitherto in a precise and comprehensive fashion. Since I was born in an excellent and most flourishing republic,[3] and since I have been staying this last winter with Mattias, that most outstanding king of the Hungarians,[4] who summoned me from the city of Rome, and since the mind cannot be idle and mine wished to exert itself in some task, I decided that I would be doing something that that prince would enjoy and that my fellow-citizens would welcome if I composed a comparison of both forms of government, bringing out into the open all the arguments both governments typically use to defend themselves and explaining the mores and institutions of both governments. I decided therefore on a disputation in the Socratic

nes utrinque afferrentur conclusionesque interrogando ac respondendo elicerentur[6] sermoque haberi coram a praesentibus videretur; ne vero cuiusquam in legendo desiderium differretur, neminem perpetua oratione utentem feci, sed ut quicquam primum ab adversario obiectum fuerat, ita primum a respondente confutari volui, ut audiret id statim quisque quod cuperet, neque minueretur intervallo pugnantium vis, sed cominus geri res et strictis mucronibus videretur.

5    Cum autem regni partes defendere nisi rex satis commode non posset, et ego apud Matthiam, ut dixi, regem essem, eum potissimum regni partes tuentem induxi. Respondentem autem ei pro republica feci Dominicum Iunium, civem nostrum, virum acris ingenii magnaeque in his rebus experientiae, quippe qui et in nostra republica esset natus et in eo regno magna cum dignitate iam pridem versaretur. Materiam porro et quasi subiectum in quo omnis eorum oratio versaretur, quoniam de republica disputandum erat, cepi nostram potissimum rempublicam, quae tum temporis vetustate, tum claritate nominis, tum institutorum bonitate videbatur omnes Italiae civitates antecedere, uberrimamque exemplorum ad disputandum copiam in omni genere posse praebere; atque hoc illustrandae nostrae reipublicae gratia consulto feci: nostros enim mores, quantum lex operis passa est, et nostra instituta descripsi.

6    Cum vero nostra consilia in medio scribendi cursu regia mors intercepisset, neque esset in rem meam in iis locis diutius commorari, me in patriam, a[7] qua puer admodum profectus fueram, magno cum desiderio recepi opusque incohatum hic, utcumque[8] per domesticas occupationes, absolvi. Cogitanti autem mihi cuinam id maxime dedicarem, tu potissimum, immo unus occurristi, Laurenti praestantissime, dignus qui tanto regi succederes, non dico

manner, to bring out the arguments on both sides and to elicit conclusions through question and answer, and also so that the discussion might seem to be held before an audience. Lest anyone should have to delay gratification while reading it, I had none of the interlocutors make long speeches, but as soon as a speaker had posited some view, I wanted him to be immediately countered by the respondent, so that each one might hear immediately what he wanted and not have the force of the combatants diminished by distance. The matter should have the air of being fought out hand-to-hand, with drawn swords.[5]

Since the royalist party could not be well defended except by a   5 king, and I was with King Mattias, as I said, I introduced him as the champion of the royalist party. I made Domenico Giugni the respondent for the republic, a citizen of ours and man of keen intelligence and great experience in these matters.[6] He after all was born in our republic and had long maintained a prominent position in that kingdom [of Hungary]. Furthermore, as the subject matter on which the whole discussion should turn, since the debate was to be about republics, I chose in particular our own republic, which seemed to excel all the cities of Italy in the antiquity and brilliance of its reputation and the quality of its institutions, and which seemed to offer the richest store of examples of every kind for discussion. I did this advisedly with a view to throwing light on our republic, for I described our mores and institutions insofar as the plan of the work allowed.

When the king's death had interrupted our plans in the midst   6 of writing, and there was no point to my remaining any longer in that place, I returned with great eagerness to the native land I had left while still a boy and here finished the work I had begun, insofar as my domestic distractions allowed. In considering to whom I should dedicate it, your name occurred to me particularly, or rather uniquely, most excellent Lorenzo, as a man worthy to take the place of that great king—I don't mean in terms of the

regio nomine, quod tu numquam expetisti, sed maiorum splendore, auctoritate tui nominis, doctrinae virtutumque omnium magnitudine, quibus rebus tu non illum regem modo,[9] sed ceteros quoque totius terrarum orbis reges ac principes provocasti. Sed te modestissimum virum ita demum maxime laudare videor posse, si modestissime laudem, ne, si pauciora quam opus est dixero, tuarum laudum splendorem, si plura meorum scriptorum fidem offendam. Huc accedebat quod, cum hi libri nostrae reipublicae mores atque instituta continerent, nemo aptior esse poterat qui eos vel iudicaret vel legeret quam qui[10] et in ea republica princeps esset et eius leges atque instituta magna ex parte restituisset.

7    Accipies itaque, Laurenti humanissime, hac conditione hanc reipublicae regnique comparationem, tribus his libris a nobis explicatam, ut in iis tuas cogitationes, tuos labores, tua consilia magna ex parte contineri putes atque ita nostra haec leges, cum per publicas occupationes licebit, ut eorum iudicem atque emendatorem, non lectorem aut laudatorem te factum existimes. Nam neque ego magnam sane harum rerum cognitionem habeo, quippe qui viginti amplius annis a patria ob rei familiaris amissionem abfuerim, et tuo iudicio tantum tribuo quantum homini ab homine tribui potest. Maximum igitur meorum laborum abs te praemium me consecutum esse arbitrabor, si tui animi iudicium sententiamque meruero. Cupio enim ut, auctore te, hi libri in manus hominum quam emendatissimi veniant.

8    Sed iam ad ipsam disputationem accedamus. Oritur autem sermo omnis a Joanne, Matthiae filio, qui triduo illo, quod ante Quadragesimam vulgo per luxum et licentiam agitur, discendi gra-

royal title, which you have never sought, but in consideration of the distinction of your ancestors, the authority of your reputation, and the abundance of your learning and universal virtue. In these qualities you have challenged, not only that king, but also all other kings and princes of the globe. But you are the most temperate of men and I think I could praise you best if I praised you temperately. I should harm the brilliance of your merits if I were to say less than needed, but the truthfulness of my writings if I said more. Moreover, since these books have as their subject matter the mores and institutions of our republic, there could be no one better fitted to read and pass judgement on them than one who is the leading man in that republic and who has largely restored its laws and institutions.

So please accept then, kindest Lorenzo, on this basis the *Comparison of Republics and Kingdoms* that we have elaborated in these three books. You will recognize that in them are largely contained your own deliberations, your own efforts and your own counsels, and please read our work, when your public duties allow, in the spirit of a critic and editor rather than that of a reader and eulogist. For I myself have really no great knowledge of the subject, having been absent from my country for more than twenty years owing to the loss of my patrimony, and I trust your judgment as much as one man can trust another's. So I think the greatest reward that I could get from you would be to have earned your judgement and opinion of my labors. For I would like to see these books come, under your authority, into the hands of mankind in the most correct possible form.

Let us now come to the disputation itself. The whole discussion arose thanks to János, Mattias' son, who during the three days before Lent, commonly spent in license and dissipation,

7

8

9

tia patrem petit eumque de imperiorum diminutione percontatur. Inde disputatio de reipublicae et regni comparatione emergit, quam legens tu ipse cognosces.

sought out his father in a spirit of inquiry, to learn from him the reasons why empires fell. That is how the disputation comparing republics and kingdoms arose, as you will see when you read it.

# Liber primus[1]

1  MATTHAEUS.[2] Gaudeo quidem omni tempore tua praesentia, fili, sed his vel maxime diebus, qui propter adventum Quadragesimae quasi Saturnalia altera ludis et lasciviis dediti sunt, iuventutemque relaxandis[3] animis solutiorem reddunt. Videris enim, cum ceterorum iuvenum consuetudinem et studia declinas, intellegere id quod est: nos, quanto ceteris hominibus dignitate praestamus, tanto studiis atque actionibus praestare oportere et tamquam in altissima specula positos ab omnibus spectari, ab omnibus iudicari, omnibus vitae et morum exemplum esse propositos, vitiaque in nobis minima a ceteris hominibus vel maxima et perniciosissima existimari. Nam ut Aquinas ait,

> omne animi vitium tanto conspectius in se
> crimen habet, quanto maior qui peccat habetur.

2  IOANNES. Ego vero, pater, cum istis quas dicis de causis ita ad te accedo, ut cupiam, quoad liceat, a tuo latere numquam discedere, tum vero ut aliquid ex te audiam quo et melior et peritior possim evadere, neque regni modo tui, sed tuae quoque virtutis et sapientiae, quantum fieri potest, heres efficiar. Regnum enim mihi auferri potest, sapientia non potest. Sed faciunt ingentes occupationes tuae ut minus saepe quam vellem ad te veniam, ne aut tibi molestus aut rebus maximis importunus atque intempestivus sim. Nunc autem, cum et te existimarem propter hos dies minus occupatum esse et ego vellem a ceterorum iuvenum vulgo studiisque differre, ob eam maxime causam ad te veni, ut te audirem de gravissimis, ut soles, rebus disserentem atque hos dies, qui a ceteris

# Book I

MATTIAS. I am always happy to see you, son, but most of all in these days, which, because of the approach of Lent, are given over to frivolity and dissipation, like another Saturnalia,[1] and make the young more licentious by relaxing its spirits. By eschewing the habits and pursuits of other youths, you seem to understand what is the case: that we must be superior to other men in our pursuits and actions to the degree that we are superior to them in rank. Placed as we are on a high eminence, we are seen and judged by all, and we are exposed to view as examples of life and morality, our smallest faults seen by other men as though they were the largest and most pernicious of vices. For as Juvenal says,

> The higher the standing of the sinner, the more public the obloquy his every vice attracts.[2]

JANOS. For my part, father, I am coming to you for the reasons you state, as I wish (so far as may be) never to leave your side, but also so that I may hear something from you that will make me better and more experienced. In this way I may become, as far as possible, the heir not only of your kingdom, but also of your virtue and wisdom. For a kingdom can be taken from me, but wisdom cannot. But so great are your preoccupations that I visit you less often than I should wish, lest I annoy you or be importunate and unseasonable amid your great affairs. But now, although I think you are less preoccupied owing to the holidays and I would like to distinguish myself from the vulgar crowd of other youths and their pursuits, I am coming to you most of all because I would like to hear you discussing the most serious subjects, as is your habit, and because I should like to channel these days, which others pass in

per luxum licentiamque aguntur, honeste tecum utiliterque traducerem.

3  MATTHAEUS. Facis ut probum adolescentem decet, cum me, quem tui amantissimum esse scis, studiose frequentas atque observas, neque mihi etiam in summis occupationibus molestus esse umquam potes. Nostrae enim occupationes ex te uno pendent omnes tuaque unius causa suscipiuntur. 'Omnis' enim 'in Ascanio cari stat cura parentis.' Nunc autem mihi, cum ociosus sim, optatissimus advenis. Nemo enim est cui omnia mea tradere, quicum omnia communicare vitamque ipsam, si queam, totam agere malim quam tecum. Proinde, si quid est quod ex me scire hoc tempore velis, age percontare ut libet; ego tibi, quantum in me erit, satisfacere conabor.

4  IOANNES. Saepenumero mecum mirari soleo, pater, hanc nostrorum temporum nescio ignaviam an infelicitatem appellem, quod omnia quae apud veteres maxima et florentissima erant, nunc labefactata et prope extincta sint, ita ut degenerare ab se quottidie mundus et ad finem quodammodo properare videatur. Nam, ut omittam artes, disciplinas studiaque omnia, quae ita debilitata atque imminuta mihi videntur esse ut eorum vix umbram exiguam retineamus, nonne regna atque imperia omnia, quae diu apud alias atque alias nationes maxima atque amplissima fuere, nunc multas in partes dispersa ac dissipata vix ulla sui vestigia reliquere? Atque, ut vetustissima illa Assyriorum, Medorum, Persarum Graecorumque omittamus, quae multis antea saeculis deleta sunt, Romani certe imperii, quod omnium longe maximum ac latissimum fuit, solum hodie nomen relictum est, imperium ipsum in multos sive regulos sive tyrannos distributum, multis iam annis extinctum est, atque ita extinctum ut neque illic neque alibi resurrecturum esse ulterius videatur. Cuius quidem rei, aliae ab aliis

licence and dissipation, into honorable and useful pursuits with you.

MATTIAS. You are acting as befits a fine young man when you wait upon me earnestly and show me respect. I love you dearly, you know, and you can never be an annoyance to me, even amid my most pressing business. Indeed, my activities all depend on you alone and are all undertaken for your sake alone. For "all the dear parent's concern was fixed upon Ascanius."[3] But your coming to me now, when I am at leisure, is very welcome indeed. There is no one to whom I would rather turn over everything I have, with whom I would rather share everything—even life itself, if I could—than you. So if there is anything you would like to learn from me at this time, go ahead and ask as you please; I shall try to satisfy you as much as I can.

JANOS. I've often wondered, father, at what I might call the feebleness or misfortune of our times: that all those things which were in their best and most flourishing state among the ancients are now corrupt and almost at an end. The world seems to be getting worse on a daily basis and hastening to its end. To leave aside the arts and disciplines and all forms of study, which seem to me to be so weakened and diminished that they keep hardly the slightest shadow of themselves, is it not the case that all the kingdoms and empires belonging to this or that nation, those which lasted a long time and were of vast extent, have left hardly any trace of themselves, being now scattered and dispersed in many places? To pass over the empires of the Assyrians, Medes, Persians and Greeks, which were destroyed many ages ago, it is surely the case that of the Roman Empire, the greatest and most extensive of them all by far, there is today left only the name. Its empire, divided up among many petty kings and tyrants, has been dead for many years, and so dead that it looks like it won't be resurrected any further, either there or anywhere else.[4] The causes of its extinction are explained differently by different people, and there are

causae assignantur, nec desunt qui christianam religionem incusent, nosque ab ea timidos atque ignavos effectos esse dicant. Cupio itaque, nisi tibi molestum est, pater, ex te audire non modo quid sentias, sed mihi quoque quid[4] sentiendum sit; illud enim verissimum existimabo quod ex te audiero.

5    MATTHAEUS. Nihil mihi antiquius ac iucundius est, fili, quam te optimis artibus praeceptisque instituere, ex quo uno omnis et senectutis meae requies et spes posteritatis pendeat. Cui quidem rei, cum te ultro deditum atque incumbentem video, incredibili profecto laetitia et voluptate afficior. Placet autem maiorem in modum te ea potissimum interrogare, quae et tuae imprimis professionis sint et non nisi a magno animo atque ingenio proficiscantur. Ego itaque cupidissime tibi morem geram, et quae hac de re mihi multorum annorum experientia comperta sunt, tibi paucis explicabo.

6    Imperia igitur, ut cetera omnia quibus artibus parta sunt, iisdem retineantur necesse est; ubi hae sublatae aut amissae sunt, illa quoque paulatim collapsa intereunt. Sunt autem artes quibus maxima imperia et facillime comparantur et diutissime retinentur, meo quidem iudicio, duae foris, domi totidem: foris disciplina militaris et gloriae cupiditas; domi, iustitia et continentia. Nam prudentia quidem, tamquam omnium virtutum regula, ita est in omni vitae parte necessaria, ut abesse nusquam possit. His igitur artibus illae quas tu paulo ante memorabas nationes maxima sibi imperia comparavere; his Romani totum paene terrarum orbem in ditionem redigere. Nam, ut vetustissimos illos reges Tanaum Scytharum et Vesorem Aegyptiorum omittamus, qui plurimas et validissimas nationes militari disciplina et gloriae studio superavere, Romulus hac disciplina fretus avum in regnum restituit, urbem

those who blame it on the Christian religion, saying that it has made us timid and feeble in spirit. So if it wouldn't be any trouble, I'd like to hear from you, father, not only what you think, but also what I should think, for I shall accept as the truest explanation the one I shall hear from you.

MATTIAS. As far as I am concerned, there is nothing more im- 5 portant and more pleasant, my son, than training you in the best arts and precepts, for on you alone depends all the tranquillity of my old age and all my hope for posterity. And when I see you of your own free will devoted to and working hard at this subject, I am filled with extraordinary happiness and pleasure; I like even more the fact that you are asking in particular about matters that are highly relevant to your calling and which only a great spirit and mind would inquire about. So I am most willing to indulge you and shall explain to you briefly what I have learned about this sub- ject from the experience of many years.

Empires, then, like other things born from good behavioral pat- 6 terns, are necessarily retained by those same patterns. When those patterns are taken away or lost, empires also fall into ruin little by little and die out. The behavioral patterns by which the greatest empires are easily acquired and kept in being for the longest possi- ble time are [four in number]: two external and two domestic. The two external ones are the discipline of war and the desire for glory; the domestic ones are justice and temperance. For prudence, being a kind of measurer of all the virtues, is so necessary in every part of life that it can never be absent. So it is through these be- havioral patterns that the nations you just mentioned acquired the greatest empires for themselves, and it was by these same patterns that the Romans brought nearly the whole world under their sway. To pass over those most ancient kings Tanaus of the Scythians and Vesoges of the Egyptians, who overcame numerous extremely powerful nations through military discipline and the thirst for glory,[5] there is Romulus who, by relying on this discipline, re-

condidit, finitimos debellavit, Martem sibi parentem vendicavit, ademptus denique rebus humanis hanc unam disciplinam posteris omni studio colendam servandamque mandavit. Ad quae quidem audenda ac perficienda, singularis profecto gloriae cupiditas eum non modo incitavit, sed per singula quoque pericula intrepidum securumque perduxit. Successit huic, singulare ac prope divinum iustitiae continentiaeque exemplum, Numa Pompilius, qui civitatem legibus, caeremoniis moribusque fundavit.

7      Quae quidem duorum regum instituta posteri diu ita servavere, ut nulla eos natio vel bellicis artibus vel studio gloriae vel domesticis virtutibus superaret. Quae enim gens disciplinis militaribus tantam umquam operam dedit? Quae gens in earum observatione tam diligens, tam severa umquam fuit? Quid enim sibi volunt aliud assiduae illae campi exercitationes, quid castra extra urbem commorantia, nisi ut tirones militari studio laborique assuescerent et veterani partam iam disciplinam consuetudine retinerent? Quibus rebus effectum est ut plures prope in ea civitate duces quam in aliis milites gignerentur; una certe urbs Roma plures imperatores produxit quam ceterae omnes toto orbe nationes. Quod quidem cum alii multi tum Plutarchus, celeberrimus apud Graecos historiarum scriptor, optime apertissimeque ostendit, qui, cum illustrium virorum res gestas conscriberet eosque inter se compararet, unius Romanae civitatis duces omnium gentium et nationum viris in comparatione opposuit; et illorum quidem etiam mediocres non reticuit, Romanorum vero multos summos viros, cum non inveniret quibuscum conferret, omisit; quod si apud aliquas nationes illis ulla ex parte similes invenisset, tantos viros profecto numquam tacuisset.

8      Singulos nominare et immensum esset et ad institutum sermonem non pertinet. Singulae enim aetates duces prope innumerabi-

stored his grandfather to his kingdom, founded a city, defeated his neighbors, avenged his father Mars, and finally, when removed from the sphere of human affairs, commanded his successors to cultivate and preserve this one discipline with the utmost zeal.[6] A unique lust for glory drove him to dare and carry out all these things and led him also through every single danger without fear or anxiety. He was succeeded by Numa Pompilius, that unique, almost divine exemplar of justice and temperance, who founded the city with respect to its laws, ceremonies and mores.

The institutions of these two kings were for a long time so well preserved by their descendents that no nation surpassed them either in the arts of war or in the desire for glory or in the domestic virtues. For what people ever devoted so much effort to military training? What people was ever so tireless and strict in observance of that training? What else was the point of those endless field exercises, those encampments outside the city, except to accustom new recruits to military pursuits and toil and to cause veterans to retain the discipline they had acquired through long practice? By these means it was brought about that there were almost more commanders born in this city than soldiers in others, and certainly the city of Rome produced more generals than all the other nations of the earth. Plutarch, the celebrated Greek historian, among many others, shows this with the utmost clarity when writing the deeds of illustrious men and comparing them with each other. He compared the leading men of all peoples and nations with the men of this one city of Rome, and he was not silent about even the mediocre figures of the former, whilst omitting many outstanding Roman men because he couldn't find men with whom to compare them. If he had found among other nations great men in any way comparable to those Romans, he would surely never have stayed silent about them.

But it would be an immense labor to name them all individually, and it would be irrelevant to the subject of our discourse.

7

8

les protulere neque quicquam eorum claritati detraxit multitudo, adeo ut si copiam inspicias, tam consummatos esse potuisse non credas; si virtutem expendas, neges esse potuisse tam multos; et quales quidem fuerint, eorum tum honores, tum res gestae facile aperteque declarant. Quid enim M. Furium Camillum totiens etiam absentem dictatorem dici coegit, nisi summa quaedam et spectata rei militaris disciplina, cuius ipse satis magna Veiis captis caesisque Senonibus praebuit documenta? Quid Q. Fabium Maximum, in summa urbis calamitate ac prope desperatione, maximo omnium consensu dictatorem fecit? Nonne eadem singularis artium bellicarum scientia, cuius quidem insigne etiam ab hoste tulit testimonium? Hannibal enim, dux omnium sua aetate peritissimus, professus est Romanos quoque suum Hannibalem habere; quod, nisi in Fabio singularem disciplinae militaris peritiam esset admiratus, numquam id de hoste dixisset, praesertim cum ipse superioribus victoriis esset elatus. Ac Fabiorum quidem familia ad debellandos hostes Romani nominis nata videbatur; ex ea enim non duces modo permulti, sed integri quoque exercitus prodiere, ita ut Veientes sibi privatim debellandos exposcere in eosque ex suis trecentos et sex uno tempore armare sint ausi. Scipionum quoque familia bellicae disciplinae peritiam sibi quodammodo hereditario iure vendicavit, quippe quae totidem imperatores quot viros produxerit; emicuere tamen inter eos, ut inter cetera sidera sol et luna, duo Africani, quorum alter subacta Carthagine praesentia tantum, alter eversa, etiam futura bella delevit. Metelli quoque, tot cognominibus e devictis provinciis reportatis se bellicam disciplinam et summo studio coluisse et exactissime tenuisse testati sunt.

There are some ages that produce nearly innumerable leaders, and their number does not detract at all from their distinction — so much so that if you consider their great number you would not believe they could be so perfect; if you weighed their virtues, you would deny that there could be so many of them. The sort of men they were is readily and plainly declared by their marks of honor and their deeds. For what made them hail Marcus Furius Camillus so often as dictator, despite his many absences, except his consummate and conspicuous mastery of military affairs, of which he himself offered great proofs in the capture of Veii and the slaughter of the Senones?[7] What was it that made Quintus Fabius Maximus dictator by universal consent at a moment of supreme calamity and despair for the city? Was it not that same unique knowledge of the arts of war, to whose distinction even the enemy bore witness? For Hannibal, the most experienced war leader of his age, confessed that the Romans also had their Hannibal.[8] This is something he never would have said about an enemy, especially in the elation of his earlier victories, if he had not admired Fabius' remarkable skills in military discipline. And the family of the Fabii seemed to be born to subdue enemies of the Roman name, for from it came not only a great many war leaders, but also whole armies. They dared to make the request that they should subdue the Veientes in a private war and fielded against them 306 of their own men.[9] The family of the Scipios laid claim to experience in military discipline by a kind of hereditary right, producing, indeed, as many generals as men. Among them gleam, like the sun and moon amid the rest of the stars, the two Africani, of whom one subdued Carthage by his presence alone, the other conquered it and wiped out future wars.[10] The many cognomina the Metelli brought back from defeated provinces bear witness to the great zeal and exacting tenacity with which they devoted themselves to the military art.[11] What of the Valerii, who were afterwards called the Corvini, our ancestors?[12] Did they not acquire

Quid Valerii, qui postea Corvini dicti sunt, gentiles nostri? Nonne hac rerum bellicarum scientia et cognomen nostrum assecuti sunt et principes civitatis semper extiterunt? E quibus fuit Marcus ille Messala, non solum maximus imperator, sed maximus[5] quoque suae aetatis orator. C. Marius, obscuro loco natus et in civitatem ex Arpinate municipio vix ascitus, hac una disciplina se tantopere nobilitavit, ut septem in urbe consolatus gereret et alterius factionis princeps nobilissimos cives proscriberet. Cn. Pompeius, in castris paene natus, omnes huius disciplinae partes ita exacte absoluteque tenuit, ita exercuit, ut ob magnitudinem rerum gestarum unus Romanorum Magni sit cognomen assecutus. Quid dicam de C. Caesare, qui et quinquagies collatis signis dimicavit et Pompeium ipsum, imperatorum omnium exercitatissimum, acie vicit? Neque patri cessit Augustus, dubium belli an pacis artibus melior, qui et bella suscipere se scire maximis victoriis triumphisque ostendit et ob id tantum, ut in pace viveretur, suscipienda esse[6] diuturna pace declaravit. Iam vero Severus Maximus aliique permulti hac una disciplina Romanum imperium sunt adepti.

9    Atque hi quidem omnes ad tantas res gerendas mira quadam et insatiabili gloriae cupiditate incitati sunt. Nemo enim fere est qui non rerum gestarum tamquam praemium appetat gloriam; quam quidem, nisi illi ante oculos propositam semper habuissent, numquam profecto tot labores perferre, tot pericula subire, tantas res gerere potuissent. Quid enim, obsecro, aliud petebat Mucius ille, cum tanto suo periculo in castra hostium ad Porsennam interficiendum proficisceretur, cum manum immotam in medio igne contineret? Quid aliud Horatius Cocles, cum solus omnem hostium impetum, donec pons[7] a tergo rescinderetur, sustineret? Quid Curtius ille, cum se in terrae hiatum armatus immitteret?

this cognomen of ours and become outstanding statesmen ever after through their knowledge of military matters? One of them was the Marcus Messalla who was not only the greatest general but also the greatest orator of his age.[13] Gaius Marius was of humble birth and was admitted to Roman citizenship only with great difficulty from the municipality of Arpino, but gained renown by this discipline alone to such a degree that he held the consulate in Rome seven times and as leader of the opposing faction proscribed the noblest citizens. Gnaeus Pompey, who was practically born in the camps, had such absolute mastery of this discipline and practiced it so well that he alone among the Romans achieved the cognomen of "the Great" for the greatness of his deeds. What shall I say of Gaius Caesar, who fought in pitched battles fifty times and defeated in battle Pompey himself, the most experienced of all generals? Nor did his son Augustus take second place to the father, and it is a matter of doubt whether the son was greater in the arts of war or of peace. His many victories and triumphs show he knew how to wage war, and the lasting peace he brought showed that he knew war should only be waged for the sake of peace. Then there was Severus Maximus[14] and many others who seized the Roman Empire through this art alone.

And all of these men were incited to perform these great deeds 9 through a kind of wondrous and insatiable lust for glory. There is almost no one who does not thirst for glory as a reward for his deeds. Indeed, if these men had not had glory before their eyes they could never, surely, have taken on so many labors and risked so many dangers and performed so many great deeds. What else was Mucius seeking when he set out in great peril for the enemy camp to kill Porsenna, when he held his hand motionless in the fire?[15] What else was Horatius Cocles seeking when he withstood singlehandedly the whole enemy attack until the bridge could be cut behind him?[16] What else did Curtius seek, the one who leaped armed into the gaping earth?[17] What about the three Decii in a

Quid tres una serie Decii, cum sua corpora hostibus pro reipublicae salute devoverent? Quid noster ille Corvinus, huius auctor cognominis, cum adversus provocantem Gallum excelso et invicto animo singulari certamine dimicaret? Quid illi quos supra memoravi aliud quaerebant, cum in ultimas usque terras armis penetrarent, omnibus se periculis laboribusque obiicerent, nisi immortalem quandam gloriam nomenque sempiternum? Quod quidem tropaea ab illis non in Urbe modo, sed per universum quoque terrarum orbem erecta facile aperteque declarant.

10    Atque his rebus foris imperium quaesiere. Domi vero iustitia et continentia, non minus quam foris arma, vigebant. Atque ut aequo inter se iure agere possent, leges non modo ipsi condebant, verum etiam ab aliis nationibus conditas ad se afferendas servandasque curabant et, quod efficacissimum exempli genus est, eas civitatis principes imprimis servabant. Quantum enim et apud viventes et apud posteros valuit exemplum illud Junii Bruti, qui, cum esset restitutae libertatis auctor, ultor regiae superbiae, primus consul, totius denique civitatis princeps, duos quos habebat praestanti ingenio atque aetate filios, quod contra senatus consultum de reducendis regibus clam egissent, securi percussit? Huius exemplum secutus multis annis post Marcus Manlius filium, quod contra imperium pugnasset, quamquam victorem, eodem tamen supplicio affecit. Quod, obsecro, potest esse maius servatae iustitiae argumentum quam, cum ipsi quoque principes civitatis intellegunt neque sibi neque suis liberis quicquam contra leges licere? Nihil enim est, mihi crede, fili, quod homines tam alliciat ad peccandum quam ipsorum principum et superiorum exemplum, quod cum sapientissimi illi viri maiores nostri plane cognoscerent, in

row who sacrificed their own bodies to the enemy to save the
republic? What about that Corvinus of ours, the originator of this
cognomen, who with a high and unconquerable spirit fought a famous battle against a Gaul who was challenging him?[18] What else
were all those I mentioned above seeking when they penetrated in
arms to the ends of the earth and exposed themselves to every
danger and labor, except immortal glory and an imperishable
name? The trophies they erected, not only in the City but
throughout the globe, give clear and ready proof of this.

They sought empire abroad through these means; at home, 10
they were strong in justice and temperance no less than they were
abroad in arms. And so that they could act on the same legal basis
among themselves, they not only laid down laws themselves, but
also took care that laws laid down by other nations should be
brought to them and followed, and — the most efficacious kind of
example — their civic leaders were the first to observe them. Think
how valuable was the example of Junius Brutus among the living
and for posterity. Though responsible for the restoration of liberty,
the avenger of royal arrogance, the first consul and the leading
man of the whole state, he nevertheless struck with an axe two
sons that he had, in the prime of their years and ability, because
they had conspired secretly against a decree of the senate about
restoring the kings.[19] Following his example many years later,
Marcus Manlius inflicted the same punishment on his son because
he had fought against the empire, even though the son had been
victorious.[20] What better proof could there be of the observance
of justice, I ask you, than when the leaders of the state themselves
understand that nothing contrary to the laws can be permitted either to themselves or to their relatives? Believe me, son, there is
nothing that entices men to sin so much as the example of leaders
and superiors, a thing that those wisest of men, our ancestors, obviously understood, since they visited severe punishment on those

auctores scelerum, quicunque illi fuissent, graviter animadverte-
bant, ne ceteri eo exemplo deteriores fierent.

11    Continentiam vero quantopere coluerint, testis est illa imprimis
consuetudo in atriis semel singulis diebus et singula tantum aut
bina ad summum fercula cenandi; testis illa C. Fabricii nobilissima
vox, qui, cum ei a Pyrrhi legatis ingens auri pondus offerretur, re-
spondit Romanos nolle aurum sed velle aurum habentibus imperare; testis illa Marci Curii voluntaria paupertas, qui, cum prae-
dam ex hostibus ingentem cepisset, nihil in domum suam nisi
ligneum scaphium[8] ad sacrificia intulisse inventus est; et quoniam
ex contrariis omnia maxime probantur, testes ante omnia sunt reges propter unam Sexti Tarquinii libidinem exacti; testes decemviri ob unius Appii Claudii incontinentiam magistratu privati.
Neque vero pietate, fide, mansuetudine, clementia, animi magnitudine ceterisque virtutibus aliis nationibus usquam cessere, sed in
his omnes longe superavere.

12    Quibus rebus effectum est ut res Romana in immensum brevi
coalesceret. Quamdiu autem ea civitas hos mores atque haec studia coluit, omnes eam nationes ut parentem et principem venerabantur eiusque imperio se subesse gaudebant, ita ut quaedam se illis ultro submitterent, omnes vero etiam remotissimae gentes
eorum amicitiam et societatem peterent. Huc accedebat quod artes, disciplinae studiaque omnia libero homine digna ibi maiorem
in modum florebant; neque ibi tantum clarissima ingenia nasce-
bantur, sed undique etiam ex toto terrarum orbe eo tamquam ad
communem omnium gentium patriam confluebant; honos enim
quo animi maxime capiuntur omnibus liberalibus disciplinis in ea
civitate ingens habebatur.

13    Ubi vero militari solertiae ignavia, studio gloriae superbia atque
avaritia foris, domi vero vis iustitiae, continentiae libido luxuriaque

responsible for crimes, whoever they happened to be, lest the rest should be made worse by their example.

A chief witness to how much they nurtured temperance is their    11
custom of dining at home just once a day and only having one or two courses at most;[21] witness too the noble saying of Gaius Fabricius who, offered an enormous sum in gold by Pyrrhus' envoys, responded that Romans did not want gold but to rule those who owned gold;[22] witness the voluntary poverty of Marcus Curius, who, although he had taken an enormous amount of plunder from enemies, was found to have brought nothing home except a wooden vessel for sacrifices.[23] And since all facts are best proved by their opposites, witness above all the kings, who were driven out solely because of the lust of Sextus Tarquinius;[24] witness the decemvirs who were deprived of their magistracy because of the incontinence of Appius Claudius alone.[25] Nor did they ever yield to other nations in piety, loyalty, gentleness, clemency, magnanimity and the rest, but far surpassed all of them in these virtues.

Through these patterns of behavior it came to pass that the Ro-    12
man state grew immensely in a short space of time. For as long as that city cultivated these mores and these pursuits, all nations venerated her as their parent and sovereign and were happy to subject themselves to her empire. Some even submitted to the Romans voluntarily, but all nations, even the remotest of peoples, sought out their friendship and alliance. Moreover, the arts, disciplines and all the pursuits worthy of a free man especially flourished there; not only were the most distinguished talents born there, but they also flowed thither from all sides, from every part of the globe, as though to the common home of all nations. Honor, by which such spirits are chiefly attracted, was considered to be in vast supply for all liberal disciplines in that city.

But when in foreign affairs sloth took the place of military re-    13
sourcefulness, pride and avarice the place of thirst for glory, and in

successit, illa imperii dignitas atque auctoritas paulatim decidere et collabi coepit. Ubi enim superbe, crudeliter atque avare imperari coeptum est, ut provinciae a magistratibus non servandae aut regendae sed expilandae ac diripiendae peterentur, neque ulla vel subditorum vel sociorum ratio haberetur, sanctissimumque illud orbis terrarum aequissimumque imperium in pessimam ac saevissimam tyrannidem esset conversum, exterae nationes, quae maiestatem Romani nominis antea venerabantur, partim contemptu, partim odio tam superbae atque avarae dominationis communi consensu tamquam ad commune incendium restinguendum ac delendum Romanum nomen insurrexere tantoque in eos odio conflagravere ut, non contentae iugum a cervicibus excussisse, Romam atque Italiam universam non semel ferro ignique vastarent, neque in homines tantum sed in aedificia quoque saevirent. Ita pulcherrimum atque amplissimum imperium, tantoque labore et industria, tanto etiam temporis spatio comparatum, brevi administrantium culpa labefactatum atque extinctum est; quod quidem ego certissimo Dei iudicio factum puto, ut quas illi nationes maxime contemnebant barbarasque appellabant, ab iis potissimum subacti vastarentur. Ignavia igitur et luxuria ceteraque foeda flagitia Romanum imperium evertere; idem antea Assyriis, Medis, Persis Graecisque contigerat: securi enim rerum suarum reges, omnia per praefectos agebant; ipsi relictis habenis gulae, somno libidinique indulgebant, adeo ut nonnulli ex iis in mulierum gregibus consenescentes raro aut viderent viros aut a viris viderentur; ita fiebat ut regna ad alias atque alias nationes transferrentur.

14     Hanc igitur eversi Romani imperii causam, qui vel ignorant vel dissimulant, temporibus Christianis assignant. Quod quidem tantum abest ut verum sit, ut dicere audeam Christianos, quominus

domestic affairs violence succeeded justice and lust and luxury re-
placed temperance, the high standing and authority of the empire
began little by little to decline and fall into ruin. For when it began
to rule with arrogance, cruelty and avarice, so that the provinces
were not kept safe and ruled by their magistrates but plundered
and robbed, and no account was taken of subjects or allies, that
holiest and most just of empires on earth was changed into the
worst and most savage of tyrannies. Foreign nations, which before
had venerated the majesty of the Roman name, partly through
contempt, partly through hatred of their arrogant and rapacious
rule, by common consent rose up to put out the fire consuming
them all and to erase the Roman name. And so much did they
burn with hatred against them that, not content with having
thrown off the yoke from their necks, they devastated Rome and
all of Italy more than once with fire and sword, their rage consuming not only men but buildings too. Thus that finest and largest of
empires, acquired with such effort and industry over so long a period of time, fell in a moment's time and was wiped out owing to
the fault of its governors. For my part, I believe this happened
through the most certain judgment of God: that the nations they
condemned and called barbarous were precisely the ones who subdued and destroyed them. Thus it was sloth and luxury and other
foul vices that ruined the Roman empire. The same had happened
before to the Assyrians, Medes, Persians and Greeks. For their
kings felt secure in their states and let everything be done by their
ministers, whilst they themselves, abandoning the reins, indulged
themselves in gluttony, sloth and lust—so much so that some of
them grew old amid flocks of women and rarely saw a male or
were seen by men. Thus it transpired that their kingdoms were
passed on to this or that other nation.

Hence those who do not know, or pretend not to know, this    14
cause for the fall of the Roman Empire impute its fall to the
Christian period. This is so far from being true that I dare say the

29

id imperium citius everteretur, magna ex parte causam extitisse.
Cui rei argumento est quod exterae nationes, cum urbem diripe-
rent, illis dumtaxat qui in sacras Christianorum aedes confugissent
(quod violari eas nefas esse ducerent) abstinebant.

15    Everso igitur imperio artes quoque et disciplinae, quae illo flo-
rente viguerant, interiere; exterae enim nationes partim odio gentis, partim rerum ipsarum ignorantia, monumenta omnia ferro
ignique vastabant. Qui vero postea rerum potiti sunt, cum neque a
natura illis artibus essent inbuti neque haberent iam viros in eo genere praestantes a quibus institui possent, defunctis prioribus
neque aliis in eorum locum succedentibus, nullum illis studiis honorem habebant. Ita paulatim eae artes ac disciplinae in quibus
Graeci Romanique plurimum insudaverant, temporum ac principum culpa periere.

16    Extincto igitur maximo illo pulcherrimoque imperio, multa regna sive, ut rectius loquar, multae tyrannides exortae sunt; singulae enim nationes atque adeo singulae civitates, sive libertatis
sive imperii cupiditate adductae, singulos sibi reges sive tyrannos
constituere;[9] paucae admodum se in libertatem vendicantes formam reipublicae retinuere. Crescente deinde paulatim ambitione
atque avaritia, cum ii qui rerum potiebantur in dies magis dubita-
rent ne ea quae ipsi occupassent quoquo modo amitterent, satis
gloriae se adeptos rati si ea quae habebant retinerent, contenti suo,
alieno abstinebant. Idem cum omnibus fere accideret, unum[10]
quasi corpus in multa membra disiectum[11] amplius coire non potuit; ita neque Romae neque alibi simile Romano imperium resur-
rexit.

Christians were in great part the cause of its continued existence, not a reason why it fell more rapidly. Proof of this is the fact that foreign nations, when they pillaged the city, spared only those who had taken refuge in the holy places of the Christians, which the pillagers believed it would be sacrilegious to violate.[26]

Thus when the empire fell, the arts and disciplines too that had flourished when it was in its prime died out, for the foreign nations, partly though race hatred, partly from their ignorance of those things, destroyed all the records of the arts and disciplines with fire and sword. Those who afterwards came to power did not honor these pursuits at all, having no natural bent for those arts and having by that time no notable men in that kind of pursuit who could educate them, as there was no one to take the place of the earlier teachers when they died. Thus the arts and disciplines to which the Greeks and Romans had devoted so much sweat gradually died out through the fault of the times and the fault of princes. 15

So when that greatest and finest of empires had died out, many kingdoms or (to speak more correctly) many tyrannies arose; for each individual nation, even individual cities, induced by a longing for liberty or for empire, set up individual tyrant kings over themselves; a very few laid claim to liberty for themselves and kept a republican constitution. Then, as ambition and avarice grew little by little, since those who were in power gradually came to harbor doubts whether they might in some way lose the lands they had occupied, they considered that they had won sufficient glory if they held on to what they had; and resting content with their own property, they spared that of others. Since practically the same thing happened to them all, the single body, as though torn apart into many members, could no longer hold together. Thus an empire similar to the Roman empire did not rise again either at Rome or in another place. 16

17    Huc accessit quod disciplina militaris, qua maxima imperia comparantur, non apud exteras nationes tantum sed in Italia quoque, magna ex parte vel amissa vel immutata est. Nam neque bellica illa virtus, quae disciplina et exercitatione perficitur, in militibus usquam est, neque, si qua est, potest exerceri. Ubi enim sunt rudimenta illa militaria quibus Graeci Romanique milites instituebantur? Illi enim nobilissimos pueros in agris plerumque et in alienis domibus magna inediae, algoris laborumque omnium patientia nutriebant; nos eos in magna rerum omnium affluentia luxuriaque educamus. Illorum pedites in itinere non solum sua arma, gladium, scutum, astam, galeam quae ipsi tamquam corporis membra in oneribus non computabant, sed vallum quoque et quindecim aut viginti dierum commeatum et si quid praeterea ad usum suum vellent portare consueverunt; nostri ne arma quidem sua omnia prae inertia ac desidia portare consueverunt. Illi vero militares exercitationes, quae non modo in castris apud exercitum, sed Romae quoque in Campo Martio, ut tirones erudirentur, assidue fiebant; hodie nullae omnino conspiciuntur. Veteres nobilissimum quemque ab ineunte aetate bellicis artibus summo studio erudiendum curabant; nos, tamquam militare turpe et ignominiosum sit, dum pax est, aut avaritiae aut ambitioni aut luxuriae indulgemus; cum bella urgent, aut rusticos ab agris ad militiam evocamus aut mercennarium militem ducemque conducimus, identidem dictitantes stultum esse nos periculis mortique exponere, cum exiguo stipendio possimus otium vitamque redimere et, quo turpius aut periculosius esse nihil potest, duces quibus nostra bella, nostra imperia, immo nostram dignitatem omnem salutemque committamus, aere mercamur, fidosque illos nobis credimus esse posse, quorum operam in auctione positam licitamur, aut existimamus eos bella sibi commissa celeriter diligenterque confecturos, quibus maxime expediat quam diutissime bella durare.

Moreover, the military discipline by which great empires are
created was in great part lost or transformed, not only among
foreign peoples but in Italy too. For the warlike virtue which
is perfected through discipline and exercise is no longer found
among soldiers, nor, if there is any, can it be practiced. For where
is the basic military training that the Greek and Roman soldiers
were taught? They indeed used to bring up the most noble boys,
in the fields for the most part and in the homes of foreigners,
to give them great endurance of hunger, cold and physical labor;
we educate our noble youths amid great affluence and luxury.
Their infantry used to carry on the march not only their arms,
sword, shield, spear and helmet — which they themselves didn't
count as burdens, being like parts of their bodies — but also stakes
for their defense-works and rations for fifteen or twenty days,
along with anything else they wanted for their use. Our infantry is
not even used to carrying its own arms out of sloth or laziness.
The Romans practiced military exercises tirelessly, not only in the
camps but also at Rome on the Field of Mars, in order to train recruits; today we see nothing of all that. The ancients took care to
train zealously each nobleman in the arts of war from his earliest
years; we wallow in greed, ambition or luxury in peacetime as
though to make war were something shameful or ignominious.
When war comes down on us we either call country folk from the
fields to military service or hire mercenary soldiers and a captain,
declaring all the while that it's foolish for us to expose ourselves to
peril and death when for a small wage we can assure our life and
leisure. Most shameful and most dangerous of all, we hire for
money the captains to whom we entrust our wars, our empires
and indeed our security and standing in the world, and we believe
that men can be faithful to us whose services we bid for at auction,
and imagine that they will execute the wars committed to them
swiftly and diligently, when it's more to their advantage for wars to
last as long as possible.

18     Quo vero pacto militaris virtus, etiam si maxima sit, in acie se
ostendere aut exercere potest, cum ignavissimus quisque tormentis
iis quae nuper excogitata sunt fortissimum plerumque eminus di-
micantem conficiat? Equites autem gravissimis armis contecti,
immo ferreis laminis omni ex parte obducti, ut ab hostium ictibus
laedi facile non possunt, ita ipsi quoque laedere alios sane ne-
queunt; ut non insulse quidam iocatus sit qui, cum se optime
omni ex parte armari munirique iussisset interrogassetque an posset usquam ab hoste vulnerari, amicis eum nusquam posse respon-
dentibus, 'Neque ego,' inquit, 'medius fidius hostem possum,' satis
ostendens id armaturae genus inutile omnino ad dimicandum esse.
Iam vero neque in castris, neque in itinere, neque in acie veterum
ordo retinetur; acies ipsae neque eodem modo instruuntur, neque
eandem pugnandi rationem habent. Quae quidem omnia cum
maxime immutata sint longissimeque ab optima illa veterum ratione discesserint, quid mirum est, si vincendi quoque et propa-
gandi imperii ratio immutata est? Causis enim mutatis, effectus
quoque ipsos mutari necesse est.

19     IOANNES. Fitne hoc, pater, apud omnes aeque nationes?
MATTHAEUS. Apud omnes quidem, sed in Italia maxime, quae
parens olim et magistra disciplinae militaris habebatur. Turcae
quidem et ab ineunte aetate armis assuescunt et disciplinam militarem aliqua ex parte observant et armis utuntur levioribus, proptereaque agiliores sunt, ita tamen ut ad excursiones quam ad pugnam aptiores habeantur; eorum vero imperium Ottomannus rex,
huius pater, ut vides, longe lateque propagavit; pater quidem meus
militarem disciplinam suo in exercitu et maxime correxit et severissime retinendam curavit; proptereaque adversus Turcas, ut audivisti, res clarissimas gessit illumque ipsum Ottomannum saepius
profligavit; ego quid in ea re effecerim aliorum iudicio relinquo:

Indeed, how can even the greatest military virtue show itself or   18
be effectual in the line of battle when the lowest knave can generally finish off from a distance the bravest fighter with those ma-
chines of war that have lately been invented? Knights are protected with the heaviest of armor, indeed covered entirely with
iron plates, so that they can't easily be harmed by enemy blows, with
the result that they themselves can't harm anyone either. There's a
rather amusing joke about a man who had ordered that he be
completely armored in the best fashion and inquired whether there
was any way he could be wounded by an enemy. When his friends
answered that he couldn't, he replied, "And so help me God I
couldn't harm an enemy, either!" — which shows well enough that
this kind of armor is entirely useless in combat. Nowadays the
methods of the ancients are followed neither in camp, on the
march or in the line of battle, nor is the line of battle itself drawn
up in the same way, nor is the same method of fighting used. Since
all this has greatly changed and has abandoned as far as possible
that best of methods the ancients used, is it any wonder that the
method of conquering and extending empires has changed as well?
For when causes change, effects must necessarily change too.

JANOS.  Is this the case, father, for all nations alike?   19

MATTIAS.  Yes, all, but most of all in Italy, which was once ac-
counted the parent and teacher of military discipline. The Turks,
to be sure, are accustomed to arms from their earliest years and
practice one part of the science of war, using lighter arms, and on
this account they are more swift and energetic, but in such a way
that they are considered more suited to raiding than to pitched
battle. Yet the Ottoman king, the father of the present one, has
extended their empire far and wide, as you see. Indeed, my father
reformed greatly military discipline in his army and saw to it that
it was kept up with the utmost severity, and on this account, as
you have heard, he performed the most famous deeds and often
put that very Ottoman to flight.[27] What I have accomplished in

35

plurimum certe ut efficerem laboravi multumque in ea re operae industriaeque consumpsi. Haec igitur disciplinae militaris sive immutatio sive amissio facit ut nemo longius queat imperii fines propagare.

20    Illud vero, de quo paulo ante dicebam, gloriae studium tanti ad eam rem momenti est, ut vel solum ad res omnes gerendas satis esse possit. Hoc enim intrepidos in periculis, in laboribus promptos, in omni re alacres et patientes reddit; hoc omnes alias cupiditates expellit et miro quodam rerum gerendarum ardore animos nostros inflammat, ita ut audeam dicere, hanc unam fuisse veteribus tantarum rerum gerendarum causam; artes vero bellicas huius tamquam instrumenta quaedam ministrasque fuisse.

21    Atque haec quidem gloriae cupiditas, quantum video, tota in pecuniae cupiditatem abiit. Pleraeque enim Italiae civitates, omissis bellicis artibus, totas se mercaturae et quaestui dedidere. Urbs quidem Roma, omni bellica laude amissa, tota in sacerdotum otio atque ambitione versatur; cives, si qui in ea sunt, qui pauci sunt, pecuariam exercent. Ferdinandus rex, socer meus, magni animi atque ingenii princeps, otium a domesticis hostibus numquam habuit; ceteri extra Italiam reges, suo contenti, aliena non appetunt. De nobis qui regnum novum accepimus nihil dico. Dedi tamen operam ut, id quod acceperam, non modo a multiplici hoste conservarem, sed aliqua etiam ex parte augerem; adieci enim ei, ut scis, ultra Danubium quidem ferocissimos Germaniae populos, quos Moravos, Slesos Bohaemosque hodie appellamus, citra Danubium vero Viennam, superioris Pannoniae, quae nunc Austria dicitur, metropolim, provinciamque eam fere totam in potestatem redegi. Sed res a nobis gestas malo te ab aliis quam a nobis audire. Illud[12] tibi ingenue fatebor, me ad eas res gerendas studio magis gloriae quam ulla imperii cupiditate esse adductum. Quod si

this regard I leave to the judgment of others; certainly I have worked very hard for what I have achieved and have spent much effort and industry on it. Thus the transformation or loss of military discipline has had the result that no one can expand the borders of empire any longer.

But what I was saying just now about thirst for glory is of great importance in this regard, as even by itself it can suffice to carry out all deeds. This desire makes men fearless in peril, ready to undertake labors, keen and uncomplaining in every undertaking; this passion casts out all other desires and inflames our spirits with a marvelous ardor to perform great deeds, so that I dare say this was the single reason why the ancients performed their famous exploits, while the arts of war were merely its instruments and ministers. 20

This desire for glory, as far as I can see, has been completely eclipsed by the desire for money. Most of the Italian cities have abandoned the arts of war and have devoted themselves entirely to trade and gain. The city of Rome, indeed, has lost all reputation for warlike spirit and is wholly taken up with the activities of idle and ambitious priests; the citizens they do have are few and spend their time grazing cattle. King Ferdinand, my father-in-law, a prince of high spirit and intelligence, has never had any peace from domestic enemies, and the other kings outside Italy are content with what they have, and do not desire the lands of others. I say nothing of myself and the new kingdom I received. But I have taken pains not only to preserve what I received against multiple enemies, but also to increase it to some extent. I added to it, as you know, north of the Danube, the fierce peoples of Germany which today we call the Moravians, Silesians and Bohemians; south of the Danube, I brought almost entirely under my power Vienna, the capital of Upper Pannonia, now called Austria, and its province. But I'd rather you hear about my deeds from others and not from me. I confess to you frankly that it was the thirst for glory, rather than any desire for empire, that motivated me. If we 21

gloriae quam pecuniae cupidiores essemus, magna nobis imperia comparare possemus.

22    Atque ea quidem quibus imperia foris parantur, quomodo sese habeant, satis, ut opinor, intellegis. Domesticae vero virtutes, quibus imperia et parari et retineri diximus, nihilo magis quam militares florent atque haud scio an etiam minus. Quis est enim qui non sui commodi studiosior sit quam alieni? Quis est iam qui dominandi gratia divina et humana iura pervertere sibi licere non putet? Quis, ut suas voluptates expleat, alienis non dico iam opibus, sed uxoribus quoque et liberis parcit? Sed non libet hac de re ulterius conqueri, ne eos quos nolo videar offendere; illud vere possum de nobis omnibus affirmare, nostra culpa accidere ut non modo imperia a maioribus accepta non augeamus, sed ne omnes quidem ea servemus. Quod, si iis quas dixi artibus domi forisque uteremur, profecto neque saecula neque imperia neque virtutes neque artes priscorum magnopere desideraremus.

Habes nostram de hac universa ratione sententiam, nisi forte quid aliud desideras.

23    IOANNES. Satis fecisti tu quidem mihi, pater, in ea re cumulatissime; universam enim imperiorum rationem ita copiose ornateque explicasti, ut nihil ulterius desiderari queat. Sed, quantum intellego, culpam hanc omnem in reges contulisti.

MATTHAEUS. Utinam, fili, utinam non id verissime fieret! Profecto aliquod imperium, quod nunc nullum est, haberemus.

IOANNES. Nonne igitur multo satius esset, pater, si omnes sub una aliqua republica viveremus?

MATTHAEUS. An nescis apologum illum qui apud Aesopum est, solem quondam uxorem ducere statuisse? Qua re commotam, terram apud Iovem esse conquestam, se unico sole ita comburi ut resistere vix posset. Quid si alii ex eo soles nascerentur? Quo tan-

want glory more than wealth we can acquire great empires for ourselves.

I think you already understand the parlous condition of those 22
virtues in foreign affairs by which empires are acquired. But the
domestic virtues by which, as we said, empires are acquired and
preserved are in no better state, possibly even in a worse one. For
who is there who is not more zealous for his own advantage than
for another's? Who is there who for the sake of domination does
not think he is allowed to twist all laws, human and divine? Who
is there who spares another man's wife and children, let alone his
property, to slake his lust for pleasure? But I don't want to continue this line of complaint lest I seem to be offending persons I
don't want to offend. I can truly state, however, concerning us
all [in modern times], that it's our fault if we don't increase the
empire we've received from others or if some of us can't even
keep what we have. But if we were to follow the patterns of behavior I've spoken of at home and abroad, we should certainly
not feel regret for bygone ages or past empires and virtues and
arts.

You have now my views on this whole subject, unless perhaps
you wish for something further.

JANOS. You have indeed satisfied me on this matter, father, and 23
abundantly so. You've laid out your whole explanation of empires
with such detail and elegance that nothing more could be desired.
But if I understand you, you've put all the blame on kings.

MATTIAS. Would that that were not the utter truth, son! Then
we might have an empire, because now we have none.

JANOS. Wouldn't it be much better, father, if we all lived under a
single republic?

MATTIAS. Don't you know the tale in Aesop about the Sun who
once decided to marry? The Earth complained about it to Jove,
saying that it could scarcely stand up to being burned by a single
sun. What would happen if other suns should be born to him?

dem pacto tantis ardoribus resistendum esset? Ita, si singuli per se reges mortalibus noxii et infesti sunt, quid coniunctos et multiplicatos facturos existimas?

IOANNES. At ego de bene instituta republica loquor.

MATTHAEUS Utrum tandem in optima republica an in optimo regno malles vivere?

24 IOANNES. Gaudeo quidem, pater, me rege natum esse et eo potissimum rege quem nostra aetas praestantissimum et prope unicum habet, cui quidem me aliquando successurum spero, quod ut quam tardissime te superstite fiat exopto! Tamen, cum ea quae de reipublicae statu vel audivi vel legi mecum reputo, profecto si rege natus et regi successurus non essem, in optima aliqua republica vellem vivere.

MATTHAEUS Qua de causa?

IOANNES. Quia multo melior mihi videtur multoque salubrior reipublicae forma quam regni.

MATTHAEUS Cur ita iudicas?

IOANNES. Quia omnia melius a pluribus quam ab uno administrantur.

MATTHAEUS. Etiam ne caelum ipsum?

IOANNES. Istud quidem non audeo dicere. Sed omittamus, obsecro, caelestia quae, ut sunt a nobis remotissima, ita dissimillimam nostris rationem habent. De nostris, hoc est terrestribus, disputemus, quae ut proxima nobis ita etiam simillima sunt; haec praeterea nobis longe sunt quam illa notiora. De his igitur, obsecro, pater, disseramus; illa in praesentia omittamus.

25 MATTHAEUS. Ita faciam. Cedo igitur: exercitus ab unone imperatore melius an a pluribus regitur?

IOANNES. Ab uno utique existimo.

MATTHAEUS. Quid navis? Ab unone rectore melius an a pluribus gubernatur?

How ever could it stand up to such intense heat then?[28] Thus, if individual kings are in themselves harmful and hostile to mortals, what do you think would happen if they are multiplied and combined?

JANOS. But I meant a well-ordered republic.

MATTIAS. Would you rather live in an excellent republic or an excellent kingdom?

JANOS. I truly rejoice, father, that I have been born to a king and especially to that king whom our age regards as most outstanding and almost peerless, and I hope I shall succeed you one day — and may your long life make that day be as far off as possible! Nevertheless, when I mull over what I have heard or read about the republican form of government, I wish, if I were not born to a king and going to succeed a king, that I lived in some fine republic.

MATTIAS. Why?

JANOS. Because the republican constitution seems to me much better and healthier than the royal.

MATTIAS. What makes you think that?

JANOS. Because everything is better governed by many than by one.

MATTIAS. Even heaven itself?

JANOS. I don't dare say that. But let's leave heavenly things aside. Things so remote from ourselves must have very different principles from our own. Let us speak of our own terrestrial affairs, which being closest to us are most similar to us, and far more knowable to us besides. Let us then speak of these things, please, father, and pass over heavenly things for now.

MATTIAS. Let it be so. I'll proceed then: is an army better ruled by one general or by many?

JANOS. Doubtless by one general, I suppose.

MATTIAS. What about a ship? Is it better steered by one steersman or many?

IOANNES. Non audeo a pluribus dicere, sed video iam quo me ducas, et pudet me ita cito de sententia esse deiectum. Proinde, nisi molestum est, pater, maiorem in modum rogo te, quando otiosi sumus et tu meae eruditionis cupidissimus es, ut hac de re latius disseras quaestionemque hanc universam discutias, ut sciam utrum in republica an in regno praestet vivere. Nihil enim mihi neque utilius neque gratius hoc tempore possem audire.

26 MATTHAEUS. Utilissima profecto res est et tua aetate ac cognitione dignissima, neque ego vel in hac vel in alia re tibi difficilem praebere me volo. Sed ea quae remissius ab uno perpetua oratione dicuntur minus movent et, quasi languidius animis immissa minus inhaerent; quae vero ad utramque partem Socratico more interrogando respondendoque disputantur, adhibitis argumentationum aculeis, efficaciora ac dilucidiora fiunt et tamquam omni dubitatione sublata acrius ac facilius animis infiguntur. Proinde ea quae tibi in hanc sententiam succurrunt, in medium affer; ego ea, ut mihi videbitur, vel comprobabo vel refellam meamque tibi sententiam exponam.

27 IOANNES. Neque mihi sane multa pro ea re in mentem veniunt (quippe qui rempublicam numquam viderim), neque ea quae veniunt apud te explicare aut defendere satis scio. Sed patronum mihi apud te, si placet, advocabo aliquem in republica versatum et illarum rerum peritum; et video peropportune hic astantem e tuorum numero quem vocare possimus, Dominicum Iunium equitem florentinum; qui, cum in optima, ut existimo, republica natus sit et in ea locum non postremum teneat, in tuo vero regno diu vixerit; poterit utraque de re tibi optime respondere.

28 MATTHAEUS. Age ut libet; hos enim dies condonavi tibi. Isto vero homine nemo est quem ego mihi ad respondendum dari ma-

JANOS. I don't dare say "by many," but I see where you're leading me, and I'm ashamed to be thrown so quickly off my opinion. Accordingly, if you wouldn't mind, father, I would earnestly entreat you, since we are at leisure and you are most eager for me to be educated, to talk some more about this subject and analyze the whole question, so I may learn whether it's preferable to live in a republic or a kingdom. There's nothing I could hear that would be more useful for me or more welcome at this time.

MATTIAS. The subject is extremely useful to be sure, and perfectly suited to your age and understanding, and for my part I don't wish to make trouble for you in this or any other matter. Opinions that are dealt with casually, however, in continuous speech are less effective and are slower to fix themselves in the mind. But views that are argued on both sides in the Socratic manner, by questioning and response, become more efficacious and clearer by using the barbs of argumentation, and are fixed more sharply and easily in the mind by having all doubt taken away. Accordingly, bring into the open the considerations which are supporting you in your opinion, and I shall endorse them or refute them, as seems good to me, and tell you my opinion. 26

JANOS. Really, there aren't many arguments that come to mind on behalf of my view (after all, I've never seen a republic), and I don't know how to explain and defend in your presence the arguments I do have. But, if you like, I'll summon an advocate for myself before you, someone with experience and knowledge of republics. By good fortune I see a man from your entourage standing here whom we can call on, Domenico Giugni, the Florentine knight. Since he was born in what I think an excellent republic and holds no lowly place within it, but has lived in your kingdom for a long time, he will be able to respond to you well concerning both forms of government. 27

MATTIAS. Let it be as you wish, for I've set aside these days for you, and there is no man whom I should better like to be given the 28

gis velim. Est enim non sane magnae doctrinae, sed magni ingenii magnaeque experientiae, quae duo, cum uni cuipiam contigere, magnae doctrinae vicem obtinent; et, ut tu dixisti, est in republica pariter regnoque versatus. Proinde hominem ad nos, si placet, voca.

IOANNES. Heus, Dominice, accede propius.

DOMINICUS. Salve rex, regum omnium praestantissime, et tu, fili tanto patre dignissime.

IOANNES. Et tu, Dominice optime, salvus sis.

29 MATTHAEUS. Nihil mihi antiquius aut iucundius est quam ut hunc filium, in quo mea omnis et spes et cogitatio sita est, optimis praeceptis institutisque erudiam; gaudeoque cum ex me aliquid et sua professione et nostra auctoritate dignum quaerit. Hodie itaque, cum multa ex me de imperiorum diminutione et administratione quaesisset, incidimus in eum sermonem ut de reipublicae et regni comparatione disputaremus. Quoniam autem te et in optima re-publica educatum et in nostro regno diu versatum esse[13] sciebamus, placuit te advocare, ut quid tu de utraque re sentires audire-mus.

30 DOMINICUS. Ego, rex, istarum rerum neque doctrinam aut ex-perientiam ullam habeo (quippe qui litteris operam nullam dede-rim) neque, etiam si haberem, obsistere sapientiae tuae possem. A philosophis potius ista petenda sunt, qui subtilius et accuratius illa conquirunt, suntque de ea re permulta, ut audio, et a Graecis et a nostris elegantissime et copiosissime scripta volumina, quae ego neque legi umquam neque, etiam si legissem, satis intellexissem.

31 MATTHAEUS. Quae a philosophis de his rebus dicuntur, ea nos et alias legimus et, cum otium dabitur, legemus. Sed illa neque omni tempore quaeri possunt, neque ab omnibus fortasse proban-tur. Ego enim exercitatum civem de republica, regem de regno multo melius quam philosophum disputare posse existimo; in qui-bus enim rebus diutissime quis versatus est, eas optime et intelle-

task of responding to me than this man. He is, to be sure, not a man of great learning, but he has great intelligence and experience, and when these two qualities occur in one man they can take the place of great learning. And, as you've said, he is equally at home in republics and kingdoms. So if you like, call the man over to us.

JANOS. Hello, Domenico, come over here.

DOMENICO. Good day to you, king, best of all kings, and you, most worthy son of a great father!

JANOS. Good day to you too, my excellent Domenico.

MATTIAS. There is nothing more important or more pleasant for  29
me than to educate this son of mine, in whom is all my hope and my solicitude, in the best precepts and practices, and I rejoice when he asks something of me that befits his calling and my authority. So today he was asking me many questions about the decline and the governing of empires, and we fell to debating the comparative merits of republics and kingdoms. Since we knew you were brought up in an excellent republic and have spent much time in our kingdom, we decided to call you over to hear what you think about the two forms of government.

DOMENICO. For my part, king, I have no learning or experience  30
in this subject — I have never devoted any effort to literature — and even if I did, I could not withstand your wisdom. On this subject you should seek out philosophers who have investigated the matter with more subtlety and care. The Greeks and our Latin philosophers have written a great many books on this subject, I hear, extremely elegant and detailed, which I've never read and couldn't understand even if I had read them.

MATTIAS. What the philosophers say on this subject we have  31
read on other occasions and shall read when we have the leisure. Such things cannot be investigated all the time, nor perhaps are they to everyone's taste. For my part, I reckon an experienced citizen can dispute much better about a republic, and a king about a kingdom, than a philosopher can. Someone who has had very long

gere et iudicare debet, quanquam Plato beatissimas fore respublicas existimabat si aut eas[14] philosophi regerent aut rectores
philosopharentur. Hoc itaque tempore, cum otiosi simus neque
philosophos habeamus, placet ex te potissimum audire quid sentias, eoque magis quod filius dixit se, si privatus esset, in republica
potius quam in regno esse victurum isque te sibi patronum defensoremque ascivit.

IOANNES. Ego quidem et ita plane me sentire profiteor et Dominicum mihi optime suffragaturum spero.

32  DOMINICUS. Neque tibi, rex, tam honestam rem postulanti repugnare audeo,[15] praesertim cum hic Ioannes me sibi socium et, ut
ipse dicit, defensorem asciverit. Neque volo ulla in re tuae sententiae adversari,[16] neque, etiam si velim, possim; tamen, quia imperanti tibi quicquam denegare non debeo, praesertim cum habeam hunc tantum meae disputationis auctorem, meam tibi hac
de re sententiam paucis explicabo, ea tamen conditione, ut quid
ego sentiam, non quid vobis sentiendum sit, me dicere existimetis.
Morem enim vobis gero, non leges praescribo; libero autem homini liberum quoque iudicium esse debet. Verumenimvero abs te,
rex, in primis quaeso et peto ut, si qua in re abs te dissensero aut
tibi veri inveniendi gratia repugnavero, mihi pro tua consuetudine
clementer ignoscas meaque dicta in bonam partem accipias. Verum enim inveniri nisi diversis omni ex parte rationibus allatis
confutatisque non potest.

33  MATTHAEUS. Immo vero istud maxime cupimus atque ista potissimum de causa te vocavimus, ut non solum quid sentires, sed
etiam cur ita sentires nobis declarares, tuamque sententiam, quibus posses modis, defenderes nostramque confutares. Verum enim
invenire volumus, non de dignitate contendimus. Age igitur, si
utrique nostrum rem gratam facere cupis, libere fateare quid sentias, uter tandem reipublicae an regni status tibi potior ac salubrior
esse videatur.

experience of these matters ought to understand and judge them best of all, although Plato reckoned that republics would be most blessed if either philosophers ruled or rulers philosophized.[29] So at this moment, since we are at leisure and have no philosophers here, we would like particularly to hear what you think — the more so as my son says that if he were deprived of the succession, he would rather live in a republic than a kingdom, and he has designated you as his advocate and defender.

JANOS. I do avow that this is absolutely my view and I hope that Domenico will give me his best support.

DOMENICO. I don't dare resist you, king, when you make so honorable a request, especially as János here has designated me his ally and, as he says, his defender. I don't want to oppose your views in any matter, nor could I, even if I would; nevertheless, since I ought not to refuse any command of yours, especially as I have this fine young man to sanction and support my argument, I shall briefly explain my views to you on this matter — with this condition, however, that you understand I am saying what I think and not what you should think. I am humoring you, not laying down laws; yet a free man's judgment ought to be free too. But first, king, I ask you, please, if I disagree with you on any matter or contradict you in the interests of finding the truth, you will forgive me with your customary clemency and take what I have said in good part. For the truth cannot be found unless differing arguments on all sides are adduced and refuted.

MATTIAS. That indeed is what we want most of all, and we have summoned you precisely for this purpose: to state not only what you think, but why you think it, and to defend your opinion in any way you can and to refute ours. We want to find the truth, not compete for personal status. Come then, if you want to do something that will please us both, tell us freely what you think: which form of government, republic or kingdom, seems to you better and healthier?

47

34 DOMINICUS. Ego quidem rempublicam regno anteponendam esse semper existimavi.

MATTHAEUS. Cur ita?

DOMINICUS. Multis ac magnis de causis. Sed volo tibi tres potissimum commemorare, quae me maxime,[17] ut ita credam, adducunt.

MATTHAEUS. Dic, obsecro, nunc istas; postea, si otium erit, dices etiam alias.

35 DOMINICUS. Ante omnia, maior est in republica quam in regno libertas; immo, si verum fateri volumus, ibi tota, hic nulla. Nos enim nemini subiicimur, nemini paremus, immo ipsi aliis imperamus; tui cives omnes tibi parent, tibi subiecti sunt, tuum imperium perferunt. Deinde maior est iustitiae in republica quam in regno observatio; nam si leges requiras, nos eas et meliores habemus et sanctius observamus; si commercia et cetera humanae societatis iura consideres, nos ea maxime, immo potius soli et retinemus et colimus. Si civium inter se aequalitatem similitudinemque intuearis, ea apud nos potissimum viget ac floret. Si praemia poenasque inspicias, nos unicuique quod debetur in utramque partem melius iustiusque persolvimus; ita ut artes ac disciplinae omnes multo magis apud nos quam in regno aliquo floreant.[18] Postremo melius ac stabilius a pluribus quam ab uno omnia gubernari certum est. Plures enim et maiorem in gubernando vim atque industriam habent et difficilius in deteriorem partem convertuntur et diutius, quod semel administrandum suscepere, numquam intermissa administratione conservant.

36 His potissimum de causis ego rempublicam regno praeferendam puto. Quas quidem magis ut tibi ac tuo filio morem gererem et te contra disserentem audirem quam ut tibi adversarer exposui. Quod si eas probabis, iuvabit me id sensisse quod tuae sapientiae consentaneum videatur, meque huius disputationis fructum non

DOMENICO. For my part I've always reckoned that a republic  34
should be preferred to a kingdom.

MATTIAS. Why so?

DOMENICO. For many reasons. But I would like to mention the
three in particular which influence me the most, as I believe.

MATTIAS. Please tell us what these are now. Later, if we have the
leisure, you can tell us other reasons too.

DOMENICO. First of all, there is greater liberty in a republic than  35
in a kingdom; or rather, to tell the truth, there is complete liberty
in a republic and none in a kingdom. For we are subject to no one
and obey no one; indeed, we ourselves command others. Your citizens all obey you, are subject to you, and submit to your command. Secondly there is greater respect for justice in republics
than in kingdoms. If you ask about laws, we have better ones and
observe them with greater devotion; if you consider commercial
relations and other relations of justice in human society, we keep
them and foster them the most — indeed, we are the only ones
who do so. If you look at the equality and similarity of citizens to
each other, this flourishes with the most vigor among us. If you
look at rewards and punishments, we pay to each person what he
is due in both respects better and more justly, and as a result the
arts and disciplines all flourish much more with us than in kingdoms. Finally, it is certain that all things are governed better and
with greater stability by many persons than by one. For many persons have greater force and energy in governing and are turned
astray with greater difficulty and preserve policies longer, once begun, without breaks in their administration.[30]

It is for these reasons in particular that I think republics are to  36
be preferred to kingdoms. I have set them out more to oblige you
and your son and to hear you speaking against them than to be
your opponent. If you endorse them, it will be a pleasure to have
views that are seen to agree with your wisdom, and I shall reckon
I've received no small recompense for taking part in this disputa-

mediocrem percepisse existimabo; sin tu[19] ab hac nostra opinione dissenties nostrasque rationes melioribus allatis confutaveris, ego in tuam sententiam non invitus concedam. Verum enim scire, non in mea sententia pertinax esse cupio.

37  MATTHAEUS. Gaudeo maiorem in modum te libere tuam sententiam explicasse et causas cur ita sentires adiecisse, ut verum investigare facilius possimus. Neque ego, qui rex sum, tibi accedere recusabo, si regni causam tutari non potero. Sed ut facilius quod quaerimus inveniamus, eas quas attulisti causas singillatim discutiamus;[20] ita verum ipsum citius, ut arbitror, dilucidiusque apparebit.

DOMENICUS. Age sane ut libet. Ego quidem tuae orationi subserviam.

38  IOANNES. Gaudeo profecto, pater, nos in hunc hodie sermonem incidisse et me potissimum esse huius disputationis auctorem, videoque mihi ex ea, in utramvis partem res cedat, fructum incredibilem proventurum. Nam si rempublicam meliorem esse constet, meam sententiam utriusque vestrum iudicio confirmabo; sin regnum anteponendum esse convenerit, me tanto errore liberatum esse gaudebo et regnum alacrius expectabo.

MATTHAEUS. Ita erit, fili; proinde ea quae dicemus attentius audi daque operam ut huius disputationis, quae tua causa suscepta est, sententias omnes memoriae commendes.

IOANNES. Ita faciam.

MATTHAEUS. Nos igitur, Dominice, ad rem nostram redeamus.

DOMINICUS. Redeamus.

39  MATTHAEUS. Rempublicam regno anteponis propterea quod libertas in ea, ut dicis, tota sit, in regno nulla.

DOMINICUS. Ita mihi sane videtur.

MATTHAEUS. Quaero igitur abs te primum quid tu libertatem appelles.

tion; but if you dissent from my views and refute my arguments with better ones, I shall quite willingly give way to your opinion. I want to know the truth, not stick stubbornly to my beliefs.

MATTIAS. I'm delighted that you have set out your views freely, 37 and have added the reasons why you hold them, so that we can investigate the truth more readily, nor shall I, king though I be, refuse to give in to you if I am not able to defend the cause of kingdoms. But in order to find what we are looking for more easily, let us discuss the reasons you've advanced one by one, for in this way the truth will reveal itself with greater speed and lucidity, I think.

DOMENICO. Do by all means; I for my part shall wait upon your speech.

JANOS. I am really happy, father, that we have fallen into this 38 discussion today and particularly that I am the begetter of the dispute. I can see that I shall glean extraordinary profit from it, whichever direction it takes. For if it becomes evident that the republic is better, I shall have my beliefs confirmed by the judgment of you both; if it turns out that kingdoms are to be preferred, I shall be happy to be freed of so great an error and shall await my reign with all the more enthusiasm.

MATTIAS. Let it be so, son. Listen carefully, then, to what we say and make sure you commit to memory all the opinions expressed in this disputation, which is being held for your sake.

JANOS. I shall do so.

MATTIAS. Let's return then, Domenico, to our subject.

DOMENICO. Let's.

MATTIAS. You prefer a republic to a kingdom because there is, 39 you say, complete liberty in it, but none in a kingdom.

DOMENICO. Yes, indeed; that is my opinion.

MATTIAS. Then I must first ask you what it is you call liberty.

DOMINICUS. Potestatem nimirum unicuique vivendi ut vult.

MATTHAEUS. Recte sentis; estne igitur apud vos ius unicuique vivendi ut vult?

DOMINICUS. Est sane.

MATTHAEUS. Potest ergo unusquisque impune hominem occidere, stuprare, spoliare, diripere, mentiri et ea quae nefaria ubique habentur flagitia committere?

DOMINICUS. Minime vero; immo multo haec omnia severius apud nos quam in regno aliquo puniuntur.

MATTHAEUS. Non potest igitur, ut video, unusquisque pro arbitrio vivere.

DOMINICUS. At ego de ratione communis vitae, non de flagitiis loquor. Licentia enim ista, non libertas appellatur.

40  MATTHAEUS. Age vero; de communi vita disputemus. Potestne unusquisque ita vestiri, ita convivari, ita exequias parare, ita nuptias celebrare, ita cetera quae ad communem vitam pertinent, facere ut vult?

DOMINICUS. Nequaquam. Habemus enim sumptuarias leges, quae omnium nobis rerum[21] modum praescribunt. Neque istud licere arbitramur, ne cives patrimonia incassum profundant.

MATTHAEUS. Iure an iniuria id faciatis non disputo. Illud disputo: vobis, ut vultis vivere, non licere.

DOMINICUS. Licet quidem, sed non in his rebus libertatem consistere arbitramur.

41  MATTHAEUS. In quibus igitur? In tributisne aut vectigalibus persolvendis?

DOMINICUS. In istis ipsis eam aliqua ex parte, sed non totam contineri putamus.

MATTHAEUS. Cedo igitur: cuiquamne tributa aut vectigalia ulla penditis?

DOMINICUS. Nulli omnino.

DOMENICO. Surely it's the power anyone has of doing what he wishes.[31]

MATTIAS. You're right. So you republicans all, then, have the right to live as you wish?

DOMENICO. Yes, indeed.

MATTIAS. Can any one of you then kill a man with impunity, rape, steal, plunder, lie and commit what are universally considered wicked crimes?

DOMENICO. Not at all. In fact, such things are all punished with much greater severity among us than in kingdoms.

MATTIAS. So you can't each one of you live as you like, I see.

DOMENICO. I was speaking about patterns of everyday life, not about crimes; the latter are called by the name "license," not liberty.

MATTIAS. Well, then, let's talk about everyday life. Can each one of you dress as you like, have banquets, hold funerals, celebrate marriages, and do the rest of the things pertaining to everyday life? 40

DOMENICO. By no means. We have sumptuary laws which prescribe limits to us in all things. We don't think it's right for citizens to squander their patrimonies uselessly.

MATTIAS. I'm not arguing about whether you are right or wrong to do this; I'm arguing that you are not allowed to live as you wish.

DOMENICO. We're allowed, but we don't believe that liberty consists in such matters.

MATTIAS. In which matters, then? In paying taxes and import duties? 41

DOMENICO. We think liberty consists partly in this, but not wholly.

MATTIAS. I'll go on then: do you pay taxes and import duties to anyone?

DOMENICO. To no one at all.

MATTHAEUS. Potestisne quaecunque vultis libere importare, exportare, mercari, possidere?

DOMINICUS. Non.

MATTHAEUS. Qua de causa?

DOMINICUS. Nobis ipsis vectigalia et quidem magna et sponte imponimus et libenter exsolvimus; aliter enim bella geri, publica opera restitui et respublica ipsa administrari conservarique non posset. Immo ob hoc ipsum nos maxime liberos appellamus, quod quae volumus nobis vectigalia et tributa imponimus. Vos vestris civibus non quae illi volunt, sed quae vos[22] vultis imponitis.

42 MATTHAEUS. De nobis postea viderimus; tu mihi hoc interea responde. Quid refert, vobisne an aliis tributa persolvatis, modo vos persolvere fateamini?

DOMINICUS. Immo permagni referre arbitror. Nobis enim sponte persolvimus, aliis inviti solveremus.

MATTHAEUS. Videamus utrum hoc quoque sponte faciatis. Quid, obsecro, dicitis 'sponte facere'?

DOMINICUS. Cum aliquid nulla vi cogente, sed sola nostra voluntate, ut agamus, adducimur. Quod quidem, cum in nobis situm sit et velle et nolle, pro arbitrio possumus.

MATTHAEUS. Licetne ergo vobis, si velitis, vectigalia non pendere?

DOMINICUS. Non licet quidem, si volumus rempublicam salvam esse, sed sponte nos ad hoc faciendum reipublicae gratia obligavimus.

MATTHAEUS. Obligati igitur ad id faciendum estis?

DOMINICUS. Sumus.

MATTHAEUS. Ergo, etiam si velitis, non potestis non pendere.

DOMINICUS. Possumus si nihil possideamus, nihil importemus, exportemus, mercemur.

43 MATTHAEUS. Poteras uno verbo dicere 'si cives non simus.'

DOMINICUS. Erimus quidem cives, sed magistratu aut beneficio reipublicae nullo perfruemur.

MATTIAS. You can import, export, trade and possess whatever you like, freely?

DOMENICO. No.

MATTIAS. Why is that?

DOMENICO. We impose import duties—and large ones—on ourselves of our own free will, and pay them willingly, for otherwise wars could not be waged, public works maintained and the republic itself administered and preserved. Indeed, this is the main reason we call ourselves free, because we impose on ourselves the duties and taxes we wish. You impose on your citizens not what they want, but what you want.

MATTIAS. We'll consider our practices later. In the meantime, tell me this: what does it matter whether you pay taxes to yourselves or to others, so long as you admit you pay them? 42

DOMENICO. I think it makes a huge difference. We pay ourselves of our own free will; we pay others unwillingly.

MATTIAS. Let's see whether you do the latter willingly too. Please, what do you mean by "acting of your own accord"?

DOMENICO. When we are led to do something with no one forcing us to, but by our own will alone. We can act as free agents when it rests with us to will or not will something.

MATTIAS. So you're allowed not to pay duties if you wish?

DOMENICO. We're not allowed if we want the republic to be secure.

MATTIAS. Are you bound then to do this?

DOMENICO. We are.

MATTIAS. Then, even if you want to, you can't not pay.

DOMENICO. We can if we have no possessions, import nothing, export nothing and trade in nothing.

MATTIAS. In a word, you can say: "if we are not citizens."[32] 43

DOMENICO. We shall still be citizens, but we'll enjoy no magistracy or privilege in the republic.

MATTHAEUS. Quid? Tu civem eum putas esse qui nullum in republica magistratum gerat, nulla eius beneficia sentiat? Ista quidem ratione nihilo magis erit civis indigena quam peregrinus. Sed esto: sit civis is qui civitatem tantum inhabitat. Nihilne is umquam in aerarium conferet?

DOMINICUS. Conferet quidem si civitatem incolat, sed admodum parum, atque hoc quidem in nostra republica evenit, in aliis nescio.

MATTHAEUS. Ergo, quantum intellego, apud vos immunis esse potest nemo.

DOMINICUS. Nemo.

MATTHAEUS. Quid si quis non solvat?

DOMINICUS. Aut cogetur aut eiicietur.

MATTHAEUS. Non estis ergo in hoc quoque, ut video, liberi, si cogi potestis, sed vobis ipsis et quidem dure graviterque servitis.

DOMINICUS. Non audeo dicere 'servimus.' Sed (quando tu me id[23] fateri coegisti) liberi inter nos a vectigalibus non sumus. Propterea autem nos liberos appellamus, quod externis, ut dixi, principibus nihil pendimus.

44  MATTHAEUS. Nostri vero cives ante omnia nihil in rebus ad usus vitae necessariis importandis exportandisque persolvunt. Liber est unicuique suarum rerum usus; deinde ordinaria quaedam nobis quotannis tributa, non sane magna, persolvunt, extra ordinem nihil omnino, atque hoc quidem non minus sponte quam vos conservandi sui gratia faciunt, immo etiam fortasse libentius. Iustis enim et ordinariis nobis vectigalibus persolutis, omnem nobis belli gerendi suique conservandi curam relinquunt; ipsi, metu omni et sollicitudine deposita, securam, quietam et liberam vitam agunt. Vobis contra, primum nulla vestrarum rerum uti, nullam omnino possidere, immo, ut verum fateamur, ne caelo quidem patrio frui sine vectigalibus fas est. Deinde, alia atque alia quottidie

MATTIAS. What? You consider that man a citizen who holds no magistracy in the republic and enjoys none of its privileges? By this reasoning a native will be no more a citizen than a foreigner is. But let that go; suppose a man to be a citizen merely by living in a city-state. Does he then never contribute anything to the treasury?

DOMENICO. He contributes if he lives in the city-state, but very little. This is what happens in our republic; I don't know about others.

MATTIAS. So if I understand you, no one is immune from taxation among you.

DOMENICO. No one.

MATTIAS. What if somebody doesn't pay?

DOMENICO. He's either compelled to pay or thrown out.

MATTIAS. So you are not free in this respect, too, I see, if you can be compelled; but you are subject to yourselves — and a hard and heavy subjection it is.

DOMENICO. I would not dare say "we are subject," but since you force me to admit it, we are not free among ourselves from duties; we call ourselves free because we don't pay anything to foreign princes, as I said.

MATTIAS. Well, our citizens, first of all, pay nothing to import 44 or export the necessities of life. Everyone is free in the use of his own property. After that, they pay ordinary taxes to us each year which are not very great, and nothing at all in extraordinary taxes, and they pay their taxes no less willingly than you do for the sake of self-preservation — indeed, perhaps more willingly. For having paid reasonable ordinary duties to us, they leave the whole task of waging war and defense to us, and having laid aside all fear and anxiety they live a secure, quiet and free life. For you, on the contrary, it is first of all unlawful to use any of your own property or to possess anything at all without payment of duties; indeed, to be frank, you can't enjoy the sky above you without duties. Then again, you keep having to pay, on a daily basis, ever more extraor-

extra ordinem tributa pensitatis. Postremo, numquam a reipublicae curis et sollicitudine quietem agitis. Et liberos vos audetis
appellare? Servitutis igitur genere a nostris aliquantulum differtis:
quia vobis mutuo servitis mutuoque imperatis, servitute certe ipsa
non differtis.

45  DOMINICUS. Servimus quidem mutuo nobis, ut dicis, rex, sed
servitutem illam, adhibita imperandi vicissitudine, aut non senti-
mus aut, id quod verisimilius est, libentius toleramus.

MATTHAEUS. Age vero; quando[24] in vectigalibus liberi non estis,
in qua tandem re estis?

DOMINICUS. In administratione reipublicae liberrimi certe sumus.

MATTHAEUS. Quo pacto?

46  DOMINICUS. Rogas? Magistratus nostros omnes ipsi creamus,
ipsi gerimus; civitatem et oppida imperio nostro subiecta ipsi administramus; senatum nostrum, hoc est liberum populi concilium,
quottidie cogimus; in eo de republica liberis sententiis disputa-
mus; eius consilio atque auctoritate bella suscipimus, percutimus
foedera, pacem componimus, leges sancimus, universam denique
rempublicam administramus. Nonne haec tibi videtur maxima et
verissima libertas? An ulla potest omnino maior excogitari?
Vestrae contra civitates omni consilio, omni iudicio, omni potestate atque administratione spoliatae, a vobis totae dependent, vestrum consilium auxiliumque expectant, omnique libertate amissa,
vestrum imperium qualecumque patiuntur; in servitute certe assidua degunt. Vos omnia per praetores et praefectos administratis,
quorum, qualis plerumque sit administratio, nolo dicere; illud dico
civitates vestras omnes multiplicem pati servitutem.

dinary levies. Finally, you can never live in quiet untroubled by the cares of the republic. And you dare call yourselves free? So you differ only minimally from us in the nature of your servitude, since, though mutually subject and mutually in command, you certainly don't differ as to the fact of servitude.

DOMENICO. We are indeed mutually subject to ourselves, as you 45 say, king, but either we are not sensible of that servitude because of the regular alternation or succession of rule, or (what seems likelier) we tolerate it more willingly.

MATTIAS. Come now, since you're not free with respect to taxes, in what respect, pray, *are* you free?

DOMENICO. We are surely extremely free in the administration of the republic.

MATTIAS. How so?

DOMENICO. What a question! We ourselves choose all our mag- 46 istrates and we ourselves fill those magistracies. We ourselves administer the city and the towns subject to our rule. Our senate, that is, the free council of the People, meets daily; in it we debate on public affairs, giving our opinions freely.[33] By its advice and authority we undertake wars, make treaties, agree on peace, pass legislation, and in short administer all public affairs. Does it not seem to you that this constitutes the greatest and truest liberty? Can any greater liberty be imagined? Your cities by contrast are stripped of all public deliberation, of all judicial and administrative power; they depend entirely on you; they dance attendance on your counsel and help; and having lost all liberty they must tolerate your power, of whatever kind it is. Surely they are living in perpetual servitude! You administer everything through governors and deputies. I won't say how they generally go about their business, but this I do say: all of your cities suffer a multifarious kind of servitude.

47 MATTHAEUS. Istud quidem an verum sit mox viderimus. Nunc qualis sit ista vestra libertas, qua tantopere gloriamini, accuratius discutiamus. Quo igitur pacto vestros magistratus creatis?

DOMINICUS. Sorte illos ducimus.

MATTHAEUS. Quanam sorte?

DOMINICUS. Habemus omnium magistratuum urnas, in quas nomina civium coniecta sunt. Cum autem comitiorum tempus appetit, sorte educuntur.

MATTHAEUS. Quomodo in has urnas nomina civium coniiciuntur?

DOMINICUS. Statis temporibus, cum exhaustae iam urnae videntur esse, aliquot cives, qui a senatu optimi iudicati sunt, replendis urnis praeficiuntur, atque id quidem novo vocabulo nos 'scrutinium' appellamus. Ii vero quos dixi cives eorum nomina, qui ad gerendos magistratus idonei vel tunc esse vel paulo post fore videntur, urnis imponunt.

MATTHAEUS. Iudicio igitur illorum standum est ut cives ad magistratus gerendos idonei esse existimentur.

DOMINICUS. Quidni?

MATTHAEUS. Quid si illi, ut fit, vel odio vel amore vel alia animi perturbatione ducantur ut quempiam vel admittant vel repudient?

DOMINICUS. Numquam id quidem facerent, si boni cives essent.

MATTHAEUS. Atqui non semper boni possunt inveniri.

DOMINICUS. Eligi[25] certe quam optimi atque integerrimi possunt.

48 MATTHAEUS. Utrum tandem tu facilius aut ad libertatem accomodatius fore existimas, si id ab uno an a pluribus petendum esset?

DOMINICUS. Ab uno profecto; sed ut facilius esset unum exorare quam plures, ita etiam facilius esset unum quam plures corrumpere.

MATTHAEUS. Atqui utrum facilius existimas unum dumtaxat optimum, an[26] multos invenire?

MATTIAS. We shall presently look to see whether this is true or 47
not. Let us now discuss with greater care the sort of liberty you
have that you boast of so much. How then do you choose your
magistrates?

DOMENICO. We choose them by lot.

MATTIAS. What kind of lot?

DOMENICO. We have urns for all the magistracies, in which the
names of citizens are put. When the time approaches for elections, the names are drawn by lot.

MATTIAS. How are the names of citizens placed in these urns?

DOMENICO. At fixed times, when the urns look to be empty,
several citizens who are judged to be excellent men by the senate
are put in charge of replenishing the urns, and we call this (using a
modern word) a "scrutiny."[34] The citizens I just mentioned place
into the urns the names of those who seem suitable to hold magistracies either at that moment or shortly thereafter.

MATTIAS. So it's by the judgment of the selectors that citizens
are reckoned worthy of holding magistracies.

DOMENICO. What of it?

MATTIAS. What if they are motivated in the usual way by hatred
or love or other passions[35] to admit or reject someone?

DOMENICO. They would never do that if they were good citizens.

MATTIAS. Yet good citizens cannot always be found.

DOMENICO. The best citizens of the highest integrity can surely
be chosen.

MATTIAS. Which in the end do you reckon will be easier and 48
more conducive to liberty: to seek integrity in one person or in
many?

DOMENICO. In one, certainly; but as it's easier to influence one
person than many, it's also easier to corrupt one person than many.[36]

MATTIAS. All the same, do you think it's easier to find one excellent person or many?

DOMINICUS. Unum sane.

MATTHAEUS. Satius igitur esset id ab uno rege petere, qui propter excellentem potentiam neque odio in suos neque invidia neque
benivolentia nimia laboraret, quam a multis civibus, qui cum ob
aemulationem et aequalitatem, tum ob cognationes et affinitates
vacui ab his perturbationibus esse non possunt.

DOMINICUS. Fateor ab uno satius fore, quicunque ille esset,
modo optimus atque integerrimus esset.

49  MATTHAEUS. Non sunt igitur, ut video, vestra comitia libera,
sed partim fortunae, partim gratiae subiecta, nisi forte vos aut for-
tunam illam in nominibus educendis aut gratiam in ambiendis civibus libertatem appellatis.

DOMINICUS. Ita est; liberum enim id existimamus esse, quod
potest unicuique contingere.

MATTHAEUS. Quam id recte faciatis, tuum iudicium sit?

DOMINICUS. Certe non recte, ut nunc quidem video; sed vulgi
iudicium immutari facile non potest.

MATTHAEUS. Concedamus tamen tibi libera esse vestra comitia.
Dic, obsecro: potestne unusquisque ita sorte eductus magistratum
gerere?

DOMINICUS. Non potest.

MATTHAEUS. Quid prohibet?

50  DOMINICUS. Multa: aetas, absentia, vectigalia non persoluta,
magistratus proxime gestus. Impediunt enim se mutuo nonnulli
magistratus neque, nisi certo interiecto tempore, geri possunt, ut
unicuique in republica sit locus neque ad unum omnia deferri videantur. Alia item obstant multa.

MATTHAEUS. Quid igitur prodest tanto labore in urnas perve-
nisse, si fortunae beneficio uti non licet? Cetera quidem impedi-
menta non improbo, sed bono civi paupertas ad gerendam rempu-

DOMENICO. One, of course.

MATTIAS. Will it then be preferable to look for such a choice from a single king, who owing to his superior power feels neither hatred nor envy nor excessive benevolence towards his subjects, or from many citizens who owing to their rivalries and equality of status, their family connections and intermarriages, cannot be free of these passions?

DOMENICO. I confess that a single person would be preferable, whoever he might be, so long as he was an excellent man of the highest integrity.

MATTIAS. As I see it, therefore, your elections are not free, but subject in part to fortune and in part to favor—unless, perhaps, you would call the luck of the draw and the exercise of influence over citizens "liberty." 49

DOMENICO. That is so: we do indeed call "free" something that can happen to anyone.

MATTIAS. And it's your judgment that you are right to do so?

DOMENICO. It's not right, certainly, as I now see, but the judgment of the common people is not easy to change.

MATTIAS. Nevertheless, we shall grant you that your elections are free. Tell me, please, can anyone at all who is chosen by lot in this way hold office?

DOMENICO. He can't.

MATTIAS. What prevents it?

DOMENICO. Many things:[37] age, absence, unpaid taxes, having recently held a magistracy—for some magistracies cannot be held jointly or only after a fixed interval of time, so that there's room for everyone in public affairs and so that everything doesn't appear to be put into the hands of a single person. There are also many other impediments to office-holding. 50

MATTIAS. What's the point of having gotten into the urns with so much effort if it's not allowable to make use of the benefits of fortune? I don't condemn the rest of the impediments, but poverty

blicam obesse non debet, si vectigal sibi impositum exsolvere non potest.

DOMINICUS. Ita fieri necesse est ut aequalitas illa et concordia reipublicae conservetur.

51 MATTHAEUS. At ista aequalitas magna meo iudicio et iniqua servitus est. Quod si bonis civibus rem publicam gerere per aes alienum, hoc est per[27] paupertatem, non licet, aut ditiorum servi cum magno libertatis et reipublicae detrimento efficiantur aut quacumque ratione cum sua summa ignominia locupletentur necesse est. Quorum utrum minus reipublicae expediat ipse iudices.

DOMINICUS. Neutrum certe expedit, sed tamen ea qua dixi de causa a nobis fit.

52 MATTHAEUS. Sed de comitiis hactenus. Videamus nunc, si placet, quae sit in magistratibus ipsis libertas.

DOMINICUS. Videamus.

MATTHAEUS. Quis est summus in vestra republica magistratus?

DOMINICUS. Novem viri, quos vulgo 'Dominos' appellamus.

MATTHAEUS. Satis unico isto vocabulo ceteros cives illorum servos esse declaratis. Dominus enim esse sine servo non potest, ut sine patre filius, maritus sine uxore, socer sine genero et quae his similia sunt, quae a dialecticis 'correlativa' sive 'ad aliquid' appellantur.

DOMINICUS. At hoc modo omnes paene cives sunt domini; bimestris enim magistratus est omnibusque communis.

53 MATTHAEUS. Immo ista ratione omnes sunt servi; prius enim ad privatam vitam, hoc est ad servitutem, redeunt, quam magistratum, hoc est libertatem, cognoscant. Sed videamus quo tandem pacto dominentur, quam sint in ipso magistratu liberi. Habentne ipsi summam rerum omnium in eo magistratu potestatem?

ought not to prevent a good citizen from taking part in public affairs, if he can't pay the taxes imposed on him.

DOMENICO. It's necessary that this be done to keep equality of status and harmony in the republic.

MATTIAS. But this kind of equality in my judgment is great and 51 unjust servitude. But if it's not licit for good citizens to take part in public affairs because of debt, that is, because of their poverty, either they are made into the slaves of the rich, to the great detriment of liberty and the republic, or it's necessary to enrich them in some way, ignominiously for them. You yourself can judge which course is less expedient for the republic.[38]

DOMENICO. Certainly neither one is expedient, yet these things are done for the reasons I've stated.

MATTIAS. Enough about elections. Let's now take a look, if you 52 please, at what liberty there is in these magistracies.

DOMENICO. Let's do that.

MATTIAS. What is the highest magistracy in your republic?

DOMENICO. The Nine, whom we call "the lords" [Signori] in the common tongue.[39]

MATTIAS. This one word is enough to show that the rest of the citizens are their servants or slaves. For there can be no lord without a servant, as there cannot be a son without a father or a husband without a wife or a father-in-law without a son-in-law. Words like these are called by logicians "correlative terms."[40]

DOMENICO. But by that token practically all the citizens are lords, since the magistracy only lasts two months and is open to all.

MATTIAS. Indeed, by this reasoning all are servants, for they re- 53 turn to private life, i.e. servitude, before they get to know the magistracy, i.e. liberty. But let's take a look at how they lord it, how free they are in that magistracy. Do they have supreme power over everything in that magistracy?

DOMINICUS. Habent quidem, sed propter eius, ut opinor, magistratus brevitatem, octo praeter eos viri sunt instituti, ad quos gravissima quaeque referuntur, quorum diuturnior est magistratus.

MATTHAEUS. Iste igitur summus dici potest, non ille.

DOMINICUS. At hic neque cum lictorum pompa et musicis instrumentis incedit, neque in publicis aedibus, quod nos vulgo palatium appellamus, publicis sumptibus commoratur, quae quidem omnia superiori illi magistratui tribuuntur.

MATTHAEUS. Ergo superior ille magistratus in publicis aedibus assidue permanet?

DOMINICUS. Permanet, et quidem summa cum dignitate publicis sumptibus lautissime vivit.

MATTHAEUS. Neque licet cuiquam, dum in magistratu est, aedes illa egredi?

DOMINICUS. Non, nisi publice et cum collegiis pompaque universa.

54 MATTHAEUS. Istos igitur potes tu, non dico dominos, sed ulla etiam ex parte liberos appellare, qui non modo summam in republica potestatem non habeant, sed ne pedem quidem e limine efferre in magistratu queant? Ista quidem meo iudicio verissima servitus, immo potius carcer quam magistratus est. Alter vero ille magistratus, qui et pompa caret et de summa republica deliberat, mihi potius supremus videtur.

DOMINICUS. Neque ille liberam rerum omnium potestatem habet. Sunt enim alii atque alii in republica magistratus inter quos ita divisa est potestas, ut omnes aliquam, nemo absolutam habeat, ne alius praeesse, alius subesse videatur, omnesque cives, quantum fieri potest, aliquam reipublicae partem administrent. Quod si possem tibi singulorum magistratuum potestatem, ordinem et coniunctionem explicare, te, ut opinor, maiorem in modum nostrae reipublicae forma delectaret.

DOMENICO. They do indeed, but owing to the brevity of that office, I think, another magistracy of Eight Men was established to whom all the gravest matters are referred, as their magistracy is longer.[41]

MATTIAS. So this is the highest magistracy, not the Nine.

DOMENICO. But the Eight do not process with the pomp of lictors and musical instruments and do not dwell in the public buildings, which we call the Palazzo in the common tongue, at public expense, while all these privileges are bestowed upon the higher magistracy.

MATTIAS. So the higher magistracy remains continuously in the Palace?

DOMENICO. They do, and they live in great luxury and honor at public expense.

MATTIAS. None of them is allowed to leave the building while they hold the magistracy?

DOMENICO. No, unless they leave for a public occasion with their colleges[42] and all pomp.

MATTIAS. So can you call these men even partly free — let alone 54 lords — who not only do not have supreme power in the republic but can't even set foot outside the palace while holding their magistracy? In my view this is servitude in the truest sense; indeed, it's more of a prison than a magistracy. The other magistracy that lacks the pomp and deliberates about the highest public affairs looks more like the supreme magistracy to me.

DOMENICO. But it doesn't have unconstrained power over affairs, either. For there are various magistracies in the republic that divide power among themselves, so that all have some power but no one of them absolute power, lest it appear that someone has preeminence and another is subject. And all the citizens as far as possible take some part in public administration. If I could explain to you the powers, order and interconnection of each magistracy, I think you would take great pleasure in our form of government.

55 MATTHAEUS. Delectant me profecto ista quae hactenus dixisti, Dominice, et aveo, cum otium dabitur, singillatim cuncta cognoscere. Sed video ex ista potestatis divisione effici ut nullus magistratus liber sit; dum enim alii ex aliis pendent, singuli per se imbecilliores fiunt.

DOMINICUS. Sic est.

MATTHAEUS. Quod si singuli magistratus parum possunt, quid singuli porro in magistratu constituti cives poterunt?

DOMINICUS. Multo minus.

MATTHAEUS. Ubi ergo est vestra ista tantopere collaudata libertas?

DOMINICUS. Non in singulis civibus aut singulis magistratibus, sed in universo reipublicae corpore continetur.

56 MATTHAEUS. Quod singuli non habent, id universi habere qui possunt? Sed satis, ut opinor, ostendimus non esse in magistratibus eam quam dicitis libertatem. Videamus nunc an in ipso senatu sit, quo respublica omnis contineri videtur. Age igitur: senatus ille quem tu liberum populi concilium esse dixisti, deliberatne de summa republica libere atque absolute, an habet alium ad quem sua consilia referat magistratum?

DOMINICUS. Habet et quidem plures pro rerum qualitate magistratus qui subtilius atque accuratius ea quae sunt in senatu tractata discutiant; nam neque omnia veniunt in senatum, neque ea quae veniunt omnia concluduntur, sed ubi audita et consultata sunt, ad alios atque alios magistratus reiiciuntur.

57 MATTHAEUS. Primum, quaero abs te cur omnia in senatum non veniant. Deinde, cur ea quae veniunt ab eo non perficiantur.

DOMINICUS. Senatus quaedam, quae infra suam dignitatem esse videntur, non admittit; alia, quae aut magna taciturnitate aut subita celeritate indigent, consulto paucis committuntur, qui et fide-

MATTIAS. I have certainly enjoyed what you have already said,    55
Domenico, and I would like to learn about them all individually
when I have the time. But I see that the result of this division of
power is that no magistrate is free. For while each depends on another, they are individually made weaker in themselves.
DOMENICO. That is so.
MATTIAS. But if single magistracies have little power, how much
power can the individual citizens in those magistracies have?
DOMENICO. Much less.
MATTIAS. So where then is this liberty of yours that you have
praised so much?
DOMENICO. It is contained, not in individual citizens or individual magistracies, but in the whole body of the republic.
MATTIAS. Can the totality have what no individual among them    56
has? But I think we have shown sufficiently that there is no liberty
such as you have described in your magistracies. Let us see now
whether it exists in that senate, which seems to encompass the
whole republic. Come then: does that senate which you have
called "the free council of the People" deliberate about the highest
public business freely and without constraint, or does it have some
magistracy to which it refers its counsels?
DOMENICO. It does have one—indeed many, depending on the
nature of the business—which discusses with greater precision
and care the subjects dealt with in the senate. For not all matters
come before the senate, nor are decisions made on all matters that
do come before it, but when those matters have been heard and
advice given, they are thrown back to the various magistracies.
MATTIAS. First, let me ask you why all public business does not    57
come before the senate; then why the matters that do come there
are not concluded there.
DOMENICO. Certain matters the senate does not hear as they
seem to be beneath its dignity; others, which require great secrecy
or great speed, are advisedly turned over to a few men who can

lius secretiora celant et facilius, cum opus est, congregantur. Sunt tamen etiam ipsi ex eorum numero qui in senatum veniunt. Non conficiuntur autem ab senatu ea omnia quae consultata sunt, partim propter negotiorum multitudinem, partim propter rerum gravitatem; melius enim omnia ab iis quorum proprium munus est quam ab senatu universo discutiuntur.

MATTHAEUS. An melius faciant non quaero; illud quaero, quae potestas aut libertas illis sit, qui neque omnia possint cognoscere neque ea quae cognoscunt pro arbitrio constituere, habeantque superiorem aliquem magistratum qui ab illis tractata et disputata diiudicet, ad quem ab illis provocatio sit?

58    Sed videamus quae tandem sit in sententiis dicendis libertas. Qua ratione de propositis rebus consultat senatus?

DOMINICUS. Proponitur sive a magistratu sive a scriba res ea quae in consultationem venit, roganturque omnes ut velint eam suis suffragiis vel approbare vel improbare.

MATTHAEUS. Quae sunt autem ista suffragia aut quo pacto illis diverse sententiae declarantur?

DOMINICUS. Apud alios aliter; nos nigris et albis fabis utimur. Qui rem approbandam sua sententia duxerit, in urnam, quae ob id ipsum circumfertur, nigram coniicit; qui non duxerit, candidam.

MATTHAEUS. Potestne animi sententia satis recte fabis exprimi? Quid si alius alia, ut fit, ratione vel dissentiat vel consentiat? Nonne in utramque partem plurimum momenti affert, qua quisque ratione ad id vel probandum vel reiiciendum adducatur?

DOMINICUS. Affert quidem, sed hoc ad brevitatem est aptius. Non enim possent omnes omnium sententiae audiri.

conceal secrets with greater trustworthiness and be assembled more easily when need be. These men, however, come from the number of those who are in the senate. The senate does not conclude all business on which it is consulted, partly because of the quantity of business, partly owing to its gravity. All business is better discussed by those whose proper task it is than by the full senate.

MATTIAS. I do not question whether they do it better; I question what power and liberty they can have who can neither take cognizance of everything nor can decide as free agents what they do take cognizance of, and who have some magistrate over them who makes decisions on the matters they've discussed and debated, to whom they make appeal.

But let's look to see what liberty there is, in the end, in the giving of views: by what method is the senate consulted on matters brought before it? 58

DOMENICO. A matter is proposed for consultation by a magistrate or an official and everyone is asked to approve or reject it on a show of votes.

MATTIAS. What exactly are these votes, and how are different views expressed?

DOMENICO. Different republics use different methods. We use black and white beans. Someone who thinks the proposal should be approved throws a black bean in an urn which is circulated for the purpose; someone opposed throws a white bean in.

MATTIAS. Can someone express his thoughts correctly with beans? What if someone agrees or disagrees for a different reason, as commonly happens? Is it not a matter of great importance for both sides what reason is given for approving or rejecting some proposal?

DOMENICO. It is, but this method is more suited to brevity; it's impossible to listen to everyone's views.

MATTHAEUS. At possent aliquae eorumque potissimum qui habentur prudentissimi.

59   DOMINICUS. Fit istud quoque nonnumquam, sed admodum raro. Cum enim res obtineri non potest eamque magistratus aliqua de causa cupit obtinere, rogat ut qui eam reiiciendam censent in pulpitum prodeant (is enim dicendae sententiae locus est) et cur ita censeant senatui exponant.

MATTHAEUS. Quid si sic quoque res non obtineatur?

DOMINICUS. Eam magistratus iterum tertioque proponit rogatque cives ut sibi assentiri velint. Quod si etiam ita non obtineat, in aliud tempus differt; interea dissentientium civium animos quacumque potest ratione in suam sententiam adducit.

MATTHAEUS. Istud quidem cogere est, non consultare, si quidem quae semel magistratui placuere, ea senatus omnino comprobaturus est.

DOMINICUS. Sed hoc, ut dixi, quam rarissime fit.

60   MATTHAEUS. Quid si res quae consultatur plures partes aut condiciones habeat, quarum alii alias, ut fit, vel admittant vel reiciant? Quo pacto singula fabis exprimi possunt?

DOMINICUS. Magistratus sententias, si potest, dividit et de his singillatim suffragia exigit. Sin id fieri non possit, propterea quod sententia una diversas habeat condiciones, liberum est unicuique vel sententiam suam dicere vel utram vult partem suffragiis sequi.

MATTHAEUS. Video ex tuis verbis cogi cives ut nonnumquam quae nolunt dicant, nonnunquam taceant quae volunt.

61   Sed illud, quod huius rei caput est, abs te quaero: suntne libera unicuique suffragia?

DOMINICUS. Liberrima.

MATTHAEUS. Palamne in urnam fabae an clanculum coniiciuntur?

MATTIAS. But they could listen to some views, especially the views of those with the greatest practical wisdom.

DOMENICO. This too is done sometimes, but it's quite rare. For 59 when they can't get approval and the magistrate wants to obtain approval for some reason, he asks those who have rejected it to step into the pulpit (that's the place for giving opinions) and explain their view to the senate.

MATTIAS. What if they can't get approval this way?

DOMENICO. The magistrate proposes the motion a second and third time and asks the citizens if they want to agree to it. If it's not approved even so, it's put off to another time; in the meantime, the magistrate brings the dissenting citizens over to his view in whatever way he can.

MATTIAS. That's compulsion, not consultation, if something that a magistrate has decided is going to be approved by the senate in any event.

DOMENICO. But this, as I've said, happens very rarely.

MATTIAS. What if the matter being considered has several parts 60 or stipulations, and different persons accept or reject different parts, as usually happens: how can opinions about individual parts be expressed through bean-counting?

DOMENICO. The magistrate divides up the different opinions if he can and takes a vote on them individually. If this is impossible, because a single opinion may contain different stipulations, everyone is free either to give his opinion or to support whichever of the two parties he likes with his vote.

MATTIAS. I see from what you've said that citizens are sometimes forced to say things they don't want to say and sometimes to be silent about things they do want to say.

But let me ask you about the nub of the matter: Does everyone 61 have a free vote?

DOMENICO. Extremely free.

MATTIAS. Are the beans thrown into the urn openly or secretly?

DOMINICUS. Clanculum.

MATTHAEUS. Cur ita?

DOMINICUS. Ut sententia extet, auctor lateat.

MATTHAEUS. Non audent igitur cives proferre quod[28] sentiunt, si volunt latere.

DOMINICUS. Audent quidem, sed invidiam ac malivolentiam cupiunt evitare.

MATTHAEUS. An debet quisquam reipublicae gratia singulorum civium odia, inimicitias invidiamque metuere? An non debet bonus civis caritatem patriae suis affectibus[29] anteponere, suaque commoda omnia minoris existimare? Quid si recte sentiat, debetne etiam latere?

DOMINICUS. Debet, ne ii[30] qui aliter sentiunt detegantur.

62 MATTHAEUS. Gratiam igitur omnem vir bonus amittet, ne malus cognoscatur, et quando utriusque sententia aeque latet, veniet vir bonus perinde ac malus in suspicionem; hac ratione fiet ut neque bono civi praemium neque malo poena debeatur. Quod si libere proferre quae sentias non licet, quae tandem in suffragiis potest esse libertas?

DOMINICUS. Immo ob hoc potissimum liberrima esse suffragia existimamus, quod unicuique sine metu ac suspicione ulla licet libere sentire quod vult. Quae quidem, tametsi reipublicae gratia magnifacienda non sunt, debent tamen cum possunt declinari, ne dissensiones in republica et factiones pariant.

63 MATTHAEUS. Immo, dum bonos praemiis fraudatis et malos ac perniciosos in republica cives toleratis atque alitis, maiores meo iudicio factiones in republica excitatis. Quae enim pestis potest esse maior, quae factio perniciosior, quam, cum malis licet impune sentire quod volunt, bonis sine suspicione non licet, quando nullum

DOMENICO. Secretly.

MATTIAS. Why so?

DOMENICO. So that the opinion may be expressed, its author hidden.

MATTIAS. Then the citizens don't dare express what they think, if they want to stay hidden.

DOMENICO. They do dare, but they wish to avoid odium and malevolence.

MATTIAS. Must someone go in fear of the hatred, hostility and odium of individual citizens for the sake of the republic? Shouldn't a good citizen put love of country ahead of his own passions, and consider all his own interests of lesser value? What if he holds the correct view: must he hide it even so?

DOMENICO. He must, so that those with different views are not revealed.

MATTIAS. Thus a good man will lose all influence so that a bad 62 man may not be known; and since the opinions of both are equally hidden, the good man will come under suspicion exactly like the bad one. By this method the good man will not receive his due reward and the bad man his due punishment. But if it is not allowed to express freely what you think, how can there be freedom in voting, pray tell?

DOMENICO. On the contrary, it's precisely for this reason that we consider our voting to be extremely free: everyone is free to hold whatever views he wants without fear or suspicion. Though fear and suspicion should not be made much of, for the sake of the republic they should be deflected when they can, in case they lead to dissension and faction in the republic.

MATTIAS. On the contrary, so long as you defraud the good of 63 their rewards while tolerating and nurturing the evil and destructive citizens of the republic, you will be inciting still greater factions, in my judgment. What plague could be greater, what faction more pernicious, than a situation where evil men can hold whatever opinions they want with impunity, good men cannot hold

inter eos discrimen est et illi sua flagitia occultare possunt, hi sua recte facta proferre non possunt? Proinde quam vos in suffragiis libertatem appellatis, ego summam et iniquissimam servitutem voco.

Sed de suffragiis hactenus. Iudicia vero quomodo exercetis? Quis vobis ius dicit?

DOMINICUS. Praetor peregrinus, quem nos, nescio quam latino, usitato certe vocabulo 'potestatem' appellamus.

MATTHAEUS. Unde eum accitis aut quo pacto iuridicundo praeficitis?

DOMINICUS. Ubicunque optimum atque integerrimum virum esse comperimus, inde eum in nostram civitatem advocamus.

64 MATTHAEUS. Tantane est in vestra civitate bonorum virorum inopia, ut aliunde advocandus sit qui vobis ius dicat, vestra vitia coarguat, vobis denique dominetur? Non potestis e vobis quemquam vobis ipsis praeficere, ne exteris nationibus vestras lites, vestra flagitia patefaciatis vosque aliis emendandos puniendosque praebeatis?

DOMINICUS. Possumus quidem et habemus optimos viros in civitate permultos, sed nefas esse ducimus civem civi mortem afferre, neque putamus civem quemquam immunem ab amore, odio, ira, invidia, misericordia ceterisque affectibus propter cognationes, affinitates, familiaritates, clientelas et alias necessitudines esse posse. Peregrinum vero hominem ob nullam nostri notitiam facile omni affectu carere et ius aequaliter omnibus dicere existimamus.

65 MATTHAEUS. Totam rempublicam magistratibus vestris committitis; singulorum civium causas et iudicia committere non potestis? Civem nullum vobis imperare vultis et externos qui imperent advocatis? Quo vero pacto ius recte dicere vobis potest qui vestras leges, vestros mores, vestra instituta non novit?

DOMINICUS. Atqui nos communibus Romanorum legibus vivimus, quarum magnam unusquisque habere cognitionem potest.

opinions without exciting suspicion, when no difference is made
between them, and the former are allowed to hide their outra-
geous views while the latter cannot bring their good deeds into the
open? Hence what you call free voting, I call the highest and most
unjust servitude.

But enough about voting. How do you run your courts? Who
has jurisdiction over you?

DOMENICO. A foreign praetor whom we call a *podestà* — a common word, though of dubious latinity.

MATTIAS. Where do you get him from, and how do you put him
in charge of giving justice?

DOMENICO. We seek out excellent men of the highest integrity
from every land and summon them to our city.

MATTIAS. Does your city have such a lack of good men that you  64
have to call them in from elsewhere to give you justice, convict you
of your vices — in short, to act as your lord? Can't you put someone from your own people in charge and not expose to the view of
foreign nations your disputes and acts of shame, and not offer
yourselves to others for correction and punishment?

DOMENICO. We can indeed, and we have a great many fine men
in our city, but we think it's wrong for one citizen to inflict death
on another, nor do we believe that any citizen can be immune to
love, hatred, anger, malice, mercy and the other passions, given his
family on both sides, his friendships, clientele and other personal
ties. But we reckon a foreigner will find it easy, thanks to his ignorance of our city, to put aside prejudice and render impartial justice.

MATTIAS. You entrust all public affairs to your own magistrates,  65
but you can't entrust the legal cases and trials of individual citizens
to them? You want no citizen to command you and you summon
foreigners to command you? How can someone give justice rightly
who doesn't know your laws, customs and institutions?

DOMENICO. All the same, we live by the common laws of the
Romans, and any person can have great understanding of those.

MATTHAEUS. Nullane alia privatim instituta, nullos maiorum mores servatis?

DOMINICUS. Immo quam plurimos mores et pulcherrima instituta habemus.

MATTHAEUS. Illorum igitur peritiam externus homo habere qui potest?

66 DOMINICUS. At facit civitatis nostrae claritas ut nostra instituta cognoscere velint quam plurimi. Multi praeterea ob hanc ipsam causam, hoc est, ut praeturam nostram gerant, illis perdiscendis dant operam.

MATTHAEUS. Quid porro ex eo magistratu consequuntur?

DOMINICUS. Maximam primum dignitatem. Quem enim praeturam Florentiae gessisse constat, omnes ad se certatim civitates advocant. Deinde etiam[31] mercedem non mediocrem quam nos[32] illi ex aerario solvimus.

67 MATTHAEUS. Ergo mercennarios praetores conducitis qui vobis ius dicant, sontes puniant, leges custodiant. Quid horum aut vos ab illis sperare aut illi praestare vobis possunt, qui vestrae pecuniae, non vestrae reipublicae gratia, magistratum gerant cupiantque et ex eo emolumentum quam maximum reportare et ad eum quam saepissime deligi? In vos vero quo pacto suo iure utentur, quos ipsi partim ob memoriam accepti beneficii vereantur, partim sibi in posterum conciliare studeant? Neque vos illos magnopere timebitis, quibus potestatem a vobis omnem et traditam esse et eripi pro arbitrio posse intellegatis.

68 DOMINICUS. At eos viros advocamus qui non mercede nostra, sed sua dignitate ad magistratum severissime gerendum adducantur, ex eoque non tam pecuniae fructum quam integritatis laudem reportare studeant; nos vero illis potestatem semel traditam ante sex menses (semestris enim magistratus est) non eripimus omnesque iis sine discrimine subiacemus.

MATTIAS. Haven't you kept any privately established institutions, any ancestral customs?[43]

DOMENICO. Indeed we do; we have numerous such customs and very beautiful institutions.

MATTIAS. So can an outsider be familiar with them?

DOMENICO. The fame of our city has made many wish to learn 66 about our institutions; many men, besides, have applied themselves to mastering them for this very reason, so that they can conduct our potestarial courts.

MATTIAS. What then are the advantages of holding the office?

DOMENICO. First of all, great honor, for when it becomes known that someone has conducted a potestarial court in Florence, all the cities compete to appoint him. Then there is the not inconsiderable salary that we pay him from the treasury.

MATTIAS. So you hire mercenary judges who give you justice, 67 punish the guilty and act as guardians of the law. But can you hope for these things from them, can they provide them to you, when they discharge the magistracy for the sake of your money, not your common weal, when they want to earn the largest possible emolument from it and to be elected to it as often as possible? How are they going to lay down the law for you, when in part they hold you in respect because of benefits received, in part they are eager to be on good terms with you in future? And you won't be afraid of *them* very much, knowing as you do that all their power comes from you and can be snatched away from them at your good pleasure.

DOMENICO. But we appoint men who will conduct our magis- 68 tracy in the severest possible way, men who are not motivated by our salary but by honor, and who are eager to earn, not a monetary profit, but a reputation for integrity. Once the office of *podestà* has been turned over to them, we don't take it away for six months (that is the term of office) and we all of us submit to them without distinction.

MATTHAEUS. Ab optimatibus tamen, si verum fateri vis, etiam severissimi abstinent.

DOMINICUS. Abstinent quidem, non quod in eos ius non habeant, sed quod illi non delinquant.

MATTHAEUS. Immo vero illorum partim auctoritatem timent, partim gratiam aucupari student.

DOMINICUS. Qui boni sunt, id profecto non faciunt.

MATTHAEUS. At quam multi boni reperiuntur? Estne, obsecro, aliquis tam severus, tam integer, qui non sibi magistratum aut prorogari aut alias dari cupiat?

DOMINICUS. Neminem puto esse aut quam paucissimos.

69  MATTHAEUS. Quo igitur pacto id consequi umquam poterit, nisi omnium civium praesertimque optimatum sibi studium benivolentiamque conciliet? Sex vero mensibus homo novus et vestrorum morum ignarus gerere quid potest? Qui tam brevi tempore vix vultus hominum causasque cognoscat, decidere certe illas non potest. Ante enim quam causas cognoscat, testes audiat, seque ad ferendam sententiam comparet, magistratu eum[33] excedere necesse est. Quod cum omnibus praetoribus accidat, fit ut causae civium in immensum protrahantur et patrimonia eorum in lites abeant. Sed rectene faciatis an non, vos videritis; illud certe negare non potestis, vos peregrino homini pulcherrimam et maxime necessariam civitatis partem, hoc est forum et iudicia, commisisse eique cives omnes esse subiectos.

Quod si neque in communi vita, neque in vectigalibus, neque in magistratibus, neque in conciliis, neque in iudiciis liberi estis, ubi sit ista vestra libertas non video, nisi forte in eo contineri arbitramini, quod exteris nationibus non serviatis.

70  DOMINICUS. An non ista tibi satis magna libertas videtur esse, quod multis imperemus, serviamus nemini praeterquam nobis ip-

MATTIAS. Yet even the most severe magistrates keep away from the optimates,[44] to tell the truth.

DOMENICO. They do keep away from them, not because they have no jurisdiction over them, but because the optimates do not commit offenses.

MATTIAS. Or rather, partly because the magistrates fear their authority and partly because they are eager to curry favor with them.

DOMENICO. The good ones certainly don't do that.

MATTIAS. But how many good ones do you find? Is there really, I ask you, anyone of such austere integrity that he doesn't want his magistracy extended or to be given other ones?

DOMENICO. There is no one, I think, or very few indeed.

MATTIAS. How then is the man ever going to get what he wants 69 unless he ingratiates himself with all the citizens, especially the optimates? How can a new man ignorant of your ways administer anything in six months? A man who in such a brief time scarcely starts to identify men and their cases certainly can't settle them. For by the time he's taken cognizance of the case, heard the witnesses, and prepared himself to give sentence, he's of necessity exceeded [the term of] his magistracy. Since this happens in the case of all *podestà*, it transpires that the court cases of the citizens are indefinitely protracted and their patrimonies are wasted in litigation. It's your business whether what you are doing is right or not, but surely you can't deny that you have entrusted the finest and most essential part of the state, i.e. the courts and legal judgments, to a foreigner, and you have made all the citizens subject to him.

But if you are free neither in everyday life, nor in taxes, nor in magistracies, nor in giving counsel, nor in the legal system, I don't see where this liberty of yours is to be found, unless perhaps you reckon it consists of your not being subject to outside nations.

DOMENICO. Doesn't this seem to you a great enough source of 70 liberty, that we rule over many and serve none except our own

sis et his quidem vicissim ac sponte? Nam quod praetori peregrino ius fori iudiciorumque tradidimus, id quidem et vitandi[34] mutui inter cives odii gratia fecimus et, ut ipse dicis, liberum est nobis eam illi cum volumus potestatem eripere, quamquam hoc non omnis respublica servat. Veneti enim non modo nullum peregrinum, sed ne cives quidem omnes magistratum aliquem gerere patiuntur. Maiores nostri, cum rempublicam constituerent, rati si iudicia singulis civibus commisissent, fore ut maxima inter eos odia nascerentur, cupientibus semper iis qui damnati fuissent iniurias ulcisci, eam provinciam peregrino homini tradendam putavere, ne quis se a cive laesum existimaret.

71    Neque in eo civitatis libertatem consistere credidere, reputantes id quod erat ius, illud ei a quibus datum esset eripi facillime posse, ministrumque iudiciorum illum esse, non dominum; ut enim in domo aliqua dispensatorem peregrinum, immo etiam servum contingit esse, cui cetera familia atque etiam dominus ipse aliqua ex parte subiaceat — illum tamen dominum esse nemo dixerit — ita in civitate iudicem peregrinum a civibus ipsis ad eam rem delectum esse quid prohibet? Illum tamen reipublicae principem esse aut ei libertatem eripere nemo debet existimare, cum eum et a civibus eligi et brevi tempore praeesse intellegat. Summa vero et verissima libertas nostra in eo potissimum consistere semper est iudicata ut nemini serviamus, nemini tributa pendamus, nostris legibus, nostris institutis vivamus. Si quid nobis ipsis[35] pendimus aut servimus, id, cum sponte faciamus, tolerabile nobis iucundumque videtur. Vestrae vero civitates, quam tandem libertatem habent?

72    MATTHAEUS. Multo profecto maiorem quam vestrae. Primum enim (id quod vos maximum et praecipuum, immo solum habetis)

selves, and we do this by turns and of our own free will? Turning over the legal system to a foreign judge is something we have done for the sake of avoiding mutual hatred among citizens, and, as you yourself say, we are free to take the power away from him, although not every republic follows this practice. The Venetians not only prohibit foreigners but even some citizens from exercising some magistracies.[45] Our ancestors, when they founded the republic, held that if they entrusted the courts to individual citizens, this would give rise to the greatest odium among citizens, as those who had been condemned unjustly would always desire to be avenged of their injury, and hence they decided to entrust that province to a foreigner, so that no one would reckon himself injured by a fellow citizen.

Nor did they believe that liberty consisted in that function of 71 the city, but they held that the legal function could be very easily taken from the person to whom it had been given, whom they thought a servant of the legal system and not its master. Just as there might be in some household a foreign steward, even a slave, to whom the rest of the household and even the master himself might in some degree be subject, yet no one would call him a lord, so in a city, what is there to prevent the citizens from choosing a foreign judge for this purpose? Yet no one should reckon that that judge is the principal citizen of the republic or that his own liberty has been taken from him, since he understands that the man has been chosen by the citizens and is in charge for a short period. Our highest and truest freedom has always been reckoned to consist particularly in the fact that we serve no one, we pay tribute to no one, and we live by our own laws and institutions. If we pay something to ourselves and serve each other, this seems to us tolerable and congenial, since we do it voluntarily. But what freedom, pray, do your cities possess?

MATTIAS. Much more than yours, surely. First of all, ours are 72 not subject to foreign nations — which is the greatest and principal

exteris nationibus non subiacent; tributa regi tantum suo et quidem parva et annua, ut dixi, persolvunt. Deinde communem vitam
liberiorem habent. Unicuique enim vestes omnis generis ferre,
convivia, nuptias, funera ceteraque civilia officia celebrare pro arbitrio licet, neque id veremur ne aut in funera aut in nuptias abeant
patrimonia; comitia et magistratus non sorti aut casui, sed principum prudentiae et iudicio subiacent, ne vel inepti admittantur vel
reiiciantur idonei; consilia sententiis, non suffragiis peraguntur, ut
libere unusquisque dicat quod sentiat.[36] Neque hoc in singulis civitatibus modo, sed apud principem quoque contingit, qui omnibus de rebus suos consulit; habet enim penes se unusquisque princeps optimum ac praestantissimum senatum e regno universo
delectum; decet enim ut qui omnibus consulturi sunt ex omnibus
eligantur. Praetores postremo, quos viros optimos atque integerri-
mos longa experientia novit, in singulas civitates destinat, ita ut ex
aliis eligat quos in alias mittat, neminem omnino ab exteris nationibus accersat, sed suorum opera et fide contentus sit.

73     Nam quod omnia per praefectos a nobis geri dixisti, scias illos
rerum ministros, non auctores esse. Omnia enim et illis ab rege
mandantur et in regis noticiam veniunt, neque vero aliter suas provincias ulla respublica potest administrare. Praefectis utique opus
est qui provincias regant; suo vel regi vel senatui omnia referant.
Sed hoc quoque nostrae vestris civitates praestant, quod rex eas vi-
sere saepe[37] potest, senatus non potest. Neque vero praefecti nostri
audent populos ullo genere servitutis opprimere, quippe qui et
alienos se ministros esse et nihil ob eam rem ad se emolumenti
pervenire certo sciant. Cives autem vestri, qui se dominos esse

liberty, indeed the only liberty you have—and ours pay tribute
only to their own king, and a small, annual one at that, as I've
said. Then, too, our everyday life is freer, for everyone is permitted
to dress as they like and celebrate banquets, weddings, funerals and
other civil functions as they wish, and we don't have to be afraid
that our patrimonies will be swallowed up in funerals and weddings. Elections and magistracies are not subject to lot or chance,
but to the prudence and good judgment of leading men, so that
inappropriate persons are not admitted to them and suitable persons are not rejected. Counsel is given by voicing one's views, not
by voting, so that everyone may say freely what he thinks. Nor is
this the case only in individual cities, but it also happens before
the prince, who consults his own counselors in all things. For the
prince has at his court an excellent, outstanding senate chosen
from the whole kingdom, it being fitting that those who are going
to be consulted about the interests of all should be chosen from
all.[46] Finally, he designates as judges for individual cities men
whom he knows from long experience to be excellent men of the
highest integrity, in such a way that men serve in cities other than
their own, but no one is brought in from foreign nations; the
prince is content with the services and loyalty of his own people.

You said before that we ran everything through governors, but 73
you should know that these men are ministers, not independent
authorities. All their orders come from the king, and everything
comes under his notice; nor can any commonwealth administer its
provinces in any other way. Governors are necessary everywhere to
rule provinces, who report everything to their king or the senate.
But in this respect too our cities excel yours: because a king can often visit them while a senate cannot. Our governors do not dare
oppress peoples with any species of servitude, as they know for
sure that they are ministers of another and that no emoluments
will come to them on this account. But your citizens, who con-

putent ditandique sui gratia provincias petant, omnibus eas bonis exhauriunt, spoliant atque expilant, omne in eas imperii genus exercent.

74 Denique rex ipse, cum provincias visit, etiam si gravior illis et molestior esse velit, tamen, quia unus est et non saepe id facit, non modo tolerabilis omnibus sed iucundus etiam videtur esse. Cives autem vestri, cum innumerabiles sint, quottidie vestras provincias permeent necesse est, quo cum veniunt, tot reges putes venire quot cives. Unusquisque enim se principem senatus et reipublicae facit. Quaecumque reipublicae subiecta sunt, sua omnia esse putat; quae provincialibus relinquit, ea tantum sibi periisse existimat. Omnibus itaque modis se locupletare studet. Quod quidem, cum et a multis et frequenter fiat, intolerabilis omnibus provinciis servitus existit. Atque harum quidem rerum innumerabilia in Romana republica exempla sunt: universus enim terrarum orbis ab illis exhaustus et spoliatus est, ut una civitas dicaretur.

75 DOMINICUS. Romanis quidem istud accidit; nobis, qui aliter provincias nostras administramus, non accidit.

MATTHAEUS. Ego quidem quid faciatis nescio; illud scio: imperia imminuta esse pecuniae cupiditatem auctam. Sed de nostra vestraque libertate satis diximus, nisi quid tu ad haec fortasse vis.

DOMINICUS. Nihil plane.

MATTHAEUS. Fateris igitur nec vobis totam libertatem esse nec nobis deesse.

DOMINICUS. Fateor nos id nomen propter imperandi vicissitudinem usurpasse, neque a servitute immunes esse, sed eam commutatione imperantium tolerabiliorem nobis minoremque videri; vestras vero civitates, siquidem ita ab aliis, ut dicis, reguntur, non modo non opprimi dura, ut audieram, servitute, sed ingenti quoque frui libertate.

sider themselves lords and seek provincial governorships for the sake of enriching themselves, drain them of all their goods, plunder them and pluck them bare, whilst practicing every kind of rule over them.

Finally, the king himself, when he visits the provinces, even if he were inclined to be more burdensome and vexatious to them, still seems not only tolerable but even a source of rejoicing to all, since he is only one man and does not often visit. Your citizens, however, being innumerable, inevitably swarm about your provinces on a daily basis, so that you'd think as many kings as citizens were coming when they arrive.[47] Each one makes himself leader of the senate and the republic; he thinks everything subject to the republic is his own property, and what he leaves behind for the provincials he regards as pure loss to himself. Thus in every way he sets out to enrich himself. When this is done time after time by many persons, an intolerable state of servitude exists in every province. There are innumerable examples of this kind of behavior in the Roman republic, for the whole world was drained and despoiled by them so that a single city might be enriched.

DOMENICO. That did happen in the case of the Romans, but it doesn't with us, who administer our provinces after another fashion.

MATTIAS. I don't know what you do, but this I do know: empires decrease as the lust for money increases. But we have spoken enough of our liberty and yours, unless perhaps you have something to add.

DOMENICO. Nothing at all.

MATTIAS. You confess then that you do not have total liberty and that we do not lack all liberty.

DOMENICO. I confess that we have appropriated this name of liberty because of our practice of ruling in turn, and that we are not free of servitude, but that our servitude seems smaller and more tolerable because of our alternating rule. I confess that your

74

75

76  MATTHAEUS. Reguntur ita ab omnibus, ut opinor, immo etiam fortasse melius. Ego enim tibi meam, non ceterorum regum consuetudinem exposui. Si qui tamen sunt qui suum regnum hoc pacto non administrent, illi mihi tyranni videntur esse, non reges. DOMINICUS. Profecto sic est.

77  MATTHAEUS. Tu vero quid ais, fili? Regnine libertatem an reipublicae, si tibi optio detur, eligendam putes?

IOANNES. Regni; respublica enim, quantum intellego, non est libera, sed sibi ipsi servit, eoque maiori servitute et sollicitudine premitur, quo melius administratur. Omnes enim communi bono invigilare necesse est, quo fit ut nulli umquam, si modo bonus civis velit esse, solida quies aut tranquillitas esse possit.

MATTHAEUS. Recte sentis. Sed satis hodie disputatum est; cras, si placet, post meridiem revertimini, ut ea quae sequuntur in Dominici propositione videamus. Tu interea, fili, quae hodie disputata sunt, memoria repetes; Dominicus se ad sequentia comparabit.

IOANNES. Ita faciemus.

cities, since they are ruled by others in the way you describe, are
not only not oppressed with hard servitude, as I had heard, but
even enjoy enormous liberty.

MATTIAS. They are ruled this way by all my governors, I  76
think—indeed, perhaps even better ruled. For I have been explaining my own practice to you, not that of other kings. If there
are those who do not rule their kingdoms this way, they seem tyrants to me, not kings.

DOMENICO. That is surely so.

MATTIAS. And what do you say, son? Do you think you would  77
choose the liberty of kingdoms or of republics, if you were given
the choice?

JANOS. That of kingdoms. The republic, as far as I understand
it, is not free but is in servitude to itself, and is oppressed by the
greater servitude and anxiety the better it is governed. For everyone has necessarily to be vigilant for the common good, with the
result that no one ever can enjoy solid peace and tranquillity so
long as he wants to be a good citizen.

MATTIAS. You are right. But we have disputed enough for today.
Tomorrow, if you agree, return in the afternoon so that we can examine what comes next in Domenico's proposed debate. Meanwhile, son, go over in your memory today's disputation; Domenico
will prepare himself for what follows.

JANOS. We shall do so.

## Liber Secundus[1]

1 IOANNES. Salve, pater. Nos, nisi tibi molesti sumus, ad clepsi-
dram venimus.

MATTHAEUS. Placet. Sed quid tu? Hesternamne disputationem
probas, fili, an postquam ad eam meditatus es, reipublicae quam
regni libertatem mavis?

IOANNES. Egone permaneo in sententia ut libertatem regni cum
reipublicae libertate comparandam esse non putem. Quis enim illa
comitia, illos magistratus, illa iudicia libera esse dicat, si nostris
contulerit? Sed nimirum ego vos interpello. Aveo enim audire, pater, quid tu ad cetera quae Dominicus proposuit velis dicere.

MATTHAEUS. Audies; placet tamen te ea quae hactenus diximus
et meminisse et probare. Nos, Dominice, pergamus ad reliqua.

DOMINICUS. Pergamus; neque enim ego minus cupio te disserentem audire quam Ioannes ipse.

2 MATTHAEUS. Sequitur, nisi fallor, iustitiae ratio, quam tu heri
multo melius in republica quam in regno coli affirmabas.

DOMINICUS. Ita nunc quoque mihi videtur.

MATTHAEUS. Quibus, obsecro, de causis ita putas?

DOMINICUS. Tum propter leges, tum propter commercia et alia
humanae societatis officia quae unicuique iure debentur, tum vero
propter civium inter se aequalitatem ac similitudinem, quae quidem omnia apud nos et potiora esse et longe melius servari existimo.

MATTHAEUS. Quibus, obsecro, legibus vivitis?

DOMINICUS. Nostris.

MATTHAEUS. Unde eas habuistis?

# Book II

JANOS. Hello, father. Let's go over by the sundial,[1] if you don't   1
mind.

MATTIAS. That is fine with me. But how are you? Do you endorse yesterday's disputation, son, or do you prefer republican to
royal liberty now that you've had time to think about it?

JANOS. I continue to believe that republican liberty does not bear
comparison with our royal liberty. How can anyone think their
elections, magistrates and courts are free by comparison with
ours? But doubtless I am interrupting you; I want to hear, father,
what you wish to say on the other issues Domenico raised.

MATTIAS. And hear you shall; but I'm pleased that you remember and endorse what we've said thus far. Let's go on with the rest,
Domenico.

DOMENICO. Yes, let's carry on. And I'm no less eager to hear you
speak than János himself is.

MATTIAS. The next subject, unless I'm mistaken, is the account   2
of justice, which yesterday you claimed was cultivated much better
in republics than in kingdoms.

DOMENICO. That also seems to me the case today.

MATTIAS. Why, please, do you think so?

DOMENICO. In part because of our laws, in part on account of
our commercial relations and other obligations of human society
which are owed to everyone by right, in part because the equality
and similarity of our citizens among themselves. All these forms
of justice I think are preferable in our state and far better practiced
there.

MATTIAS. What laws do you live by, please?

DOMENICO. Our own.

MATTIAS. And where did you get them from?

3   DOMINICUS. Partim ex Romanis accepimus, partim ipsi condidimus.

MATTHAEUS. Quibus nos porro vivere arbitraris?

DOMINICUS. Utique vestris.

MATTHAEUS. Unde acceptas putas?

DOMINICUS. A maioribus vestris.

MATTHAEUS. Quo igitur pacto vestras iudicas meliores esse quam nostras? An vos sapientiores estis?

DOMINICUS. Minime. Sed vestrae a singulis hominibus, nostrae ab universo senatu sunt conditae; multos autem plus in omni re sapere quam unum te dubitare non arbitror.

4   MATTHAEUS. Istud quidem postea viderimus; hoc interim ex te quaero: quis Romanas leges condiderit?

DOMINICUS. Eas partim ab Atheniensibus accepere, partim ipsi condidere.

MATTHAEUS. Atheniensium porro leges quis condiderat?

DOMINICUS. Priores Draco, posteriores Solon.

MATTHAEUS. Singuli ergo isti fuere, non universi. Romanis vero quis primus leges instituit?

DOMINICUS. Numa Pompilius.

MATTHAEUS. Iste quoque, ut vides, unus fuit et quidem rex.

DOMINICUS. Emendavit tamen eas atque illis alias addidit postea senatus.

MATTHAEUS. Quas addidit?

DOMINICUS. Primo, Duodecim Tabulas, deinde eas quas consules ac ceteri magistratus de integro sanciebant.

5   MATTHAEUS. Atqui Duodecim Tabulae unius Solonis sunt, ceterae omnes singulorum hominum, ut inscriptiones ipsae declarant. Dicuntur enim Leges Juliae, Corneliae, Puppiae, Rosciae a singulis auctoribus, non ab universo senatu, quod si eas senatus condidisset, non singulis hominibus ascriberentur. Quid Servius

DOMENICO. Partly we had them from the Romans, in part we invented them ourselves.

MATTIAS. By what laws do you think we live, then?

DOMENICO. Surely by your own.

MATTIAS. Where do you think we acquired ours?

DOMENICO. From your ancestors.

MATTIAS. Why then do you think yours are better than ours? Do you have more wisdom?

DOMENICO. Not at all. But yours were instituted by individual men; ours were laid down by the whole senate. I don't think you can doubt that many men are wiser than one.

MATTIAS. We'll examine that issue later. Meanwhile, let me ask you this: Who founded the laws of Rome?

DOMENICO. They received them in part from the Athenians and in part they founded them themselves.[2]

MATTIAS. Who founded the laws of the Athenians, then?

DOMENICO. The first set was founded by Draco, the second by Solon.

MATTIAS. They were individuals, then, not collectivities. And who was the first to institute laws for the Romans?

DOMENICO. Numa Pompilius.[3]

MATTIAS. He too was a single individual, as you see, and a king at that.

DOMENICO. The Senate however corrected them and added others to them later.

MATTIAS. Which did they add?

DOMENICO. First, the Twelve Tables; then those that were sanctioned originally by consuls and other magistrates.

MATTIAS. Yet the Twelve Tables were Solon's work, a single man, and all the rest were laws of single men, as their titles show, for they were called the Lex Julia, the Lex Cornelia, the Lex Puppia, the Lex Roscia after their individual authors, not after the whole Senate. If the Senate had instituted them, they would not have

Sulpicius, Mucius Scaevola, Pomponius, Ulpianus, Paulus ceterique iuris consulti quorum hodie legibus utimur? Nonne singuli suarum auctores extitere? Quis porro eas in eum quem habemus ordinem digessit et in concinnam hanc brevitatem redegit? Nonne Iustinianus, qui et unus et imperator fuit? Quibus rationibus efficitur ut Romanae leges, quibus vos, ut affirmas, utimini, ab uno semper et conditae et reformatae fuerint.

6     Neque vero aliarum nationum leges a pluribus conditae sunt. Hebraeorum enim leges, quae sacrae a nobis divinaeque habentur, ab uno Moyse illis sunt traditae atque ab ipso Deo, ut affirmabat, institutae; Cretensium leges, quae ab Iove conditae putabantur, unus Minos composuit; Lacedaemoniorum item leges, quae per universam Graeciam optimae ac sanctissimae habebantur, rex eorum Lycurgus instituit; omnium denique nationum leges ab uno aliquo institutae atque illis traditae sunt. Vestras quoque, si recte inspicies, ab uno aliquo semper institutas invenies, sed quia nomen eius fortasse satis celebre non est, in tuam cognitionem non venit.

7     DOMINICUS. Fateor quidem esse leges nostras a singulis civibus institutas, et ego nonnullos memini qui leges aliquot me praesente sanxerunt, sed eas omnes senatus suo iudicio atque auctoritate confirmavit, quod si factum non esset, eas populus ratas non haberet.

MATTHAEUS. Nos quoque senatum habemus et quidem ex universo regno delectum, cui leges, quas ipsi sancimus, ostendimus eiusque iudicio atque auctoritate comprobandas tradimus. Legum tamen latio, ut etiam Plato affirmat, ad regiam dignitatem proprie pertinet. Quod si tam vestrae quam nostrae leges ab uno conditae sunt et multorum postea iudicio comprobatae, cur vestrae potiores esse possint non video.

been ascribed to single individuals. And what of Servius Sulpicius, Mucius Scaevola, Pomponius, Ulpian, Paulus and the other juris-consults whose laws we use today?[4] Weren't these individuals the authors of their own laws? Furthermore, who digested the laws into the order we have them and created this brief, elegant redaction? Wasn't it Justinian, who was both an individual and an emperor? By this account the laws of Rome, which you affirm that you use, were founded and reformed always by single individuals.

Nor were the laws of other nations founded by pluralities, for    6
the laws of the Hebrews, which we hold to be sacred and divine, were handed down to them by Moses alone and instituted by God himself, as he affirmed. The laws of the Cretans, which were believed to be laid down by Jupiter, Minos alone drew up; likewise those of the Spartans, which were considered throughout Greece as the best and most holy laws, King Lycurgus instituted.[5] In short, the laws of all the nations were laid down by a single individual and passed down to them. And if you examine the question correctly, you will find that your laws too were always instituted by some one person, but that his name is not known to you, perhaps because he was not famous enough.

DOMENICO. I admit that our laws were instituted by individual    7
citizens, and I remember some men who enacted several laws when I was present, but all of these were confirmed by the judgment and authority of the senate. And if they had not done so, the people would not have considered them valid.

MATTIAS. We too have a senate, and one chosen from the entire kingdom at that, to which we show the laws we have ourselves enacted, turning them over to be endorsed by their considered judgment and authority. Yet legislation, as even Plato affirms, pertains properly to the royal office.[6] But if your laws and our laws alike are founded by a single individual and afterwards endorsed by the judgment of many, I don't see how yours could be preferable.

8 DOMINICUS. Possem tibi multa earum capita recitare et cum vestris conferre, sed volo tibi concedere non esse nostras vestris potiores. Melius certe nostrae a nobis quam a vestris vestrae servantur.

MATTHAEUS. Quo tandem pacto?

DOMINICUS. Primo, quia plures legum custodes magistrosque habemus, qui delinquere plebem non sinunt; delicta autem omnia a pluribus et citius deprehenduntur et facilius corriguntur. Deinde, quia nos in sontes gravius et severius animadvertimus quam vos. Unus enim vel exorari vel corrumpi quoquomodo potest, multi non possunt; sublata porro veniae spe, peccandi quoque licentia tollitur.

9 MATTHAEUS. Existimatis fortasse reges solos legum custodes esse neque alios habere custodes? Quid vero tot praetores, tot provinciarum praefectos, tot iudices, tot magistratus in regno toto facere arbitramini? Uni huic rei omnes incumbunt atque ad nos de singulis delictis referunt. Omitto alios quos ipsi exploratores submittimus, ne quid nobis ignotum sit, ita ut ne minima quidem, quae usquam fiunt, latere nos queant. Nos, qui non solum legibus, sed legum etiam custodibus praesumus, delicta ipsa, omni animi perturbatione submota, quippe qui ab illis ut plurimum longe absimus, liberrime atque aequissime iudicamus. Neque vero, cum necesse est, quisquam nobis severius in reos graviusque animadvertit; verum id non nisi maximis de causis et quam rarissime facimus, Aquinatis illud nobis semper proponentes,

nulla umquam de morte hominis cunctatio longa est.

Exorari vero aut corrumpi nos non ita facile possumus, quippe qui neque multos nobis sanguine coniunctos habeamus. Nam soli su-

DOMENICO. I could cite you many specific provisions and com-  8
pare them with yours, but I will concede to you that ours are not
preferable to yours. But ours are certainly better observed by us
than yours are by you.

MATTIAS. Why do you say that?

DOMENICO. First, because we have many guardians and teachers
of the laws who don't allow the plebs to misbehave; all infractions
are more quickly caught by many people and more easily corrected. Second, because we take more serious and severe punitive
action against the guilty than you do. For one person can be influenced or in some way corrupted; many cannot. Furthermore,
when expectation of being indulged in wrongdoing is removed,
freedom to do so is taken away too.

MATTIAS. Do you perhaps suppose that kings are the sole  9
guardians of the law [in kingdoms] and that it has no other guardians? What then do you think that all those judicial ministers, all
those provincial governors, all those judges and magistrates are doing all over the kingdom? They are all devoting their energies to
this one purpose and reporting back to us on individual offenses. I
omit the others whom we ourselves send out secretly as spies, lest
something be hidden from us, so that not even the smallest act
that is committed can be hidden from us. We, who are set over
not only the laws, but also the guardians of the laws, judge these
very offenses in the freest and most equitable way, dispassionately,
being as far removed as possible from them. Nor is there anyone
more serious and severe than we are in taking punitive action
against the guilty when necessary. Yet this we do only in the rarest
circumstances, and only in exceptional cases, keeping before us always that dictum of Juvenal,

No delay can be too long where a man's life is concerned.[7]

But we cannot be so easily influenced or corrupted, not having
many blood relations—we are [socially] isolated and usually form

mus et matrimonia ut plurimum cum externis contrahimus, neque opibus aut muneribus indigeamus, quippe qui et ditissimi simus et alios nostris opibus locupletemus.

10    Vos autem multo facilius meo iudicio flecti corrumpique potestis. Nam, cum multi sitis, multas quoque sanguinis coniunctiones, affinitates, clientelas necessitudinesque habeatis necesse est, quas quidem deserere sine summo ac nefario scelere non potestis. Multos itaque defendatis, iuvetis, amplectamini necesse est, si crudeles in vestros et impii esse non vultis. Quo fit ut multa apud vos crimina inpune abeant. De vobis ipsis, qui magistratus geritis ‹et› rempublicam administratis, nihil dico, quos, cum plurimi sitis et ab humana fragilitate nequaquam immunes, labi nonnumquam, errare, nescire, decipi necesse est. Quis porro in vos animadvertere audeat et, ut Aquinas ait,

> quis custodiat[2] ipsos
> custodes?

Nonne alter sibi metuit quod molitur in alterum,[3] neque audet quisquam in alium facere quod ipse mox ab alio pati possit? Nobis hoc contingere non potest, qui neque imperii socium habemus neque quicquam timemus; ab aliquo libera nobis in omnes potestas est, vobis non est.

11    Vos, praeterea, cum multi sitis, minus opum singuli habeatis necesse est. Quod enim in multos distribuitur, etiam si per se amplissimum sit, ipsa divisione minuitur. Itaque cum magnas opes singuli non habeatis, et omnes mortales, praesertim in quibus aliqua aemulatio est, sint habendi cupidi, multo facilius corrumpi potestis quam nos, qui et opes regni universas obtinemus et ab omni non modo invidia, verum etiam aemulatione liberi sumus.

marriage alliances with foreigners — and we have no need of money or gifts, as we are extremely rich ourselves and enrich others with our wealth.[8]

You, however, can be influenced or corrupted much more easily, 10 in my judgment. For since you are many, you necessarily have many blood relations, marriage alliances, relations of clientage and personal ties which you cannot abandon without the greatest and foulest villainy. So necessarily you defend many, you help many, you embrace many if you do not wish to be cruel and wicked towards your own. Which is how so many crimes go unpunished among you. I say nothing about you yourselves who hold magistracies and govern the republic. Since you are many and by no means immune to human weakness, you will necessarily be corrupted, make mistakes, overlook things or be deceived from time to time. Furthermore, who would dare take punitive action against you, and as Juvenal says,

> who is to guard
> the guardians themselves?[9]

Does not one person fear that what is being plotted against another will be his own fate? Will someone dare do to another what he himself could presently suffer from another? This could not happen in our case, as we have no associate in our power, nor do we fear any such thing. Our power over all is free from another's power; yours is not.

You, moreover, being many, necessarily as individuals have 11 fewer resources, for what is divided among many, even it if is very large in itself, is diminished by its very division. Thus, since you as individuals do not have great resources, and all mortals, especially in matters where there is some rivalry, must be regarded as [presumptively] greedy, you can be much more easily corrupted than we, who have all the resources of the kingdom and are free not only from all envy, but all rivalry. If we ourselves do not keep

Leges autem si ipsi non servamus, puniri ab homine non possumus; aliis certe ad unguem servandas curamus, ita tamen curamus ut quam leges in criminibus puniendis prudentiam habere non possunt, ipsi habeamus, habitaque nunc rerum, nunc personarum ratione, clementiae potius laudem quam severitatis affectemus amarique a subditis quam timeri malimus. Quo fit ut leges a nostris multo quidem melius, ut ego sentio, sed, ut tu etiam fateberis, non deterius quam a vestris serventur.

12   DOMINICUS. Esto. Hoc quoque, quando tu ita vis, tibi concedamus et cetera omnia aequa faciamus. Praestat certe sub optima lege quam sub optimo rege vitam ducere.

MATTHAEUS. Quamobrem?

DOMINICUS. Primo, quia lex omnibus quid agendum sit tamquam optimus dominus artifexque praescribit. Rex vero, quasi minister atque instrumentum, quoddam legem aliis proponit, interpretatur et summo studio servandam curat. Ob id enim vel maxime reges instituuntur, ut populum sub legibus aequo iure contineant, legesque ipsas et ab hostibus, si opus est, armis defendant et a civibus intactas inviolatasque conservent; denique se legum, ut dixi, ministros instrumentaque praebeant. Optabilius autem est domino quam ministro, artifici quam instrumento subiacere. Ita fit ut legi quam regi praestet esse subiectum. Deinde rex, homo cum sit, amori, odio, irae, invidiae, cupiditati ceterisque affectibus obnoxius est. Lex, cum sensu careat, omnis affectus ac perturbationis est expers; ipsa quidem omnibus semper aequa atque eadem est. Rex idem semper esse non potest, ex quo efficitur ut optimae legi quam regi, quamvis optimo, parere satius ducam.

13   MATTHAEUS. Acute mehercule et subtiliter arguis, Dominice, ostendisque te et dialectices et philosophiae esse non ignarum. Sed quid tu 'sub lege vivere' appelles, non intellego. Nam si id dicis ut

the laws, we cannot be punished by man. Certainly we see to it that others observe them to the letter, yet we are careful that the prudence the laws cannot possess in punishing crimes, we ourselves possess, and taking account, now of circumstances, now of persons, we aim at a reputation for clemency rather than severity, and prefer to be loved by our subjects rather than feared.[10] Hence I believe that the laws are much better kept by us, but as even you will admit, they are at least kept no worse by us than by you.

DOMENICO. Let it be so. We shall concede this to you as well, 12 since you wish it so, and let's call it equal for all the rest. But it is surely better to spend one's life under an excellent set of laws than under an excellent king.[11]

MATTIAS. Why is that?

DOMENICO. First, because law prescribes to everyone what they must do, as though it were the best lord and best craftsman.[12] But a king, like a kind of minister or tool, promulgates the law to others, interprets it and with the greatest zeal makes sure that it is observed. This is in fact the main reason kings were established, to restrain the people fairly under laws, and he both defends the laws with arms from enemies if need be, and keeps them intact from the citizens and inviolate. In the end, they offer themselves as ministers and tools of the laws, as I've said. But it is more desirable to be subject to a lord than to a minister, to a craftsman than to a tool. Hence it is better to be subject to law than to a king.

Second, a king, being a man, is subject to love, hatred, anger, envy, lust and the other passions. Law, since it lacks the power of sense, is free of all passion and strong emotion, and is always the same and equal for all.[13] A king cannot always be the same, hence I believe it is preferable to obey excellent laws than to obey a king, however excellent.

MATTIAS. By Hercules, you argue with acuteness and subtlety, 13 Domenico, and you show that you are not ignorant of either dialectic or philosophy! But I don't understand what you call "living

homines sine magistratu, sine monitore, sine rectore aliquo legibus sua sponte obtemperent, vide quid dicas. Si enim ita boni, ita moderati erunt, ut quae legibus praescribuntur omnia ultro servent (si quidem tales umquam reperientur), ii legibus non indigebunt. Ipsi sibi lex erunt, immo aliis praescribere leges poterunt. Sed neque hactenus, quod ego quidem sciam, multi reperti sunt, neque, ut arbitror, in posterum reperientur. Sin erunt humanis cupiditatibus perturbationibusque obnoxii, quales vulgo homines esse videmus, hi profecto leges contemnent et tamquam ranae illae quae trabem pro rege acceperant, suis legibus insultabunt. Sin autem id intelligis, ut homines ita sub legibus vivant, ut habeant legum ipsarum custodes ac defensores magistratus, a quibus coerceantur et inviti, si opus sit, legibus parere compellantur (quod quidem magis consentaneum est), quaero ex te, primum, cur reges potius quam magistratus legum ministros atque instrumenta esse dicas, aut si soli reges legum ministri ac defensores sunt, qui magis dicatur 'sub legibus vivere' is qui sub magistratibus vivit quam qui sub regibus? Quod si utrique eodem modo leges custodiunt ac defendunt, quodnam ius in leges magistratus quam reges magis habeant, ut qui sub ipsis vivunt 'sub legibus vivere' dicantur, qui vivunt sub regibus non dicantur?

14 Deinde, si leges ab hominibus conditae sunt praesertimque ab regibus, cupio abs te scire quo pacto opus ipsum artifice et auctore suo melius ac nobilius esse possit? Reges vero et legum latores, cur potius ministri atque instrumenta legum quam domini atque auctores appellari debeant, cum ipsi et eas quibus praesunt leges condiderint et conditas ab aliis possint emendare, immo etiam quottidie emendent? Eoque magis homo ipsa lege[4] melior atque optabilior sit quod ipse legem et componere et emendare potest, lex se ipsam non potest. 'Atqui lex optima emendatione non eget.'[5]

under the law." If you mean that men obey the laws spontaneously without a magistrate, a watchdog or some kind of ruler, look what you're saying. For if men will be so good and self-controlled that they observe willingly all that the laws prescribe (if indeed such men could ever be found), they won't need laws. They will be laws unto themselves,[14] indeed, they will be able to prescribe laws for others. But hitherto, so far as I am aware, not many such persons have been found, nor shall they be in future, I think. But if men continue to be subject to human desires and emotions, as we commonly see they are, they will assuredly despise the laws, and like those frogs who took a log for a king, they will jeer at his laws.[15] But if you realize that men live under laws only insofar as they have magistrates as guardians of these laws and as police by whom they are coerced and unwillingly, if need be, compelled to obey the laws (which is the more consistent view), my question for you is, first, why you would say that kings are any more ministers and tools of the laws than magistrates are; or if kings alone are ministers and protectors of laws, why the man who lives under magistrates is said "to live under the laws" any more than the man who lives under kings? But if both kings and magistrates guard and defend the laws in the same way, what greater legality do magistrates have than kings, such that men who live under magistrates are said "to live under law," while those who live under kings are not said so to live?

Secondly, if laws are laid down by men and especially by kings, 14 I would like to know from you how a work can ever be better or nobler than its craftsman or author? And why should kings and legislators be called ministers and tools of the laws rather than their lords and authors, since they themselves laid down the laws over which they have charge and can amend laws laid down by others — indeed, they amend them on a daily basis. And all the more so as a man is better and more desirable than the law itself, because he can lay down and amend a law, but a law cannot do this for itself. "But [you say] the best law needs no amendment."

Immo vero nulla tam distincta, tam accurata, tam cauta lex est, cui non quottidie aliquid addere, detrahere, immutare, interpretari, propter ea quae quottidie nova atque insperata eveniunt, necesse sit; plura enim singulis diebus re ipsa accidunt, quam quae aut cogitari ab homine aut lege ulla caveri potuerint.

15    Leges praeterea non nisi in universum loquuntur; quod nisi singulis aut rebus aut personis ab homine accommodentur, insulsae plane atque inutiles videbuntur. Quid cum aut ambiguae aut contrariae inter se aut obscurae sunt? Quid cum voluntas scriptoris cum scripto ipso videtur dissentire? Nonne eas declarare, componere, dilucidare interpretarique[6] ab homine et quidem prudentissimo ac peritissimo necesse est? Quod si et emendatione et interpretatione sine dubio indigent, ut docuimus? Quis eas melius vel emendare vel interpretari potest, quam is qui de integro condidit? Hunc autem unum fuisse et illum quidem regem satis abundeque declaratum est. Regem ergo non legum ministrum aut instrumentum esse, sed legibus praeesse dominarique perspicuum est. Quod cum ita sit, multo satius est regibus obtemperare quam legibus.

DOMINICUS. Cur igitur inventae sunt leges, si omnibus prospicere semper non possunt?

16    MATTHAEUS. Ut et quam plurimis et plerumque prospiciant; quemadmodum enim qui multos aliquam artem docent universalia illis praecepta tradunt, etiam si non omnibus aut semper utilia esse sciant, sed ut plurimis et plerumque conducant, ita legum latores, quae plurimis et ut plurimum conferre intellegunt, ea legibus in universum cavent. Quoniam autem multiplices et variae sunt hominum actiones, neque, ut ait Plato, fieri potest ut simplex et certus ordo ad res varias et incertas sit accommodatus, rex quibus leges prospicere satis non possunt, iis sua sapientia et cura prospiciat necesse est. Ne vero, id quod fieri non potest, singulis

On the contrary, there is no law so clear, so careful and so prudent that it is not necessary to add to it, subtract from it, change and interpret it on a daily basis, since new and unhoped-for events occur daily. For in reality many things happen every day which no man could have imagined and no law could anticipate.

Moreover, laws address only the general; and if they are not 15 adapted by a man to particular situations or persons, they seem stupid and useless. And what about when the laws are ambiguous, contradictory or little known? What about when the will of the writer seems to disagree with what is written? Isn't it then necessary for them to be made known, put in order, clarified and interpreted by a man, and an extremely prudent and knowledgeable one at that? What if they need amendment and interpretation beyond any doubt, as we have shown? Who is better able to amend or interpret them than the person who originally laid them down? That this was a single person, and a king at that, has been shown abundantly enough. It is clear therefore that a king is not a minister or tool of the laws, but has charge of them and lordship over them. And since this is the case, it is preferable by far to obey kings than to obey the laws.

DOMENICO. Why then were laws invented, if they can't always foresee everything?

MATTIAS. So that they could foresee most things at most times. 16 Just as a man who teaches an art to many people hands universal precepts down to them, even if he knows they are not always useful for everyone but are helpful to most people most of the time, so legislators anticipate in their laws the general conditions which they understand will apply to most people in general. Since the actions of mankind are many and various, and it is not possible, as Plato says, to adapt a simple, fixed order to things that are various and unfixed,[16] a king necessarily foresees by his care and wisdom things which the laws cannot sufficiently foresee. But lest he be forced to set out and command what every individual has to do,

quae agenda sunt voce proponere et iubere cogatur, leges, quae in universum omnibus aeque praecipiant omnesque pertinaciter et severe compellant, scriptas proponit; ipse autem pro cuiusque necessitate, utilitate, casu, tempore eas moderatur, emendat, abrogat atque restituit. 'At rex, cum homo sit, animi affectibus obnoxius est et ab amore, ira, cupiditate facile vinci potest; lex, cum sensu careat, non potest.' Eodem recidimus, ut dicamus legem per se hominibus imperare et se ipsam sine humana ope tutari atque ulcisci posse. Quod quam absurdum sit, quam fieri non possit, ipse considera.

DOMINICUS. Minime vero istud dico. Quis enim nescit leges sine humana ope vim per se nullam habere? Sed illud dico: regem utpote unum a perturbationibus facile vinci posse; legem, hoc est magistratum, utpote multos non posse.

17 MATTHAEUS. Primum nos de rege optimo loquimur, qui motus animi vincere et cohibere sciat, non se ab illis vinci patiatur, quales et apud Graecos et apud Romanos extitere permulti. Deinde, etiam si nemo a perturbationibus immunis aut invictus reperiatur, uni quam pluribus legum tutelam potius committendam esse censeo. Multos enim non solum invictos non esse, sed multo etiam facilius quam unum vinci posse existimo. Nam si unus affectibus vacuus non reperitur, ne multi quidem reperiuntur; porro multos plus perturbationum atque affectuum quam unum habere, proptereaque facilius vinci posse necesse est. Ubi enim vitii plus est, ibi profecto virtus minus potest. Quemadmodum autem, ubi materiae ad ardendum idoneae copia maior est, eo ignis immissus et maius et facilius incendium excitat, ita, ubi plures sunt qui flecti ab affectibus et corrumpi queant, illic profecto maior et facilior labes exo-

which is impossible, he sets out written laws which prescribe what is fair to all generally and which compel everyone with strictness and severity; while he himself moderates, amends, abrogates and makes restitution in proportion to the necessity, utility and context of each case. "But [you say] a king, since he is a man, is subject to passions and can be overcome easily by love, anger or desire; law, since it has no faculty of sensation, cannot." This comes back to the same thing: that we are saying that law commands men by itself and itself can protect and avenge them without human aid. Think for yourself how absurd that is, how impossible it is.

DOMENICO. I wouldn't say that at all. Who doesn't know that the laws have no intrinsic power without human aid? But this I do say: that a king, being a single person, can easily be overcome by emotions; while the law, that is the magistracy, being many people, cannot.

MATTIAS. First of all, we are talking about an excellent king who 17 knows how to conquer and control his emotions and not allow himself to be conquered by them — the kind of king of whom there were many examples among the Greeks and Romans. Secondly, even if no one may be found who is immune to or unconquerable by emotions, I still think that protection of the laws is better entrusted to one person than to many. In fact I believe that many persons are not only not unconquerable [by emotions], but can even be conquered much more easily than one person. For if you can't find one person free of passion, you surely won't find many; furthermore, many people have more passions and desires than one, so they will necessarily be more easily conquered by them. For where there is more vice, there can surely be less virtue. Where there is a greater abundance of inflammable materials, a fire burns more fiercely and more readily when lit. In just this way, where there are more people who can be influenced or corrupted by their emotions, there, surely, more dishonest conduct arises with greater ease. Once one person is infected, since cupidity will

ritur. Uno enim infecto, cum longe lateque cupiditates serpant, ceteri contagio ipso facile inficiuntur, ut

> grex totus in agris
> unius scabie perit et prurigine[7] porci
> uvaque conspecta livorem ducit ab uva.

Unus autem, cum neque per se morbi multum habeat neque ab alio possit accipere, profecto non ita facile corrumpi a morbis animi violarique potest. Si cui igitur legum custodia committenda est, uni qui virtutis plurimum, minimum vitiorum atque affectuum habet, committenda est. Quod si quis penitus ab omni affectu invictus et liber inveniri posset, unum profecto quam plures invenire facilius esset. Igitur, cum et legum tutela uni potius quam pluribus committenda sit, quoniam[8] se ipsam tueri non potest et facilius sit unum optimum invenire quam plures, praestat sub uno rege optimo quam sub aliquo magistratu legibus praesidente vitam ducere.

18  DOMINICUS. Obruis profecto me tua facundia, rex, et mentem meam tuis argumentationibus perinde ac Circe carminibus facere dicebatur pervertis. Nam, cum nihil mihi rectius ac sanctius videretur quam sub legibus ac magistratibus vivere, effecisti tuis rationibus ut regium imperium non deterius esse cogar existimare. Et quamvis id non facile natura concedat, cum sim in libera civitate natus et sua cuique patria optima videatur, tuae tamen rationes me id prope iam fateri compellunt. Sed audire cupio quid ad reliqua responsurus sis, ut totus libensque in tuam sententiam traducar.

MATTHAEUS. Placet te paulatim in nostram sententiam accedere, neque id orationis nostrae, sed ipsius veri vi et potentia effici putes; nam nostra quidem oratio, apud te praesertim, vim tantam non habet. Sed quae tandem sunt ista quibus me adhuc respondere vis?

gradually creep in far and wide, the rest are easily infected by the contagion, so that

> the whole herd in the field
> is ruined by the mange and itching of just one pig,
> and one bunch of grapes is discolored by the sight of another.[17]

An individual, however, since he would not have much sickness by himself and can't get much from someone else, surely cannot be so easily defiled and corrupted by mental sicknesses. Therefore if custody of the laws is to be entrusted to anyone, it should be entrusted to the one person who has the most virtue and the least vice and passion. And if someone unconquerable by and free of all passion can be found at all, it is surely easier to find one such person than many. Therefore, since protection of the law is to be entrusted rather to one than to many persons, since the law cannot protect itself and since it is easier to find one excellent person than many, it is better to spend one's life under a single excellent king than under some magistracy presiding over the laws.

DOMENICO. You certainly overwhelm me with your eloquence, 18 king, and lead my mind astray with your arguments, just as Circe was said to do with her magic charms. When it seemed to me that nothing was more right and holy than to live under laws and magistrates, your reasoning compelled me to reckon that royal power is no worse. And although nature does not easily give way in this, as I was born in a free city and everyone's homeland seems best to him, your reasoning already nearly compels me to admit this. But I want to hear what you will respond to the rest, so that I may be completely and willingly brought over to your opinion.

MATTIAS. It pleases me that you are yielding gradually to my views and do not think this is happening because of my rhetorical power rather than the force of the truth itself. For my speech does not have so much power, especially with you. But what, please, is it that you still wish me to respond to?

19 DOMINICUS. Quae ad ius humanae societatis et civitatis conservationem pertinent, quae quidem omnia nos sanctius colere et
servare melius videmur.

MATTHAEUS. Quaenam ista sunt?

DOMINICUS. Commercia imprimis, quae apud nos multo, ut
mihi quidem videtur, liberiora multoque frequentiora quam apud
vos sunt. Nam et nostri cives libere cum omnibus nationibus commercia et societates contrahunt totumque terrarum orbem suis
mercibus sibi patefaciunt mortalesque omnes sua industria suisque
artibus iuvant, et nationes omnes undique in nostras civitates tamquam in communia omnium gentium emporia confluunt, ut multo
plures quandoque in nostris civitatibus peregrini quam cives reperiantur. Vestri autem cives suis finibus, suo caelo contenti, ad exteras nationes non commeant; venientes ad se non satis benigne sus-
cipiunt, quasi eorum opes alii consumpturi atque asportaturi
veniant, non suas illis vicissim allaturi. Neque vos sine multis et
magnis vectigalibus in vestra regna peregrinas merces admittitis et,
quasi parum sit ad vos ea quibus indigetis ultro ab aliis nationibus
afferri, immunia a vectigalibus esse non vultis; immo antequam
vestra sint, ab illis ipsis qui deferunt pretio redimi cogitis. Quae
quidem gentium inter se commercia dirimunt et humanae societatis iura pervertunt.

20 MATTHAEUS. Videris tu quidem mihi non in universum de
omni regno atque republica, sed de nostro tantum regno et de vestra republica disputare; ita non ceterarum inter se civitatum mores, sed nostros tantum vestrosque comparasti. Nam, si contra re-
putes, invenies neque omnium rerum publicarum cives per orbem
passim vagari, ut vos facitis, neque omnium regum subditos intra
suos se fines, ut nostri faciunt, continere. Nam et Galli atque
Hispani, qui sub regibus vivunt, non minus quam vos atque haud

DOMENICO. That which pertains to the justice of human society and the preservation of the state, all things which, it seems to me, we [republicans] cultivate more devotedly and preserve better.

MATTIAS. And what things are these?

DOMENICO. Commercial relations, principally, which seem to me much freer among us and much more widespread than among you. For our citizens contract commercial relations and partnerships with all nations freely and open up the whole world to their merchandise and help all mankind with their industry and crafts, and all nations everywhere flood into our [republican] cities as though into common emporia of all peoples, so that sometimes more foreigners are to be found in our cities than citizens. Your citizens, however, rest content with their own borders and their own skies, don't travel to foreign lands and are not overly welcoming to the people who come to them, as though others were coming to consume and carry off your wealth and were not in their turn going to import valuable goods of their own. And you don't admit foreign goods to your kingdom without imposing numerous large duties on them. As though it were some small thing that other nations willingly bring you the things you need, you don't want to grant them immunity from duties; indeed, before imported goods become your property, you try to make good their cost from the very people who have brought them to market. This is tantamount to dissolving commercial relationships among peoples and subverting the rights of human society.

MATTIAS. You seem to me not arguing generally about all kingdoms and all republics, but only about our kingdom and your republic; thus you are not comparing the customs of other states among themselves but only ours and yours. If you were to think it over, you would find, on the contrary, that the citizens of other republics do not all wander the globe, as you do, and the subjects of other kings do not all stay within their borders, as ours do. For the French and the Spanish, who live under kings, range over the

scio an etiam magis, universum terrarum orbem peregrinationibus navigationibusque collustrant et Senenses Lucensesque, qui sub reipublicae forma vivunt, non ferme Italiae fines egrediuntur.

21    Verum ego tibi ostendam, primum, haec, quibus tu iuvari mortales putas, commercia magna ex parte illis noxia et perniciosa esse; deinde, quae utilia sint neque nos, ut dicis, repellere neque vos omni ex parte admittere. Nam si verum ingenue fateri volumus, quid, obsecro, est aliud quod bene institutas civitates corrumpat et ex optimis pessimas reddat, nisi peregrini mores mutuaque commercia? Haec enim adolescentium mores pervertunt, haec patriam linguam adulterant, haec bene informatos animos illecebris lasciviisque effeminant et de ipso quasi modestiae et constantiae gradu deturbant; haec cum peregrinis opibus ac mercibus avaritiam pariter, ambitionem, gulam, libidinem et cetera foeda ac nefaria flagitia invehunt. Adolescentes enim domi pudice, parce liberaliterque educati, ubi mercaturae gratia ad exteras nationes se conferunt, liberius vivendi potestatem nacti, patriam sensim continentiam parsimoniamque[9] deponunt, affluenteque illis omnium rerum copia, cum socii atque auctores scelerum praesto omnibus locis adsint, facile teneros adhuc et molles animos, ut proni semper ad vitia sumus, in deteriorem partem deflectunt proclivesque in omne flagitii genus impellunt; mutatis moribus, linguam porro retinere non possunt. Ita post aliquot annos in patriam redeuntes, suorum civium mores ac disciplinam serpente passim labe contagioque corrumpunt.

22    Quid illa omnium gentium ac morum in una civitate permixtio atque colluvio, quantum civitati detrimentum affert? Dum enim se peregrini legibus illis astrictos esse non censent, cives quoque sua societate adductos, ad earum contemptum violationemque alliciunt; ita leges ab omnibus deseruntur. Diversissimis vero omnium gentium moribus in unam civitatem coeuntibus, mores patrii servari aut retineri qui possunt? Linguarum porro tanta varietas,

whole world with their travels and voyages no less than you do, possibly even more, while the Sienese and Lucchesi, who live under republican constitutions, usually do not leave the confines of Italy.

But let me show you, first, that these commercial relations 21 which you think helpful to mankind are mostly harmful and pernicious to them; secondly, that those commercial relations which *are* useful we neither reject, as you say, nor fully allow. If we will confess the truth to you frankly, what else is it, I ask you, that corrupts well-ordered cities and makes the best of them into the worst, except foreign ways and mutual trade? These things pervert the mores of the young, adulterate the native language, make well educated minds effeminate with wanton allurements, and undermine modesty and constancy. These things carry along with them, besides foreign wealth and foreign wares, avarice, ambition, gluttony, lust and other foul and wicked sins. Young men who were brought up at home to be decent, frugal and generous, when they betake themselves to foreign nations for the sake of trade, encounter an ability to live with greater freedom, and insensibly they discard their native self-control and parsimony. Awash in opulence of every kind, surrounded by companions and agents of wickedness everywhere, their soft and tender minds (and we are always prone to vice) are twisted into following the worse course, and they are driven to slide into every form of sin, changing their mores and even their language. Thus, returning after many years to their country, they gradually corrupt and infect the customs and orderly conduct of their fellow citizens everywhere.

How does that mixing and jumbling together of all peoples and 22 ways of life in a single city-state bring so much harm to it? When foreigners believe themselves to be unconstrained by those laws, the citizens too who are attracted by their society are enticed to despise and violate them as well; thus everyone abandons the laws. When the utterly diverse mores of all nations come together in a single city-state, who can observe or preserve their native mores?

nonne patrium sermonem adulterat et pervertit omnino? Legibus
porro et moribus de civitate sublatis linguaque immutata, nonne
ipsum civitatis nomen tollitur? Quid illa externarum opum mer-
ciumque invectio, nonne omnes cupiditates, omnia scelera, omnia
flagitia secum advehit? Quae enim mortales non norunt, ea numquam ferme cupiunt; ubi vero res sibi antea ignotas vident, facile
earum cupiditate capiuntur. Divitiae praeterea et copiae libidinis,
gulae, avaritiae, ambitionis vitiorumque omnium fomites et altri-
ces sunt.

23     Atque harum quidem rerum omnium, ne de aliis civitatibus dicere cogamur, satis idoneum nobis exemplum praebere potest Romana respublica quae, quamdiu fuit suis moribus et paupertate
contenta, omnes Italiae Graeciaeque civitates gloria rerum gestarum et virtutum magnitudine superavit; ubi vero Graeciae primum, deinde Asiae mores, opes deliciasque admisit, omnia scelera
flagitiaque admisit. Dilabente vero parsimonia, continentia civi-
lique disciplina, paulatim ex optima deterrima facta est. Qua quidem ex immutatione quid postea consecutum sit cernis: concitatis
enim in se ob ingentia atque intolerabilia sua vitia exterarum gentium odiis atque armis, omne non modo imperium, verum etiam
nomen, genus, linguam omnem decusque amisit, atque ita amisit
ut numquam e tanta ruina resurrectura aut sui similis futura videatur. Hodie quoque illae quae remansere reliquiae, propter multarum gentium quae ad sacra confluunt colluvionem, proprios mores linguamque non habent.

24     Qua quidem ex re satis, ut opinor, apparet quantum obsint peregrini mores et commercia civitatibus. Quod si haec mores corrumpunt, linguam invertunt, omnia vitia et cupiditates invehunt,
civitates denique ipsas evertunt, quid humano generi prosint aut
quam ob causam sint admittenda non video. Plato quidem, philosophorum omnium sine controversia princeps, cum optimam rem-

Furthermore, doesn't such a variety of languages adulterate and entirely pervert the native speech? With its laws and mores destroyed and its language altered, isn't the very name of the city destroyed? And what of that importation of foreign products and wares? Doesn't it bring with it all lusts, all crimes, all sins? The things of which mankind has had no experience they generally never desire; but when they catch sight of things formerly unknown to them, they are easily captivated by desire for those things. Moreover, riches and plenty ignite and feed lust, gluttony, avarice, ambition and all the vices.

The Roman republic offers us a suitable enough example of all 23 this (not to speak of other states). So long as it was content with its own mores and poverty, it excelled all the cities of Italy and Greece in the glory of its deeds and the greatness of its virtues; when it allowed in the customs, wealth and pleasures, first of Greece, then of Asia, it let in every crime and every sin. As its thriftiness, self-restraint and civil discipline faded away, Rome, which had been the best of states, gradually became the worst of all. You may see this in the change that followed afterwards: for once it had aroused the hatred and the arms of all outside peoples against it on account of its enormous and intolerable vices, it lost not only its empire, but also its reputation, its ethnic identity, its whole language and its honor, and lost it in such a way that it seems it will never rise again from so great a collapse and be like itself again. Today too the remnants of it that remain, thanks to the jumbling together of many peoples who stream to Rome for its sacred sites, have no mores or language of their own.

From this case it is evident enough, I think, how much foreign 24 ways and trade are harmful to states. But if these things corrupt morals, subvert languages, bringing with them all vices and lusts, in the end destroying those very cities, I don't see what advantage they bring to humanity or why they should be allowed. Plato, the undisputed prince of the philosophers, when he wished to found

publicam constituere vellet, hoc imprimis cavit, ut civitas ea procul
a mari sita esset, ne aut peregrinis in eam quottidie confluentibus
aut civibus ad alias frequenter navigantibus mores civitatis cor-
rumperentur. Quod si Plato utilia civitati commercia existimasset,
non ea profecto legibus prohibuisset.

25     'At indiget externis rebus vita: non enim omnia nasci omnibus
locis possunt.' Ego vero provinciam nullam esse[10] puto quae non
omnia ad usus vitae necessaria abunde producat. Deum enim ipsum, optimum ac beneficentissimum parentem nostrum, incusare
videremus, si quicquam ad vitam degendam necessarium singulis
locis deesse diceremus, quasi ipse non satis prudenter humano generi prospexisset, qui terram ita constituisset[11] ut nusquam in ea
homines sine aliarum terrarum praesidio possent vivere. Prospexit
quidem nobis omnibus prudentissime ac liberalissime optimus ille
opifex et parens Deus, terramque universam ita produxit, ita con-
stituit, ut in omnibus eius partibus ali homines et servari possent,
alii tamen in aliis melius et salubrius viverent. Nam cum omnibus
in rebus singularem suam providentiam sapientiamque ostenderit,
in hac una, supra quam credibile est, eam nobis perspicue declaravit. Cum enim singulas caeli terraeque partes incredibili rerum
omnium varietate distingueret, non modo ut alia aliis locis nascerentur, sed ut alia quoque caeli temperies et salubritas esset, ita
hominum quoque corpora naturasque accommodavit, ut quibus in
locis nati essent, in illis optime ac facillime viverent. Natura enim
nostra, parvo admodum contenta cum sit, quibus ab initio rebus
assuevit, illis facile sustentatur atque alitur. Quibus vero ali natura
sustentarique posset, quae quidem ad traducendam vitam necessaria Deus esse cognovit, ea omnibus passim exposuit, ut non modo

the best commonwealth, first made sure that the city would be founded on a site far from the sea, lest the mores of the state be corrupted by foreigners streaming into it on a daily basis or by its own citizens voyaging repeatedly to other cities.[18] If Plato had thought commercial relations useful for his city, he would surely not have prohibited them by law.[19]

"But [you will say] imported goods are necessary for life, for   25 not everything can be found in every place." But I think there is no province that does not produce in abundance all things necessary for life's use.[20] We would be laying charges against God himself, our best and most beneficent parent, if we were to say that there is anything lacking in a given place that is necessary for the conduct of human life — as though He had not taken forethought for the human race with sufficient prudence, as though He had so ordered a given land that men could never live in it without the aid of other lands. But God, that best creator and parent, did indeed take thought for us all in the most wise and generous way. He created and designed the whole earth in such a way that in each of its parts men might be nurtured and kept safe, though other men in other lands might live in a better and more salutary condition. For since in all things He shows His singular providence and wisdom, in this particular matter He has clearly made known His providence to us in an incredible way. For when He marked out the individual parts of the earth and sky with an unbelievable variety of all things, not only in such a way that different things arose in different places, but also so that there should be different climates and degrees of wholesomeness, He adapted the bodies and natures of men so that they would be born in the places where they might live best and with the greatest ease. For our nature, content as it is with very little, is easily sustained and nourished by the things to which it becomes accustomed from the outset. As nature can be nourished and sustained by those things which God knew to be necessary to live out one's life, He made them available to everyone

non quaerenda longius, sed ne magno quidem labore aut sumptu comparanda essent. Verum nos necessariis rebus contenti non sumus, sed naturae fines egressi, ultra quam satis est semper appetimus. Ita fit ut praesentibus et domesticis rebus non contenti, externas ingenti labore ac periculo, blandiente nobis cupiditate, conquiramus.

26    Dices fortasse: 'At deest aliis vinum, aliis oleum, aliis unicum illud humanae vitae praesidium, triticum. Nonne haec tibi ad vitam degendam necessaria esse videntur?' Mihi vero non. Quo enim pacto vel mortales omnes tot saeculis ante panis, vini et olei inventionem vixerunt, vel hodie multa hominum milia, quibus eorum usus omnino ignotus est, vitam ducunt? Quod si essent haec necessaria, carere illis natura non posset. Quid enim tanta fructuum atque animalium varietas et copia, tanta lactis ubertas? Nonne nobis ad vitam commode traducendam satis esse posset, si modo iis quae satis sunt vellemus esse contenti? Sed modum cupiditatibus nostris imponere nescimus; prolapsi iam omnes in hunc luxum atque incontinentiam sumus, ut sine panis, vini et olei usu vivere nullo modo posse videamur.

27    Sed esto; hoc nostrae fragilitati concedamus. Pauca certe admodum erunt quae ab exteris nationibus petenda sint, eaque a finitimis, qui a nostris moribus non magnopere discrepant, accipere possumus. Quae vero malum dementia est ad Ethiopicum aut Indicum Oceanum, ut gemmas inde et margaritas eruamus, navigare? Quae insania est universum terrarum orbem gulae aut luxuriae gratia peragrare? Quod, quia nostri non faciunt, eos desides esse et commercia societatemque ex humano genere tollere arbitraris? Non commercia tollimus aut odimus societatem, sed pecuniae cupiditate vacamus; contenti sumus iis quae partim apud nos gignuntur, partim ab externis mercatoribus ex Italia, Gallia,

everywhere, not only so that did they not have to be sought c
far-away places, but also so that they might be gathered with s.
labor and expense. But we are not content with necessities; we
beyond the bounds of nature and always desire more than enoug
hence we are not content with the things we have before us ?
home, but, coaxed by our desires, we seek out foreign goods with
immense labor and risk.

Perhaps you will say "But some of us lack wine, others oil, others that special safeguard of human life, wheat. Don't these things
seem to you necessary for living one's life?" But they don't to me.
For how did human beings survive for so many centuries before
the discovery of bread, wine and oil, how do so many thousands
of men even today live their life in entire ignorance of these
things? If they were necessities, nature could not lack them. Why
then the great variety and abundance of fruits and animals, the
great richness of milk? Is it not possible they could suffice us to
pass our lives with ease, if only we would be content with what is
enough? But we don't know how to place limits on our desires; we
have all now fallen into this state of self-indulgence and unre-
strained appetite, so that it seems to us impossible to live without
the use of bread, wine and oil.

But let that go; let's allow this much to our weakness. Surely    27
there are very few things indeed that must be sought from outside
countries, and these we can get from our neighbors, whose mores
do not differ much from our own. What the devil is this madness
anyway, sailing to the Ethiopian or Indian Ocean to pluck gems
and pearls from those shores? What insanity is this, traversing the
whole globe for the sake of gluttony and dissipation? Why do you
think we are lazy for not doing this, that we are destroying the
commercial and social relations of the human race? We're not taking away trade, we don't hate human society, but we are free of the
lust for money. We are content with the things our land produces
in part and in part with the things imported from Italy, France and

Germania nobis non petentibus afferuntur, non quod illis indigeamus, sed ne venientes ad nos exteras nationes repellere ac repu-
diare videamur.

28      Nostri quoque homines suis finibus egrediuntur et in easdem
quas modo dixi provincias, sed litterarum, non pecuniae gratia se
conferunt, qua quidem peregrinatione dignior atque honestior esse
nulla potest. Vos autem non finitimas modo, sed remotissimas
quoque provincias et omnes mundi angulos quaestus unius gratia
peragratis; nihil cupiditati vestrae invium atque inaccessum est;
usque ad inimicissimas Christiano nomini gentes, quod dictu nefarium est, penetrare audetis, contemptisque summi pontificis et
Christianae reipublicae imperiis communique omnium nostrum
salute neglecta, ferrum, arma, tela et cetera bellica instrumenta,
quibus nos expugnare mox queant, ad hostes nostros pro nimia
pecuniae cupiditate defertis. Utrum tandem hoc est, humanam societatem conservare an bellum fovere, cives prodere, rempublicam
Christianam evertere? Quae, quia nos non facimus, ignavi sumus,
commercia non amamus? Vos potius, ut vides, commercia dirimi-
tis, vos societatem dissolvitis, vos Christianam rempublicam nomenque evertitis, qui hostes nostros armatis, ad bellum instruitis,
in nostram perniciem concitatis. Neque vero hoc de vestra civitate
tantum dico, quae inter ceteras moderatissima est, sed de aliis
quoque Italiae civitatibus, quae sibi reipublicae nomen asciscunt.

29      'At vos,' inquis, 'peregrinis mercibus vectigalia imponitis, quod[12]
si peregrinos non odissetis, eos libere omnia importare atque exportare pateremini.' Quam liberi sint apud nos mercatores et
quam immunes, ne mihi ipsi blandiri videar, nolo dicere; illud tantum dico, eos, si non hospitaliter a nostris amiceque susciperentur,
si non maius hic quam alibi lucrum facerent, non tam frequenter
et tam cupide ad nos esse venturos. Si quid autem in portubus aut

Germany without our asking for them—not that we need them, but to prevent it looking like we are rejecting and repudiating the outside nations that come to us.

Our people too leave our borders and betake themselves to 28 what I just called the provinces, but for the sake of learning, not money. This indeed is the most worthy and honorable form of travel. You however scour not only nearby provinces but the most remote ones as well, and every corner of the globe, for the sake of gain. There is nowhere too trackless and inaccessible for your greed; you dare penetrate as far as those peoples who are most hostile to the Christian name, a thing wicked even to say; and showing contempt for the commands of the Supreme Pontiff and the Christian commonwealth and setting at nought the common security of us all, you bring our enemies swords, armor, spears and other instruments of war that could presently be used to defeat us, all from excessive love of money. What in the end is this behavior? Is it preserving human society, or is it fostering war, betraying citizens, subverting the Christian commonwealth? And we are spiritless and indifferent to trade relations because we don't do this? It is rather you, you see, who are breaking up trade relations, you who dissolve partnerships, you who ruin the Christian commonwealth and its good name when you arm our enemies, equip them for war and incite them to our undoing. But I don't say this about your city only, which is the most restrained among the rest, but of other cities of Italy that appropriate for themselves the name of republic.[21]

"But you impose duties on foreign merchandise," you say; "if 29 you didn't hate foreigners, you would allow them to import and export everything freely." Just how free and immune merchants are among us I don't want to say, lest I seem to be flattering myself. But this I do say: if they were not being received hospitably and in a friendly way by us, if they weren't making more profit here than elsewhere, they wouldn't be coming to us so often and with such avidity. If they do pay something in the ports and on the road to

in itinere publicanis nostris conservandi regni gratia persolvunt, quadruplum mox in mercium venditione recipiunt. Quod si quid nobis, qui tutos illis portus accommodamus, tuta itinera praestamus, salutis suae gratia persolverent, cum ipsi sua sponte et sui tantum quaestus gratia ad nos veniant, non iniuste persolverent.

30    Vos vero, quid? Immunesne omnes merces ad vos deferri permittitis?

DOMINICUS. Immo nullas.

MATTHAEUS. Quam ob rem?

DOMINICUS. Quia, cum imperium exiguum habeamus, tutari id, nisi nos vectigalium iuvaret magnitudo, non possemus.

MATTHAEUS. Vultis ergo ut etiam peregrini suis mercibus imperium vestrum tutentur?

DOMINICUS. Aequum est, si volunt apud nos suis mercibus quaestum facere, ut nos, cum ad eos commeamus, pendere illis vectigalia non recusamus.

31    MATTHAEUS. Quid illi qui ex aliis in alias provincias per vestram regionem iter faciunt, suntne a vectigalibus immunes?

DOMINICUS. Non sunt, si modo quicquam quod alicuius momenti sit secum ferant.

MATTHAEUS. Quare?

DOMINICUS. Ob eandem quam tu paulo ante dixisti, tutandi itineris et servandae regionis causam.

MATTHAEUS. Merces vero permittitisne omnes ad vos undecunque, etiam cum vectigalibus, deferri?

DOMINICUS. Nequaquam.

MATTHAEUS. Quas vero non admittitis?

32    DOMINICUS. Eas quae apud nos fiunt, ut lanicia omnia et quae serica vulgo vocant.

MATTHAEUS. Cur non?

DOMINICUS. Ut nostras vendamus, ne nostris alienae pretium atque auctoritatem minuant.

our tax collectors for the security of the kingdom, they soon make four times that from the sale of their merchandise. But if for their own safety they pay something to us, who keep the ports open for them and supply them with safe roads, there is no injustice in that payment, since they come to us of their own free will and solely for the sake of gain.

But what do you do? Do you permit all merchandise to be im- 30 ported free of duty?

DOMENICO. Actually, none.

MATTIAS. Why is that?

DOMENICO. Because we couldn't protect our empire, given its small size, without the help of large duties.

MATTIAS. So your wish is to have foreigners protect your empire with their merchandise?

DOMENICO. That's fair, if they want to make money in our country from their merchandise, just as we do not refuse to pay them import duties when we go to them.

MATTIAS. What about those who are travelling from one prov- 31 ince to another through your territory: are they not liable to duties?

DOMENICO. They are, but only if they are conveying something of value with them.

MATTIAS. Why is that?

DOMENICO. Because of what you said just now, in order to pro- tect the territory and keep the roads safe.

MATTIAS. You permit all kinds of merchandise to be imported (even with duty), from every source?

DOMENICO. By no means.

MATTIAS. Which kinds do you not allow in?

DOMENICO. Those that we ourselves manufacture, all woolens 32 and silks (as they are called in Italian).

MATTIAS. Why not?

DOMENICO. So that we can sell our own, and to prevent foreign wares bringing down the price or reputation of ours.

MATTHAEUS. Cur magis veremini ne alienae vestris quam ne vestrae alienis in vestra civitate a vestris civibus praeferantur?

DOMINICUS. Quia nova et inusitata omnia magis placent, et earundem mercium copia vilitatem parit.

33 MATTHAEUS. Vultis igitur ut vestri cives quae vos vultis et quanti vultis inviti emant. Quid si vestra aut non aeque bona sint aut illis aeque non placeant, peregrinas autem merces in vestram civitatem non admittitis, ut vos vestras ab aliis admitti vultis? Quid si alii vobis idem faciant? Estne hoc humanae societatis et commerciorum iura conservare, an civium et peregrinorum coniunctionem dissolvere et utrisque vendendi et emendi libertatem eripere? Nos quidem et omnium gentium merces admittimus et liberum unicuique per provincias nostras iter concedimus et ea quae apud nos sunt exportari ab omnibus tuto libereque permittimus. Vos igitur estis qui commercia non colitis, vos estis qui gentium iura perfringitis, vos estis qui humani generis communionem tollitis.

34 DOMINICUS. Memoria tenere te arbitror, rex, illud non modo tritum sed verum quoque probatumque proverbium, omnes sibi malle quam alteri. Nos, cum magna ex parte mercaturae dediti simus profiteamurque nos aliis vestium omnis generis copiam posse sufficere, iniurii profecto nobis ipsis videremur esse, si artis nostrae quaestum in nostra civitate aliis tribueremus, praesertim cum habeamus in eo genere tantam non modo copiam, verum etiam bonitatem atque praestantiam, ut nemo neque plura neque pretiosiora possit desiderare. Quod si peregrinas eius generis merces admitteremus, nostris non modo pretium, verum etiam auctoritatem minueremus. Videremur enim externis accipiendi nostrarum vel inopiam vel vitia aperte arguere, quae cum contra sint, nullo modo peregrina lanicia censuimus admittenda, neque propterea vel civibus vel peregrinis iniuriam facimus. Nam, cum plerique mercato-

MATTIAS. Why are you so afraid that foreign wares will be preferred to yours by your own citizens in your own city?

DOMENICO. Because they always prefer exotic novelties, and because an abundance of the same merchandise makes it cheap.

MATTIAS. So then, you want your citizens, unwillingly, to buy 33 the things you want at the price you want. What if your goods are not of equal quality and equally desirable to them, and you don't allow foreign goods into your own city — why do you want your goods to be allowed in by others? What if others do the same thing to you? Is this preserving the just rights of human society and economic relations, or is it breaking up the bond between citizens and foreigners and taking away the freedom to buy and sell from both of them? For our part we let in the merchandise of all peoples and allow them all free passage through our territories, and we permit what is ours to be exported safely and freely by all. It is you, therefore, who do not nurture trade relations, you who infringe the rights of nations, you who destroy the unity and shared interests of the human race.

DOMENICO. I think you remember, king, that familiar but tried 34 and true proverb, "Everyone prefers his own betterment to another's."[22] Since most of us devote ourselves to trade and we claim that we can supply an abundance of clothing of all types to others, we should assuredly seem to be doing ourselves an injury if we allowed others the right to profit from our own craft in our own city, especially when we have, of that type of goods, not only great abundance but the most excellent quality, so that no one could wish either for more or for more valuable wares. If we admit foreign wares of this type, we reduce not only the price but also our reputation. We would seem to outsiders to be openly conceding either that there was a shortage of our goods or that they were lacking in quality. Since the opposite is the case, we hold that foreign woolens should be no means be admitted, and we do no injury to foreigners or our own citizens on this account. Since most

res sint, cives ipsi hanc legem sanxerunt, neque ei a quoquam de-
rogari patiuntur. Peregrini vero, apud quos eadem ars in pretio aut
in honore est, eodem adversus nos iure utuntur, estque inter nos
tacito gentium consensu ita propter communem utilitatem comparatum, ut neutri ad alteros ex eo quo illi quaestum faciunt genere
merces deferant. Qui autem vel nullas omnino vel admodum paucas eius generis et viles habent, nimirum eos ab omnibus quae de-
feruntur accipere necesse est. Atque haec vobis, qui bellicis rebus
dediti estis, causa est ut omnes omnium gentium merces admitta-
tis: excludere enim eas, si commode vivere vultis, non potestis.
Nos admittere, si modo volumus civitatem nostram conservare,
non possumus. Quod, cum ab omnibus eiusdem artis fiat, conser-
vantur hac ratione commercia et societates non dirimuntur.

Sed de his hactenus; non enim vereor ne tu institutum nostrum
non probes.

35 MATTHAEUS. Ego vero, si id in rem vestram est atque ita inter
omnes maxime convenit, non improbo. Censeo tamen commercia
inter homines maxime libera esse oportere, sed in his unusquisque
suo utatur arbitrio; nos ad reliqua transeamus. Cupio enim scire
quid aliud sit ex hac tota ratione iustitiae in quo vestrum statum
nostro anteponatis.

36 DOMINICUS. Sequitur res in tota civili vita dignissima et in
omni civitate, ut ego sentio, maxime necessaria: civium aequalitas,
de qua imprimis cupio audire quid sentias. Haec enim una res civitatem et a principio condit et conditam diu servat; haec cives
omnes mira inter se benivolentia concordiaque devincit; haec invidiam, lites, factiones, mala denique omnia a civitate depellit. Hanc
Lycurgus, cum leges Spartanis conderet, ita in omni re, in omni
vitae parte servandam colendamque praecepit, ut, cum agrum
Spartanum messis tempore quondam perambularet, videretque in
areis acervos tritici omnes aequales, Spartam videri sibi patrimo-

of them are merchants, the citizens themselves have endorsed this law, nor will they suffer it to be set aside by anyone. And foreigners who value and honor the same craft rightly use the same law against us, and there is between us an arrangement for the common utility, by tacit consent of all peoples, that neither party will export to the other goods from which the other party makes its income. Parties that make no goods of this kind at all, or few or cheap ones, of course must necessarily take what is brought to them by everyone else. And this is the reason why you, who are devoted to military affairs, admit all the goods of all nations: because you cannot exclude them if you wish to live comfortably. We cannot do this if we wish to preserve our city. Since this pattern is followed by all who practice the same craft, commercial relations are preserved and businesses are not broken up.

But enough of this; I have no fear that you will not approve of our practice.

MATTIAS. In fact I do not condemn it if it is in your interest and 35 there is general agreement about it. Yet I do hold that commercial relations ought to be as free as possible among men, but in these matters each man may use his own judgment. Let us go on to the rest. For I wish to know what else there is, on this general subject of justice, wherein you prefer your state to ours.

DOMENICO. The next subject is the most excellent in all of civil 36 life and the most necessary in every city, in my opinion: the equality of the citizenry, a subject on which I would particularly like to hear your views. For this one principle stands at the foundation of a city from the beginning and long preserves it after its foundation. This principle binds citizens to each other with marvelous harmony and good will; this principle casts out from the city envy, lawsuits, factions — in short, evils of every kind. Lycurgus, when he laid down the laws of the Spartans, taught that this principle should be so preserved and cultivated in everything and every part of life that, when he was once walking through Spartan territory

nium multorum fratrum paulo ante divisum affirmaret. Atque
hanc quidem aequalitatem civitates vestrae non modo non servant,
sed ne cognoscunt quidem; summa inter omnes omnium rerum licentia est, qua quidem nulla meo iudicio perniciosior pestis civitatibus potest accidere.

37 MATTHAEUS. Est quidem ut dicis aequalitas in civitate maxime
necessaria, si modo rite servetur: in eo enim, ut cives aequo inter
se iure vivant, maximum iustitiae munus continetur. Sed vos in
qua potissimum re eam servatis? Habetisne ex aequo divisas inter
vos possessiones?

DOMINICUS. Minime vero. Que enim iustitiae ratio haberetur, si
suo cuique perfrui non liceret aut si cives aliis, non sibi quaestum
facerent et, non modo maiorum suorum censu atque hereditate,
sed suorum quoque laborum fructu et mercede privarentur?

MATTHAEUS. Quo igitur pacto possessiones inter vos divisae
sunt?

DOMINICUS. Unusquisque, quod sibi vel hereditate obvenit vel
ipse aliquo pacto acquisivit, id possidet.

MATTHAEUS. Quid qui neque a maioribus quicquam acceperunt
neque ipsi parare potuerunt, nihilne habent?

DOMINICUS. A republica quidem nihil.

MATTHAEUS. Quid si optimi cives sint, nihilne illis sua virtus
opitulatur?

38 DOMINICUS. Nihil ad aliena quidem possidenda, sed subvenitur
iis, a cognatis atque amicis, si modo tam tenues sunt ut illorum
ope indigeant. Dantur praeterea illis a republica magistratus et
provinciae quibus non modo ad praesens sustentari, sed in posterum quoque sibi providere facile queant.

during the harvest and saw that the piles of wheat were all equal
on the threshing-floor, he declared that Sparta looked to him like
a family estate which shortly before had been divided among many
brothers.[23] Your cities not only do not observe this principle of
equality, but are not even aware of it. There is the greatest license
among you all in all things, than which no more destructive
plague, in my judgment, can ever infect cities.

MATTIAS. Equality is, as you say, extremely necessary in a city, 37
so long as the principle is properly observed. For the greatest task
of justice lies in all citizens living among themselves with equal
justice. But in what particular way do you observe equality? Do
you have possessions divided equally among you?

DOMENICO. Not at all. For what kind of justice would it be if
everyone was not permitted to enjoy his own property, or if citizens should earn income for others, not themselves, and if they
should be deprived not only of the economic standing and inheritance of their ancestors, but of the fruits and wages of their own
labors too?

MATTIAS. How then are possessions divided among you?

DOMENICO. Everyone owns what either comes to him from his
inheritance or what he himself has acquired in some way.

MATTIAS. What? Do those who get nothing from their fore-
bears and can't earn anything for themselves have nothing?

DOMENICO. The get nothing from the republic, certainly.

MATTIAS. What if they are excellent citizens: is their virtue of
no service to them?

DOMENICO. They don't get possession of someone else's goods, 38
but they are assisted by relations and friends so long as they are so
poor that they need their help. The republic furthermore gives
them magistracies and provincial posts, thanks to which they can
not only support themselves in the present but also provide for
themselves in the future.

MATTHAEUS. Atqui, si recte memini, vestri magistratus sorte creantur, non ad cuiusquam arbitrium dantur; sed concedamus dari posse nonnullos. Primum, in eo ceteris fit iniuria, quod his magistratus dantur, illis non dantur. Deinde, si quid acquirunt, suo labore, non beneficio reipublicae acquirunt. Postremo, si boni viri esse volunt, multum ex magistratu reportare non possunt.

39    Sed omittamus haec omnia; ad id quod caput est veniamus: suntne inter vos alii ditissimi, alii pauperrimi?

DOMINICUS. Quidni? Nonne in omni civitate sic evenit?

MATTHAEUS. Atqui ille, quem modo commemorabas, Lycurgus non sic rempublicam Spartanam instituit, sed aequas omnium possessiones esse voluit, proptereaque acervos tritici aequales vidit. Consideravit enim prudentissimus legum lator lites, furta, rapinas, caedes et quae mala in civitatibus oriuntur, ea omnia ab hac una habendi cupiditate proficisci; hac sublata, cetera e vestigio tolli omnia. Et profecto, si recte reputemus,[13] sic est. Quod est[14] enim inter homines malum quod non ab hac tamquam a fonte quodam et principio oriatur? Propone tibi ante oculos scelera ac flagitia omnia quae inter homines patrari solent, quaeque ab illis foeda ac nefaria existimantur. Nullum omnino invenies quod aut opum gratia aut earum adiumento ac ministerio non conficiatur. Quod, obsecro, periculum, quis labor vel terra vel mari invenitur, qui non unius pecuniae gratia cupidissime subeatur? Percurre libera cogitatione omnes mortalium artes, omnia studia, omnes denique actiones. Nullam profecto invenies quae non ad pecuniae cumulationem tamquam ad unicum suae vitae finem dirigatur. Quod si essent ita respublicae ab initio institutae ut aequa omnium civium possessio esset, neque liceret cuique plus habere quam aliis, profecto neque furta in civitatibus neque lites neque discordiae ullae

MATTIAS. Yet if I remember correctly, your magistrates are chosen by lot, not on the basis of someone's decision; but let us concede that some of the needy could be given offices. First, injury is done to the rest by this, because magistracies are given to the needy but not them. Second, if they do make something [as magistrates], they make it through their own labor, not by public service. Finally, if they want to be good men, they can't profit too much from their magistracy.

But let's pass over all this and come to the nub of the matter: are there not among you some who are very rich and others who are extremely poor? 39

DOMENICO. Of course. Doesn't this happen in every city?

MATTIAS. Yet that Lycurgus whom you mentioned just now did not establish the Spartan republic this way, but wanted the possessions of everyone to be equal, and that's why he took note of the equal piles of grain. For that most prudent of legislators believed that lawsuits, thefts, seizures, murders and like evils that arise in cities all came from this one lust for possessing things; take that away, and you would altogether take away the rest. And surely, if we consider the matter rightly, that is the case. For what human evil is there that does not spring from this as from its source and principle? Place before your eyes all the crimes and sins that men commonly commit against each other, all the things men reckon to be foul and wicked. You won't find any of them that are not committed for the sake of riches or in aid and service thereof. What risk, I ask you, what labor is encountered on land or sea which is not undergone with the utmost avidity for the sake of money alone? Run over in your mind all the arts of mankind, all the pursuits, all actions in short: you'll surely find none that are not directed to piling up money as though it were the one end of human life. But if republics were so founded from the beginning to equalize possessions among the citizenry, and no one were allowed to have more than others, neither, surely, would any thefts, lawsuits

nascerentur omnino, cives vero non tam multam operam in mercatura, navigatione, agricultura et ceteris quaestuariis artibus prae
insana lucri cupiditate consumerent; non tantopere cognatorum
atque amicorum vitae hereditatis gratia insidiarentur; non suum
denique caput, suam vitam tot periculis obiectarent, totiens mani-
festissimae morti opponerent.

40 DOMINICUS. At si desereretur mercatura, magno ornamento ac
praesidio humana vita privaretur.

MATTHAEUS. Immo vero magno gulae, luxuriae atque avaritiae
instrumento ⟨privaretur⟩, et (ut in commerciis diximus) modico
suoque contenta, quietius ac salubrius ageret.

DOMINICUS. Quid ii qui quottidie nascuntur, quas possessiones
sortirentur?

MATTHAEUS. Eas utique quas morientes relinquerent.

DOMINICUS. Quid cum plures nascerentur quam interirent?

MATTHAEUS. Quid cum plures interirent quam nascerentur?
Nimirum utrisque respublica provideret.

41 DOMINICUS. Quid vero si nulla mercedis ac lucri cura aut ex-
pectatio esset? Artes, quibus humana vita continetur, quo tandem
pacto aut a quibus exercerentur?[15] Nonne omnes e vestigio cessarent? Quis enim tantos labores suscipere incassum vellet? Sublatis
porro artibus, nonne non modo civitas, sed universa quoque humana societas et vitae degendae ratio tolleretur?

42 MATTHAEUS. Atqui deesse artibus pretium et honos non posset;
cum enim nemo sibi ipsi ad vitam traducendam satis esset ege-
retque alter alterius ope atque artificio ad res sibi necessarias com-
parandas, mutua illa utilitas ac necessitas artes et studia omnia in
civitate retineret. Si quem autem haec necessitatis ratio minus cogeret, ut aliis sua industria prodesset, propterea quod ipse solus esset minusque aliis rebus indigere videretur, hunc, si civis esse vel-

and discords at all arise in cities, and citizens would not expend so much effort on trade, voyages, agriculture and the rest of the arts of gain out of an insane lust for profit. They wouldn't plot so much against the lives of their relatives and friends for the sake of an inheritance; they wouldn't, finally, throw themselves and their lives into so many risks and face manifest death so many times.

DOMENICO. But if they gave up trade, human life would be deprived of a great embellishment and a great protection.   40

MATTIAS. Rather, it would be deprived of a great instrument of gluttony, luxury and avarice and (as they say in trade) it would rest content with its own measure, and would be conducted more peacefully and wholesomely.

DOMENICO. What of those who are born each day, what possessions would they be allotted?

MATTIAS. Those of course that the dying leave behind.

DOMENICO. What if more are born than die?

MATTIAS. What if more die than are born? The commonwealth will of course plan for both cases.

DOMENICO. But what if there is no concern for or expectation   41
of reward and profit? How, pray, will the crafts by which human life is preserved be practiced, and by whom? Won't they all vanish without a trace? For who would undertake such great labors without profit? Furthermore, if you take away the crafts, won't not only the state, but also all of human society, the whole reason for living life, be destroyed?

MATTIAS. But the recompense and honor associated with those   42
crafts could not be lacking; since no one can survive on his own and each person needs the help and skills of others to acquire the things necessary for himself, that mutual utility and need would keep all crafts and pursuits within the city. If this reason of necessity were to motivate someone to benefit others by his industry to a lesser extent, because he was solitary and seemed to need other things less, the commonwealth would use force on this person, if

let, aut cogeret aut[16] remuneraretur ipsa respublica pensaretque cum illis qui pluribus rebus indigerent quam ipsi aliis possent praestare, atque hoc pacto non solum civitas, sed illa etiam quam quaerimus aequalitas optime servaretur.

43    Nunc autem, quae potest inter vos aequalitas esse, cum alii ditissimi, alii pauperrimi sint? Divites enim superbire, praeesse ac dominari volunt; pauperes contra submitti, obtemperare ac servire necesse est. Hi praeterea multis illorum iniuriis propter imbecillitatem obnoxii sunt; illi ab his accipere nullas possunt. Iam vero, quanta inter eos in victu, habitu moribusque diversitas! Divites et plurimis et lautissimis cibis pascuntur, immo maxima etiam patrimonia nonnulli in gulam congerunt; pauperes et modico et vili ac facili cibo contenti sunt. Illi plurimas et pretiosissimas vestes habent; hi unica et simplici operiuntur. Illi in luxu, delitiis atque inertia educati, neque laborem ullum neque incommodum umquam pertulere; hi algori et[17] inediae, vigiliis ac laboribus ab ineunte aetate, immo ab ipsis incunabulis, assueti, neque luxum neque delicias neque otium ullum norunt. Aliter etiam natales, nuptias, ludos, dies festos, funera hi atque illi celebrant. Aliter aedificant, aliter habitant, aliam denique omnibus in rebus hi ab illis vitam ducunt. Et tu ullam inter eos aequalitatem esse posse existimas? An nescis aequalitatem similitudine quadam vivendi et virtutis studio contineri? Virtutem autem, cum mediocritas sit, in extremis esse non posse; extrema enim omnia vitio dari. Quomodo igitur hi qui in extremis opum atque inopiae finibus positi sunt et tota inter se vitae ratione dissentiunt, ullo virtutis aut aequalitatis vinculo iungi et connecti queunt? Quod si mediocres omnibus opes essent, ita ut alter alterum non multo excederet, omnes invidiae et contentionum causae cessarent et illa quam volumus aequalitas servaretur.

44    DOMINICUS. At leges nos aequales reddunt.
       MATTHAEUS. Quonam pacto aut quibus in rebus?

he wanted to be a citizen, or it would compensate by counterbalancing him with those who needed more things than they themselves could offer others, and in this way not only the city, but also that principle of equality we seek would be preserved.

Now how can there be equality among you when some are extremely rich, others extremely poor? For the rich are minded to take precedence, to lead and to dominate; the poor on the other hand necessarily submit, obey and serve. The latter moreover are subject to many injuries from the former owing to their weakness; the strong can receive no injuries from the weak. And how different they are in way of life, dress and morals! The rich feed upon numerous sumptuous foods; indeed, some of them pour huge patrimonies down their gullets. The poor are content with a small amount of humble food, easily obtained. The rich have much clothing of the greatest value; the poor cover themselves with a single, simple garment. The rich are brought up in luxury, pleasure and idleness and never experience labor or inconvenience; the poor are used to cold, hunger, sleepless nights and labors from their earliest years, indeed from the very cradle, and never know luxury, pleasures or leisure. The two classes celebrate births, weddings, games, holidays and funerals differently. The build differently, dwell differently; in short, they live different lives in all things. And you reckon that there is any equality between them? Don't you know that equality is a kind of similarity in living and in the pursuit of virtue? Virtue, however, since it is a mean, cannot exist in extremes; all extremes are vicious. How then can those who are placed at the extreme limits of wealth and want, who disagree with each other completely in their way of life, be joined and connected by any bond of virtue or equality? But if everyone had average resources, so that one person did not much exceed another, all ill will and the causes of contention would cease, and that equality we seek would be preserved.

DOMENICO. But the laws make us equal.

MATTIAS. How do they do that, and in what respect?

DOMINICUS. Ante omnia is nobis habitus est, quo neque pauperes extolli neque deprimi locupletes multum possint. Habet enim
et gravitatem et honestatem et eam, quam tu modo commemorabas, mediocritatem. Eum ita communem omnibus et aequalem leges atque instituta nostra effecere, ut summi ab[18] imis interdum
discerni non queant. Argentum et aurum ferre nobis non temere
concessum est; mulieres modico admodum nec sane pretioso or-
natu per universum corpus utuntur, ita ut sponsae nuptis, nuptae
viduis quam simillimae sint; uniones et margaritas omnino non ferunt; gemmas, non nisi nuptae et in digitis dumtaxat ferunt; eas
gestare paucis admodum viris licet. In conviviis, nuptiis, funeribus,
sepulcris et ceteris publicis actionibus magna quoque parsimonia
est, ita ut nemo fere tam tenuis sit, qui se ditissimis aequare non
possit. Aedificare quidem intra extraque urbem unicuique pro arbitrio et facultate licet, ita tamen ut tenuiorum aedificia a ditiori-
bus neque per vim occupentur neque per iniuriam debiliora obscu-
rioraque reddantur. Iura porro omnibus ex aequo redduntur,
neque potentiores in plebem iuris quicquam habent, neque ipsi a
iudiciis ac poenis per opes aut potentiam immunes sunt, ita ut
neque cuiquam ad ius suum obtinendum vel obsit paupertas vel
opes prosint. Quibus rebus magna in nostra civitate aequalitas
concordiaque efficitur.

45     Huc accedunt artes, disciplinae studiaque omnia quae libero
homine digna existimantur, quae quidem ob hanc aequalitatem in
nostra republica magis quam in regno ullo vigent ac florent. Dum
enim nemo aliis inferior esse vult, omnes ad summum certatim
pervenire contendunt. Ita fit ut et optima apud nos educentur ingenia et plurimi in omni artis ac disciplinae genere praestantissimi
reperiantur. Cui quidem rei argumento est, quod plures e nostra
republica, ut de aliis taceam, in omni genere praestantes per universum terrarum orbem quam ex ullo regno commeare cernuntur;

DOMENICO.  Above all our condition is such that paupers cannot be raised up nor the rich brought much down. It preserves both gravity and honor and that principle of the mean that you just mentioned. Our laws and institutions create this condition that is common and equal for all, so that sometimes the highest cannot be distinguished from the lowest. We are not allowed to display gold and silver without good cause; our women use only modest amounts of inexpensive ornament on their bodies, so that engaged women are very similar in appearance to married women, and married women to widows. They do not wear pearls or pearl ornaments at all; they wear no gems except on their wedding-rings; their contact with men is limited. Great parsimony is used in banquets, weddings, funerals and other public displays, so that almost no one is so poor that he cannot match the very richest people. Everyone is allowed to build inside and outside the city as he wishes and as his resources allow, yet the dwellings of the poor are not forcibly seized by the rich, nor are they made flimsier or dingier through acts of injustice. Justice, furthermore, is administered equally to all, and the more powerful have no rights over the plebs, nor does their wealth and power give them immunity from the courts and from punishment. As a result, poverty is no obstacle nor wealth of any benefit in obtaining justice. By these means great equality and harmony is achieved in our city.

Add to this the arts, disciplines and all the pursuits reckoned worthy of a free man. Thanks to our equality, these things grow strong and flourish more in our republic than in any kingdom. For so long as no one wishes to be inferior to others, everyone competes to reach the summit of achievement. Hence the finest minds are nurtured among us and numerous outstanding persons in every art and discipline are found in our city. A proof of this is that numerous outstanding men from our republic (to say nothing of others) in every field of endeavor are observed to crisscross the globe — far more than from any kingdom. If the finest minds did

45

quod, nisi apud nos optima ingenia coalescerent studiaque optimarum artium imprimis florerent, tam multi in omni virtutum
atque artium genere clari e nostra civitate non prodirent. Nam, si
permulti inde ultro egrediuntur, magnam ibi eorum copiam esse
plurimosque ibidem remanere credibile est. Quae cum ita sint,
permagnam esse in nostra civitate aequalitatem summamque haberi iustitiae rationem manifestum est.

46 MATTHAEUS. Magna mehercule voluptate me affecit ista vestrorum morum explicatio. Nam et ipsi sunt ad gravitatem, ut dicis,
modestiamque compositi et ego vestram civitatem praecipuo quodam studio atque amore complector. Sed vereor ne in qua re vos
maxime discrepare conveniret, in ea maxime similes atque aequales
esse studeatis; in qua vero maxime pares esse oporteret, in ea
maxime discrepetis. In censu enim et possessionibus, quae civibus
momenti plurimum ad vitia et virtutes afferunt, in quibus vos
maxime pares esse deberetis, discrepatis plurimum; in cultu vero
corporis, in sepulcris et ceteris rebus quae hominem nihilo meliorem reddere aut deteriorem possunt et sunt virtutis ac nobilitatis
testimonia, quibus alterum ab altero maxime distingui necesse esset, vos maxime convenitis. Nam cum iustitia sit aequitas, ius
suum unicuique tribuens, quod aliud summae virtuti aut nobilitati
ab homine testimonium aut praemium potest expectari quam honos, quam amplitudo, quam dignitas? Quis porro honos homini
ab homine tribui potest, nisi ut eum viventem habitu ab aliis do-
moque distinguat, defunctum statuis, imaginibus monumentisque
exornet? Quod si nulla virtutis nobilitatisque est in civitate facienda distinctio, cuius, obsecro, rei facienda est aut quanam alia
ratione facienda est, si hac qua dixi non est facienda? Summum
enim civem ab infimo, probum ab improbo, nobilem ab ignobili
discernere qui possis, si habitu, domo et sepulcro non possis?
Quae vero causa bono viro erit ut domi forisque se per virtutem

not grow up among us, if zeal for the liberal arts did not flourish there above all, so many famous men in every genus of virtue and the arts would not emerge from our city. For if very many such men leave Florence spontaneously, one must believe that a great abundance of them exist there and that most of them remain behind. This being the case, it is clear that there is very great equality in our city and that the best model of justice is maintained there.

MATTIAS. This explanation of your mores has given me great 46 pleasure, by Hercules. They are, as you say, so ordered as to produce gravity and modesty, and I embrace your city with particular zeal and love. But I'm afraid you try to be the most egalitarian in the areas where it would most benefit you to make distinctions, yet where you ought to be most equal is where you most make distinctions. For with respect to economic status and possessions, which have the most weight in bringing citizens to embrace virtue or vice, you have the most differences, while you equalize the most in personal appearance, funeral monuments and the rest, which can't make a man any better or worse but are marks of virtue and nobility necessary for distinguishing one man from another. Since justice is fairness, rendering to each his due, what other witness or reward can a man expect for his virtue or nobility than honor, prestige and rank? Besides, what honor can be paid a man by other men except to mark his eminence over others while alive by means of his dress and dwelling, and to decorate him after his death by means of statues, images and monuments? If no distinctions for virtue or nobility are to be made in the city, what will distinctions be made for, on what other basis will distinctions be made if not the ones I mentioned? Who can tell the highest citizen from the lowest, the decent from the indecent, the noble from the ignoble if it can't be done from his dress, dwelling and tomb? What cause will a good man have to act with virtue at home and abroad, fight for his country, remain loyal, help friends, maintain

exerceat, pugnet pro patria, fidem servet, amicos iuvet, vincat affectus, omni denique virtuti incumbat, si nulla eum laus, nullus honos, nulla gloria, nullum praemium consequatur, si ne habitu quidem ipso ab ignavo et scelesto distinguendus sit? Quid porro adolescentes ad virtutem et bonas artes incitabit, si maiorum suorum honos, splendor et monumenta non incitent? Qua enim de causa claris viris funerum pompas exhiberi, statuas, arcus monumentaque ingentia erigi existimatis? Putatisne defunctorum animis ista ad salutem immortalitatemque prodesse? Nihil haec profecto illi curant qui ex hac vita excessere. Maioribus enim aut cruciantur poenis aut praemiis perfruuntur quam ut exigua haec curare aut possint aut velint. Viventium haec, mihi crede, viventium, inquam, et posterorum partim solacia, partim exempla sunt, ut excellentem defunctorum virtutem et qui amiserunt retinere videantur et qui admirati sunt imitari queant. Magna igitur est meo iudicio in civium habitu et sepulcris pro virtute cuiusque et nobilitate facienda distinctio.

47    Nam quod de nuptiis conviviisque dixisti, placet mihi quidem illa mediocritas, ne cives omnem in his rebus censum consumant; plurimum tamen in his quoque claros ab obscuris, probos ab improbis velim differre, nisi forte vos nobilitatem plebi, splendorem obscuritati in matrimoniis permiscetis.

DOMINICUS. Immo vero maximum in his rebus delectum habemus.

48 MATTHAEUS. Idcirco diversam quoque par est nuptiarum celebrandarum esse rationem. Legibus autem vos omnes pariter subiacere et aequo inter vos iure vivere, ut tu paulo ante affirmabas, quomodo possitis non video. Primum enim genere, opibus copiisque differtis quae superbiam alunt, mores corrumpunt, legibus subesse indignantur. Deinde, qui vos ad parendum legibus cogant,

bonds of affection — in short, devote himself entirely to virtue — if he wins no praise, honor, glory or reward, if he is not distinguished from knaves and scoundels even in his dress? What, furthermore, will incite the young to virtue and the liberal arts if the honor, splendor and monuments of their ancestors will not? Why do you suppose that funeral exequies are celebrated, and statues, arches and huge monuments are erected to famous men? Do you think these things are of any profit to the souls of the dead for their salvation and immortality? Those who have departed this life surely care nothing for such things. For they are being tortured with greater pains or enjoying greater rewards; they neither can nor should care about these small ones here. It is for the sake of the living, believe me — the living, I repeat — that these things are done, as solace and example, so that those who feel the loss of the excellent virtue of the dead may seem to have it still, and so that those who admired it might imitate it. Therefore, in my judgment a great distinction is to be made in the dress and the tombs of citizens in proportion to the virtue and nobility of each.

Now regarding your remarks about weddings and banquets, I 47 like that moderation that prevents citizens from consuming all their wealth on these things; yet I would make distinctions here too between the famous and the obscure, the decent and the disgraceful, unless perhaps in matrimonial affairs you would confound the noble with the commoner, fame with obscurity.

DOMENICO. In fact, we take the greatest pleasure in such distinctions.

MATTIAS. Then it is fair to employ diverse modes of celebrating 48 weddings. But I don't see how you can all be equally subject to the laws and live on a basis of equal right, as you were maintaining a little while ago. First of all, you make distinctions of descent, wealth and resources which nourish pride, corrupt morals, and create resentment at submitting to laws. Second, you have no one to compel you to obey the laws. Your judicial magistrates, because

non habetis. Nam praetores quidem, quod et a vobis ultro delecti atque acciti sint, et sciant se a vobis tum eiici tum confirmari posse, vestram partim potentiam metuunt, partim gratiam aucupari student, vos itaque cogere nec audent nec possunt. Leges vero vos ipsi quottidie et antiquatis et conditis, ita ut quae placeant servetis, quae displiceant abrogetis.

DOMINICUS. At cogunt nos illas servare magistratus.

49   MATTHAEUS. Qui vero sunt isti magistratus? Nonne vos ipsi potissimum estis? An est credibile vos eos velle offendere, a quibus mox graviter puniri possitis? Nonne, cum illos offenditis, vos ipsos offenditis? Quis, obsecro, est tam demens, qui civem in magistratu positum multare aut damnare velit, a quo ipse paulo post sive iure sive iniuria multo gravius damnandus sit? Vobis igitur leges parcunt, in vilem tantum plebeculam saeviunt. Nam, ut Aquinas ait,

dat veniam corvis, vexat censura columbas.

Cui quidem rei argumento est, quod numquam fere locupletes ac potentes capite damnantur, numquam in crucem tolluntur, immo numquam furti, numquam caedis, numquam stupri aut adulterii accusantur, aut si quando accusantur, per pecuniam et gratiam absolvuntur. Inopes contra et abiecti quottidie in vincula rapiuntur, trahuntur in Gemonias, multorum ac magnorum criminum accusati damnatique legibus, graves sine ulla miseratione poenas expendunt.

50      Dices fortasse: 'Nobiles et locupletes non peccant.' An illos credibile est non peccare, qui et peccandi tum facultatem tum materiam summam habeant et maximam peccatorum veniam atque impunitatem sperent? Inopes vero tantum ut peccent committere, qui neque ullam peccandi opportunitatem habeant et sciant se nequaquam impune abituros? Immo vero multo frequentius mul-

you freely select and appoint them and because they know that they can be expelled or confirmed by you, are in part afraid of your power and in part desirous of currying favor, so they neither dare to nor can place you under compulsion. You yourselves abrogate and institute laws on a daily basis: you keep what you like and reject what you don't.

DOMENICO. But there are magistrates who do compel us to observe the laws.

MATTIAS. But who are these magistrates? Aren't they, precisely, 49 you yourselves? Is it credible that you would want to give offence to those who could presently punish you with severity? Don't you harm yourselves when you harm them? Is there anyone so out of his mind, I ask you, that he would fine or punish a citizen holding a magistracy who could a little later, rightly or wrongly, punish him much more severely? Thus the laws spare you, and are cruel only to some low little prole. For as Juvenal says,

he pardons the crow and vexes the dove with his censure.[24]

Proof of this is the fact that the rich and powerful are almost never condemned to death, never crucified, indeed they are never even accused of theft, murder, rape or adultery, or if they are accused, they are found innocent thanks to money and influence. The poor and humble, on the other hand, are taken off in chains on a daily basis, or dragged down the Gemoniae,[25] accused and condemned by the laws of many great crimes, and suffer the hardest punishments without any mercy.

Perhaps you will say, "The nobles and the rich don't commit 50 offenses." But is it credible that they don't, when they have the ability and every resource to commit them, and may hope for forgiveness and impunity for their offenses? Is it only the poor who commit offenses, who have no opportunity to do so and know that they will never get off without punishment? In fact, the rich

toque gravius divites potentesque delinquunt, 'sed illos,' ut Aquinas ait,

defendit numerus iunctaeque umbone phalanges.

Proptereaque haud insulse Solon, unus ex septem Graeciae sapientibus, leges aiebat aranearum telis persimiles esse, quas quidem minora animalia subirent, maiora perrumperent. Effugiunt enim divites, mihi crede, legum nexus earumque vincula non una ratione perrumpunt; tenuiores autem, omnis gratiae pecuniaeque expertes, legum nodis irretiuntur earumque poenas et severitatem subeunt; immo parva tenuiorum delicta magnorum scelerum nomen assumunt poenisque etiam gravissimis subiacent, maxima vero ditiorum flagitia virtutum nomen sortiuntur et laudem plerumque gloriamque merentur. Pirata quidam, cum ab Alexandro Macedonum rege[19] esset captus et capite, quod praedabundus in homines grassaretur, damnatus, regi dixisse fertur se propterea quod exiguo navigio paululum praedaretur, piratam appellari et in crucem tolli; illum, qui ingenti exercitu et classe omnia terra marique vastaret, in omnes saeviret, omnibus vim afferret, ducem atque imperatorem legitimum esse et praemiis ingentibus dignum iudicari. Non sunt igitur minora divitum quam pauperum peccata, sed hi legibus cogi possunt, illi non possunt. Quod si e vobis alii tum opibus, tum potentia, tum gratia ita fulti ac muniti sunt ut neque ab homine neque a lege ulla compelli queant, alii contra ita[20] fortunis potentiaque nudati ut omnibus magistratibus ac legibus sint obnoxii, quo pacto aequo inter vos iure vivere possitis non video.

51      Quod autem de vestris ingeniis studiisque dixisti, fateor quidem apud vos et optima esse ingenia et studiis bonarum artium erudiri; sed vel florere apud vos magis quam in regno ullo artes disciplinasque liberales, vel plures e vestra civitate quam ex aliis

and powerful commit much more serious and frequent crimes, "but they" as Juvenal says,

> are defended by their numbers, and the tightly locked shields of the phalanx.[26]

Hence Solon, one the seven wise men of Greece, was no fool when he said that the laws were like spiders' webs, which caught small creatures, but which the larger creatures broke through.[27] Believe me, the rich escape the bonds of the laws, and they break their chains without any justification; but the poor, lacking all influence and money, are captured in the nets of the law and are subject to its severity and punishments; indeed, their tiny delicts acquire the reputation of great crimes and are heavily punished, but the greatest sins of the rich are allotted the name of virtues and generally earn praise and glory. A certain pirate captured by Alexander the Great, when he was condemned to death for having prowled the seas to prey on men, is reported to have said to the king that he was called a pirate and crucified because he had taken a little plunder in a small ship, but that the king, because he had laid waste to everything on land and sea with a great army and fleet, was judged to be a legitimate leader and general and deserving of enormous rewards.[28] The sins of the rich, then, are not less than those of the poor, but the latter can be compelled by the law, the former cannot. But if some of you are so fortified by wealth, power and influence that you can't be put under compulsion either by a man or by any law, and others, by contrast, are so naked of the goods of fortune and of power that they are exposed to all magistrates and laws, I don't see how you can be living among yourselves on a basis of equal right.

Regarding what you said about the talents and pursuits of your 51 people, I confess that you have the most excellent talents and are educated in the liberal pursuits; but I don't admit that the arts and liberal disciplines flourish more among you than in any kingdom,

claros in omnibus disciplinis viros prodire, non fateor. Nam ut de nostro Viennensi gymnasio taceam, in quo, quamquam nos bellicis artibus maxime dediti sumus, omnis tamen liberales disciplinae non in postremis sunt, quid Neapolis regia Ferdinandi soceri mei? Nonne ingenia, ut audio, maiorem in modum in omnibus disciplinis exercet, ita ut nunc demum eam iure optimo appellare liceat Parthenopem 'studiis florentem ignobilis oci,' ut sua aetate Maro appellavit. Quid urbs Roma, quae sub pontificibus agit? Nonne et ipsa disciplinas omnes summo studio complectitur? Et habet Perusinum celebre Italia tota gymnasium, in quo omnium liberalium disciplinarum studia floreant.[21] Neque Ticinum sive, ut nunc appellatur, Papia, quae sororio[22] tuo subiacet, fili, aliis Italiae civitatibus usquam cedit; in ea enim est eximium omnium disciplinarum frequensque gymnasium. Sed una Parisiensium civitas, Gallorum regi (quam gentem vos barbaram appellatis) subiecta, omnes Italiae civitates optimarum artium studiis longe antecellit. In ea enim semper fere viginti, nonnumquam etiam triginta, auditorum ac studiosorum in omnibus disciplinis milia reperiuntur, quae quidem eo non e Gallia modo, sed ex Italia quoque, Hispania, Germania, Britannia, Europa denique universa tamquam ad communem omnium disciplinarum parentem altricemque conveniunt.

'At pictura', inquis, 'et sculptura in nostra civitate magis florent.' Florent quidem hae artes etiam in aliis, sed illi fortasse artifices minus illustres sunt, propterea quod e patria minus prodeunt.

52  DOMINICUS. Prodirent profecto, si usquam essent, si non emolumenti, laudis certe et gloriae cupiditate adducti.

MATTHAEUS. Sed concedamus tibi non solum has artes, sed ceteras quoque ingenuas disciplinas in vestra potissimum civitate et florere et coli: ista profecto unius vestrae civitatis, non omnium rerumpublicarum virtus est. Nam si esset, omnes profecto civitates,

or that your city produces more famous men in all the disciplines than any other. I'll say nothing of our University of Vienna, which is by no means the least in all liberal disciplines, despite our being devoted above all to the arts of war. But what about the palace of my father-in-law, Ferdinand of Naples? Does it not find exceptional employment for talents in all the disciplines, as I hear, so that nowadays one may with perfect right call Parthenope "flourishing in the pursuits of ignoble ease," as Vergil called it in his time.[29] What about the city of Rome under the popes? Has it not too embraced all the disciplines with the utmost zeal? Perugia has a university celebrated throughout Italy, in which all the liberal disciplines flourish. Nor does Ticinum, or as it's called today, Pavia—which is subject to your brother-in-law,[30] my son—yield second place to the other cities of Italy, for in that city is a famous and much-frequented university of all disciplines. The single city of Paris, subject to the French king, which you [Italians] call barbarous, excels all the cities of Italy in the best studies; in it there are always to be found 20,000, sometimes 30,000, students and men of learning in all the disciplines, who gather not only from France, but also from Italy, Spain, Germany, Britain—all Europe, in short—as though to a common parent and nurse of all the disciplines.

"But," you will say, "painting and sculpture flourish more in our city." These arts also flourish in other cities, but the craftsmen in those places are perhaps less famous, because they are less inclined to leave their country.

DOMENICO. [Our Florentine artists] surely do leave, if they are  52 of any account, drawn by the desire for praise and glory, certainly, if not of emolument.

MATTIAS. But I'll concede to you that not only these arts, but the rest of the liberal disciplines too flourish and are cultivated especially in your city. This surely is owing to the excellence of your one city, not of all republics generally. For if that were the case,

quae reipublicae formam servant, vobis hac in re pares essent. Quod contra est, nisi forte unam vestram rempublicam bene institutam esse, ceteras omnes pessime vultis affirmare.

53 DOMINICUS. Nobis quidem, rex, hoc non arrogamus; immo alias omnes melius institutas esse credimus. Sed id accidere omnibus existimamus, ut studia literarum artesque omnes, quae libero homine dignae sunt, complectantur ac colant, ob eam quam habent omnes respublicae in suis civibus instituendis diligentiam.

54 MATTHAEUS. Aliae profecto his studiis non ita incumbunt, sed obmittamus rerumpublicarum inter se comparationem. Illud quod ad nostram disputationem attinet, si placet, concludamus, artes disciplinasque liberales non magis apud vos quam apud reges principesque vigere. Plures autem in una vestra civitate quam in universo aliquo regno praestantes in omnibus disciplinis viros reperiri, si cum uno nostro regno illam conferas, facile concedo. Nos enim bellicis studiis magis dediti, otiosas istas atque umbratiles disciplinas minus curamus, quamquam et clari nobis viri non desint et ego aliquanto diligentius quam maiores mei studia literarum in hac nostra Pannonia curaverim frequentanda, et in eam, ut apud vos liberius de me ipso praedicem, ex ipso quodammodo Parnaso mansuetiores Musas invexerim et Viennam nunc nostram claris quottidie viris disciplinisque exornem.

55 Sed si cum aliis regnis vestram rempublicam conferas, invenies nullum omnino regnum, ne dicam oppidum, vestrae civitati virorum non modo multitudine, verum etiam splendore et claritate concedere. Neapolis enim, quam uxoris meae gratia et libenter et saepe commemoro, tum iuris consultos tum poetas et quam plurimos et quam optimos habet, neque quicquam aut numerus claritati aut numero claritas detrahit. De urbe Roma, omnium virtu-

surely all cities that have a republican constitution would be your equals in this respect. But the contrary is true — unless perhaps you want to maintain that your republic alone is a well-ordered one, while the rest are all badly ordered.

DOMENICO. I would certainly not claim that for ourselves, king;  53
in fact I believe all the others are better ordered. But I do reckon it happens in all republics that the study of literature and all the arts worthy of a free man are embraced and cultivated, thanks to the careful attention all republics devote to educating their citizens.

MATTIAS. Surely other republics are not so assiduous in these  54
studies; but let's avoid a comparison of republics among themselves. Let us come to the conclusion, if you please, relevant to our debate: that the arts and liberal disciplines are not more vigorous among you than among kings and princes. However, I might concede to you readily that more outstanding men in all the disciplines can be found in your one city than in the whole of any kingdom, [certainly] if you compare it with our one kingdom. We are more given to warlike pursuits and take less care with those retiring disciplines of peacetime — although we do not lack for famous men. And I have taken somewhat more care than my ancestors did that the study of literature should become popular in this Hungary of ours. I have imported into it (if I may praise myself somewhat freely with you) the gentler Muses in a certain sense from Parnassus itself, and I am embellishing our city of Vienna with famous men and with the disciplines every day.

But if you will compare your republic to other kingdoms, you  55
will find that there is no kingdom at all, not to say town, that yields to your city, not only in the multitude, but also in the brilliance and fame of your men. For Naples, which I often call to mind with pleasure thanks to my wife,[31] has both law professors and poets, numerous and excellent ones, too, nor does their number take away from their fame, nor their fame from their number. I say nothing of the city of Rome, parent of all virtues and disci-

tum disciplinarumque parente, nihil dico. Est enim in ea praestantissimorum in omni artium ac disciplinarum genere virorum tanta copia, ut exhaustum universum terrarum orbem omnesque qui usquam erant eo confluxisse arbitrere, adeo ut, qui alibi summi ac praecipui sunt, ibi nullo fere in pretio habeantur. Quid dicam de Mediolano, Ferraria, Mantua et totius quondam Etruriae principe Bononia, quae singulis principibus subiacent? Nonne, cum eo veneris, tantam clarissimorum virorum ac doctissimorum hominum copiam videas, ut ex illis quemquam aliis in locis esse non putes? Cum vero ad alias Europae civitates te conferas, tantam clarorum virorum ex his, quas modo nominavi, civitatibus copiam reperias, ut nullum in patria credas remansisse. Singulos tibi viros nominare nec possum, qui omnes non norim, neque, etiam si possim, volo; operis enim immensi atque infiniti esset. Illud tantum dixisse satis sit, quod etiam me tacente apparet, non esse plures vestrae reipublicae quam cuiusquam regni claros viros.

56    Quod quidem, etiam si tibi concederem, non tamen a vestra illa institutione et aequalitate, ut tu vis, sed a vestrorum ingeniorum tum multitudine tum bonitate proficisceretur. Atque hoc non reipublicae beneficio, sed caeli tenuitati et clementiae ascribendum esset.

57    DOMINICUS. Atqui neque omnia sub tenui caelo acuta ingenia nascuntur (sunt enim etiam apud nos obtusa permulta), neque ea quae nascuntur omnia ad frugem claritatemque perveniunt. Quod si a caelo, ut ais, acumen illud proveniret, in omnes ibi nascentes aeque diffunderetur pariaque ingenia omnia procrearet, nisi forte caelum ac Deum ipsum huic quam illi magis favere[23] et factionem quodammodo retinere censemus, quod quidem etiam cogitare nefas est. Educatio igitur atque institutio reipublicae, non caeli tenui-

plines. There is in that city such an abundance of outstanding figures in every kind of art and discipline that you would think the
whole world had been drained and anyone of consequence had
streamed there — so much so that men who were of high eminence
in other places were not valued at all when they came there. What
shall I say of Milan, Ferrara, Mantua and Bologna, once the leader
of all Etruria — all of which are subject to single princes? Is it not
the case that when you go to those places you see a great abundance of famous and learned men, so that you wouldn't think anyone could have left those cities for other places? But when you betake yourself to the other cities of Europe, you discover such an
abundance of famous men who come from the cities I've just
named that you'd believe not a single one had remained in his
country. I can't name individuals to you since I don't know all of
them, nor would I if I could, since the task would be endless. Let
it suffice to say this: there are not more famous men in your republic than there are in any given kingdom.

And even if I were to yield to you on this matter, your abun- 56
dance of famous men would not be a consequence of your educa-
tional practices and equality, as you would have it, but rather a result of the multitude and fine quality of your minds. And this is
not to be set down to the beneficial effects of your republic, but to
your rarified, gentle climate.

DOMENICO. All the same, not every mind that is born in this 57
rarified climate is sharp (even we have many dullards among us),
nor do all those minds that are born achieve merit and fame. But
if, as you say, our mental acumen came from the climate, it would
be distributed equally among all those born there, and it would
make all minds equal — unless perchance we were to conclude that
the climate and God favor this man more than that one and belong to a faction, as it were, which is wicked even to imagine. It is
therefore republican education and institutions, not a rarified cli-

tas, ingenia et acutiora ad discendum et ad cogitandum reddit, et ad maturitatem frugemque perducit.

58 MATTHAEUS. Quo pacto istud fieri possit non video. Nam si aciem ingeniis educatio ulla conferret, omnes qui aut molliter aut tenuiter educarentur ingenio valerent, ceteri qui non ita educarentur non valerent. At contra passim videmus evenire. Nam neque omnes quibus educandis ars et diligentia adhibetur sunt ingeniosi, neque omnes quibus non adhibetur hebetes atque obtusi sunt. Permultos enim videmus agrestes aut inopes, qui nullo umquam cultu sunt usi, immo nullo uti vel scivissent vel potuissent, ingenio tamen optimo et perspicacissimo esse; alios contra omni in ea re diligentia et arte consumpta esse obtusissimos. Immo, si verum fateri volumus, neminem umquam vidimus quem cultu atque industria hominum ingeniosum effectum esse constaret, sed potius quosdam qui, cum ingeniosi essent, custodia illis et cura in victu studiisque adhibita ingenium omne perdiderunt. Quod si domestica iis educatio et cura non confert, publica institutio conferre qui potest? Si tamen aliquid haec quoque conferret, omnibus civibus, immo omnibus civitatibus, aeque conferret. Quod quidem perspicue falsum esse, neque omnes civitates studiis ingeniisque florere, tu ipse potes optime iudicare.

59 Nihil igitur ingeniis meo iudicio confert industria, sed ea natura procreat et producit ad alias atque alias res pro caeli qualitate accommodata, at non omnia paria procreantur. Deumne iniquum esse censendum est? Minime vero. Sed alia, ut dixi, aliis rebus habiliora sunt. Omnia tamen vim aliquam et virtutem habent. Eam quia non omnes cognoscimus et sumus liberorum institutionis cupidiores, eorum saepe ingenia pervertimus atque in contraria studia repugnante eorum natura detorquemus. Proptereaque non inscite facere videntur ii qui liberos, cum primum per aetatem

mate, that makes wits sharper in the tasks of learning and thinking and leads to ripeness and fruitfulness.

MATTIAS. I don't see how this can be. For if any form of educa-   58
tion sharpens the mind, everyone with a fine and supple education would have an able mind, while the rest who were not so educated would not. But we see everywhere that the opposite is the case. For not all those educated with skill and care are intelligent, and not all uneducated persons are weak-minded and thick. We see many rustic and resourceless people, completely uncultivated— who indeed never knew or could have known how to be cultivated—who nevertheless are persons whose intelligence is excellent and extremely perceptive. On the other hand there are others upon whom skill and care has been lavished who are extremely dense. To tell the truth, I've never seen anyone who has evidently been made smart by the training and effort of human beings, but I have seen certain people who were intelligent but who lost all their intelligence once care and supervision had been applied to their nurture and studies. But if domestic care and education doesn't make them smart, how are public institutions going to do so? If nevertheless the latter does sharpen the intellect somewhat, it would do so equally for all citizens, nay, for all [republican] cities. And this is obviously false. You yourself can be an excellent judge of the fact that not all [republican] cities flourish in intellectual pursuits.

In my judgment therefore hard work contributes nothing to in-   59
telligence, but nature creates minds and leads them to this or that purpose, adapting them according to the quality of the climate; but it does not create all minds equal. Must we then conclude that God is unjust? Not at all. Different minds, as I've said, are better adapted to different purposes. Yet all have some strength and excellence. Since we don't all recognize that excellence and are over-zealous in the education of children, we often wreck their minds and twist them to follow pursuits contrary, even hostile to their natures. For this reason it seems by no means an ignorant practice

cognoscere aliquid possunt, per urbem totam circumducunt omnibusque illis artibus studiisque propositis iubent quod potissimum velint eligere — quamquam ne ii quidem satis recte, meo iudicio, faciunt; decipitur enim saepenumero aetas illa varietate atque ignorantia rerum omnium, neque semper naturae affectionem sequitur.

60    Sed missa haec in praesentia faciamus. Illuc redeamus unde digressi sumus, nihil ad optima procreanda ingenia posse vestram educationem institutionemque conferre; caelo et naturae vis illa mentis aciesque debetur. Quae quidem, ut tenuissimum ac levissimum corpus est sortita, ita se maxime effert atque exercet.

DOMINICUS. Istam vero ipsam corporis habitudinem dicebam ego educatione et cura posse comparari.

MATTHAEUS. Adiuvari quidem victu et exercitatione potest, comparari non potest. Ex humorum enim et qualitatum sive elementorum quibus constamus compositione provenit, ut corpus ipsum vel obesum vel macilentum vel alio quovis modo affectum sit, atque hoc ex conceptu ipso accipitur, non aliqua industria comparatur. Nihil igitur existimanda est ingeniis afferre vestrae institutionis diligentia.

61    Aequalitatis vero cupiditas claritati confert, ut ego quidem existimo, multo minus. Animus enim bene informatus supremum semper gradum petit et antecellere omnibus atque extare affectat. Parem vero et aequalem generosus spiritus pati nullo pacto potest; aemulari semper proximum et superare contendit. Quod quidem pulcherrimum honestissimumque certamen, cum fere semper inter eiusdem rei studiosos oriatur, non potest in eo non aliquis superior esse, neque vos in hac re aequalitatem servare par esset; nam, cum unicuique ius suum ex iustitiae ratione debeatur, summae profecto virtuti summus honos praemiumque debetur. Quod quidem cum ille, quisquis est summus, domi non invenit, patria exce-

when fathers take their sons, as soon as they are old enough to understand, through the whole city and show them every craft and pursuit, then bid them choose the one they particularly want to do. Although not even these fathers are entirely correct, in my judgment. For it often happens that youth is deceived by the very variety of pursuits and by its general ignorance, and it doesn't always follow its natural bent.

But let's set this aside for now and return where we left off: that 60 your education and [republican] training can contribute nothing at all to making excellent minds; that climate and nature are responsible for power and acuteness of mind. It emerges and performs best of all when it is allotted a body that is very slender and light. DOMENICO. I would say that this same habit of body can be acquired by care and upbringing.

MATTIAS. It can be helped along by nurture and practice, but it can't be acquired. It comes from the combination of humors and qualities or elements of which we are composed, as a result of which the body is inclined to be fat or thin or what have you. This inclination is received at conception, not acquired by effort. The care taken in your education therefore must be reckoned to add nothing to your intelligence.

But the desire for equality in my view contributes much less to 61 personal distinction. A well-formed mind always seeks the highest rank and strives to stand out and excel everyone. A noble spirit can in no way bear an equal or peer; it always strives to emulate or surpass its neighbor. When such a fine and honorable contest arises between men who are zealous in the same pursuit, as it nearly always does, there cannot but be a superior, and it wouldn't be fair for you to preserve equality in such a case. For since each person is owed what is his right on grounds of justice, the highest honor and reward is surely due the highest virtue. When someone comes highest, whoever he is, and does not find that preëminence honored and rewarded at home, he is compelled to leave his country and

dere et quaerere id decus apud alias nationes compellitur. Atque haec est, ut video, praecipua causa multis e vestra civitate commigrandi, quia domi fortasse pretium virtutis non habent. Vide itaque ne quod tu argumentum copiae clarorum virorum vestrae civitatis esse voluisti, quod multi e vestris per totum terrarum orbem passim inveniantur; id vestrae potius iniustitiae argumentum sit, quod iis neque honorem neque praemium tanta virtute dignum statuatis eosque aequales deterioribus esse velitis. Quae quidem si facitis, quam sit aequalitas ista laudanda aut quae tandem sit apud vos iustitiae ratio, ipsi iudicate.

62    Nos cives nostros, quibus in rebus maxime opus esse iudicamus, in iis potissimum aequales reddimus. In ceteris ⟨non⟩ parvi referre diversitatem illam arbitramur, immo in quibusdam aequales esse non patimur, sed alios aliis anteponimus. Nam in possessionibus quidem et opibus, in quibus mediocritas atque aequalitas illa magni momenti est, neminem alios usque adeo excedere sinimus, ut vel iniuriam aliis afferre vel factionem in civitate excitare possit. Sed ita omnium opes et vires moderamur, ut nemo necessariis rebus egeat, nemo affluat supervacuis. Iura item unicuique ita ex aequo distribuimus, ut ad ius suum obtinendum, neque tenuiori obsit inopia, neque potentiori gratia aut opulentia aut auctoritas prosit. Nemo nimis vel potentia confidere vel diffidere imbecillitate apud nos potest; licet unicuique ius suum, etiam adversus nos ipsos, si sit opus, obtinere. Nos enim non alios modo, verum etiam nosmetipsos[24] legibus iustitiaeque subiicimus, ne quis nos, propterea quod reges simus, velle a communi iure liberos esse existimet. Licet praeterea non modo per alios, verum etiam per nos ipsos unicuique suis rebus tuto ac libere pro arbitrio perfrui. Nos vim aeque ab omnibus et iniurias propulsamus. Habitum autem, convivia, nuptias, monumenta et quae sunt generis

seek honor in other nations. And this, as I see it, is the main reason why so many emigrate from your city: because, perhaps, they do
not get the reward of virtue at home. So have a care that what you
take to be a proof of the abundance of famous men in your city —
that many of your citizens are found scattered around the globe —
does not rather amount to a proof of your own injustice, in that you
have accorded them neither honor nor reward worthy of their virtue and you want them to be equal to their inferiors. If you do act
this way, you can see for yourself how much your equality deserves
praise, or what in the end your principles of justice amount to.

We make our citizens equal especially in regard to those mat- 62
ters wherein we judge equality necessary. In other matters we
reckon diversity to be of no small moment, indeed in certain matters we don't allow them to be equal, but assign them ranks. For in
possessions and resources, where moderation and equality is of
great importance, we let no one exceed others to such an extent
that he could injure somebody else or incite civil strife. We control
the resources and powers of everyone so that no one stands in
need of necessities and no one is awash in superfluities. Also, we
distribute to each his rights on such a fair basis that penury is no
obstacle to the poor man, nor is influence, wealth and authority of
advantage to the powerful man, in obtaining what is due to each of
them by right. No one can either trust overmuch to his power or
despair of his weakness in our presence; each man may obtain
what is due him by right, even against our own interests if need
be. For we subject not only others, but also ourselves to justice and
the laws, lest anyone reckon that we wish to be free from common
justice because we are kings. Each person is permitted to enjoy the
free and safe use of his own property as he wishes, not only by
other persons, but by us ourselves. We ward off violence and injustice equally from all. We allow to each person, in accordance
with his or her personal worth, a form of dress, banquets, weddings, monuments and things of that sort that we think should

eiusdem, quae indiscreta esse non putamus oportere, unicuique pro dignitate concedimus, rati et viventes honoribus et posteros exemplis ad virtutem excitari. Ingenia vero non modo nostra summis praemiis ornamentisque extollimus, sed alia etiam ad nos undecumque confluentia fovemus, alimus et ornamus; immo etiam ad nos permulta maximis praemiis atque honoribus evocamus, ita demum summam iustitiae rationem haberi existimantes si unicuique praemium pro virtute et dignitate tribuatur.

Sed satis abundeque videmur de iustitiae ratione disputasse, nisi quid tu fortasse habes quod adhuc velis dicere.

63 DOMINICUS. Habeo quidem alia permulta quae pro ea re possim dicere, sed ita sum iam tua eloquentia tuisque rationibus debilitatus ac fractus ut dicere amplius nihil audeam. Multum praeterea temporis disputando consumpsimus, neque fas esse duco vos ambos diutius detinere, et aveo reliqua quomodo dissolvas audire. Proinde satius esse duco disputandi hodie finem facere et quae dicenda supersunt in diem crastinum reservare.

64 IOANNES. Ego quidem, Dominice, vestris sermonibus ita delector, ita afficior, ut neque cibi neque somni meminerim cupiamque stare solem diemque geminari, ut Iosue illi apud Hebraeos contigisse ferunt, ne qua vestrae disputationis fiat intermissio. Sed vereor ne patrem ita defatigemus, ut absolvere cras hoc disputandi munus non possit; eius itaque valitudini et quieti consulendum censeo.

65 MATTHAEUS. Ego quoque non minus hac disputatione delector, praesertim cum te, fili, et audientem libenter et non nihil proficientem video. Sed valitudinis meae ratio citius me a vobis distrahit quam vellemus. Proinde cras eadem hora, si placebit, adsitis.

IOANNES. Aderimus.

not be treated in an egalitarian way, believing as we do that the living should be stimulated to embrace virtue by honors and posterity by good examples. We not only raise up our own men of talent with the highest prizes and decorations, but we foster, nurture and honor the other talents that flow to us from every source. Indeed we even summon many talented persons to us with the greatest rewards and honors, believing that the principles of justice are only maintained if a reward is given to each person in accordance with his virtue and worth.

But we seem to have debated enough, indeed abundantly, about the principles of justice—unless perchance you have something more you would still like to say.

DOMENICO. I have many other things I could say on the subject, 63 but I am now so weakened and broken down by your eloquence and arguments that I wouldn't dare say anything more. Moreover, we've spent much time debating, and I think it wouldn't be right to keep you two any longer, and I'm anxious to hear how you will refute the rest of the points I raised. Accordingly, I think it would be preferable to put an end to today's debate and reserve for tomorrow what is left to discuss.

JANOS. For my part I've so enjoyed your speeches, Domenico, and 64 have been so impressed by them, that I've forgotten about food and sleep, and might wish the sun would stand still and double the day, as they say happened to Joshua and the Israelites,[32] to prevent any break in your debate. But I'm afraid we've tired father out so that he might not be able to finish his task in the debate tomorrow. So I think we should consider his health and his need for rest.

MATTIAS. I too have taken no less pleasure in this debate, espe- 65 cially when I see you, son, listening to it with such good will and profiting from it. But reasons of health take me from you more quickly than I should like. Accordingly, please come here tomorrow at the same hour.

JANOS. We shall be here.

# Liber Tertius[1]

1   DOMINICUS. Quantopere nos proximi bidui disputatio delectaverit, rex, ut etiam pro Ioanne hoc loquar, hinc vel maxime potes deprehendere quod hodie non expectata hora, maturius fortasse quam tuae valitudinis ratio postulabat, ad te venimus; sed nimiae cupiditati nostrae ignosces[2] eamque tua sapientia moderabere.

MATTHAEUS. Nihil est quod valitudinem nostram impedieritis; quietior enim solito ab ea nunc eram et mecum nostrae disputationis sententias reputabam, non multo post affore vos huc sperans. Sed quid, obsecro, est quod a me tantopere cupiatis?

DOMINICUS. Aveo maiorem in modum id, quod reliquum est ex tribus quae proposueram, quo pacto dissolvas, ex te, si placet, audire. Proposueram enim tertio loco rempublicam a pluribus quam ab uno, ut cetera omnia, melius gubernari, quod quidem nostrae disputationis ego caput esse existimo. Ob id enim vel maxime rempublicam regno anteponendam esse censebam. Hac igitur etiam de re cupio te audire disserentem et tuas rationes sententiamque expecto.

2   IOANNES. Hoc vero est quod ego quoque iam diu expecto. Nam cum omnia quae hoc biduo dixistis mihi iucunda grataque fuere, tum hoc, a quo ego disputandi initium sumpseram, mihi iucundissimum imprimis et gratissimum est futurum. Hoc enim potissimum me in eam sententiam adduxerat, ut rempublicam regno anteponerem, quod existimarem a pluribus omnia melius quam ab uno gubernari, atque hinc omnis nostra defluxit oratio. Proinde, Dominice, si me amas, hanc partem diligenter exsequere, tibique persuade me quidem non modo nullo audiendi taedio, sed summa

# Book III

DOMENICO. How much the debate of the last two days has de- 1
lighted us (if I may speak for János too) you can best appreciate,
king, from the fact that we come to you today not at the expected
hour, but perhaps sooner than your health demanded; but you
will forgive our excessive eagerness and restrain it in accordance
with your wisdom.

MATTIAS. You aren't hindering my health at all. I am now better
rested than usual and was just thinking over my views on the subject of our debate, hoping you would be here soon. But what is it
that you are so eager to hear from me?

DOMENICO. I am extraordinarily anxious to hear from you, if
you will, how you will resolve the last of the three issues I proposed. I had stated as a third point that a commonwealth, like everything else, is better governed by many than by one, a point that
I take to be the key one in our debate. It was chiefly for this reason
that I believed a republic should be preferred to a kingdom. It is
therefore on this subject that I wish to hear what you have to say,
and I look forward to your views and arguments.

JANOS. And this is what I too have now been long waiting to 2
hear about. For while everything you've said over these last two
days has pleased and gratified me, this issue, which I took as the
starting-point of the debate, is the one that will be the most pleasant and gratifying to hear about. It was this point in particular
that brought me over to the view that republics were preferable to
kingdoms, because I reckoned that all things were better governed
by many than by one, and hence our whole discussion arose. Accordingly, Domenico, if you love me, do be careful to follow up on
this aspect, and be assured that I am not at all tired of listening,
but am going to take the greatest pleasure in it. I believe also that

quoque voluptate affectum iri. Credo item patri, qui universam hanc disputationem mea causa suscepit, non molestum fore.

3 MATTHAEUS. Ego quidem, fili, tametsi nihil mihi grave potest esse quod tibi commodum aut iucundum sit, hoc tamen, quod ad me ipsum pertinet, munus etiam mea causa libenter obibo. Nam si constiterit melius a pluribus civitatem quam ab uno administrari, iniurius subditis nostris esse videar, si non aut eos in libertatem restituam aut mihi socios administrationis assumam, ut illi quam optime gubernentur. Sin unius administrationem optimam esse perspicuum fuerit, tibi pariter mihique gratulabor, quod et ego sim optimum inter mortales potestatis genus consecutus et tu te paulo post consecuturum speres. Age igitur, Dominice; tuam istam sententiam latius explica mihique hoc primum edissere: censeasne omnia melius a pluribus, an quaedam tantum gubernari?

4 DOMINICUS. Non audeo dicere omnia, ne tu mihi continuo caelum obiicias, cogarque primo congressu aut de mea sententia decedere tibique victas manus praebere aut, id quod maxime stultum et nefarium dictu est, caeli administrationem, hoc est Deum ipsum, damnare. Sed quae in hominum potestate sunt sita et humano consilio regi possunt, ea melius a pluribus quam ab uno regi puto.

MATTHAEUS. Navis nonne hominum potestati subiecta est?

DOMINICUS. Est quidem, cum non a ventis et a³ fluctibus vehementius agitatur.

MATTHAEUS. Quid⁴ cum non agitatur: regiturne humano consilio?

DOMINICUS. Regitur.

MATTHAEUS. Tunc ergo a pluribusne rectoribus an ab uno melius gubernatur?

DOMINICUS. A pluribus temonem vicissim regentibus. Unus enim, nisi quandoque quiescat, diu durare non potest.

it won't be tiresome for my father either, who undertook the whole debate for my sake.

MATTIAS. As far as I am concerned, son, although anything that is useful and pleasant for you is no burden to me, the task that falls to me is one that I undertake willingly for my own sake as well. For if it should be established that a state is better run by many than by one, I would seem to be doing our subjects an injustice if I did not restore them their liberty or if I did not accept some associates in governance, so that they could be governed as well as possible. But if it should become clear that the governance of one person is the best, I shall congratulate you and me equally, because I have been employing the best kind of power among mortals, a power you hope to employ hereafter. Come then, Domenico, explain your views more fully and tell me this first: do you think that all things, or only some, are better governed by many persons?

DOMENICO. I don't dare say all, or you'll immediately bring up against me the case of heaven, and I'll be forced to retreat from my opinion at the first clash and surrender, or condemn the government of heaven, that is God himself, a thing which it would be foolish and wicked to do. But I do think that what is placed in human power and can be ruled by human counsel is better ruled by many than by one.

MATTIAS. Isn't a ship subject to human power?

DOMENICO. It is indeed, when it is not violently acted upon by wind and seas.

MATTIAS. But when it is not so acted upon, it is ruled by human counsel?

DOMENICO. It is so ruled.

MATTIAS. Is it then better governed by many helmsmen or by one?

DOMENICO. By many, who take the helm by turns. For a single helmsman cannot last long unless he rests sometimes.

5 MATTHAEUS. At isto quidem modo etiam regnum a pluribus regitur, sibi suo ordine succedentibus. Unus enim rex vivere semper non potest. Ego vero, num eodem tempore navem plures rectores temonesque an unum tantum habere satius sit, ex te quaero.

DOMINICUS. At isto modo plures ne capere quidem posset.

MATTHAEUS. Quid si posset?

DOMINICUS. Non regeretur etiam satis recte, nisi omnes eandem mentem peritiamque haberent.

MATTHAEUS. Istud vero quo pacto fieri potest?

DOMINICUS. Difficile admodum esset.

MATTHAEUS. Egeret ergo alter consensu atque auxilio alterius.

DOMINICUS. Utique.

6 MATTHAEUS. Unus autem egetne cuiusquam auxilio?

DOMINICUS. Minime.

MATTHAEUS. Potestne a se ipso dissentire?

DOMINICUS. Non si sanus est.

MATTHAEUS. Commodior igitur et expeditior ad regendum est unus quam plures.

DOMINICUS. Ita videtur.

7 MATTHAEUS. Quid exercitus? A pluribusne imperatoribus an ab uno rectius gubernatur?

DOMINICUS. A pluribus puto, si inter se concordes sint.

MATTHAEUS. Poteruntne autem omnes[5] et semper et in omnibus esse concordes?

DOMINICUS. Si non omnes, at plerique tamen poterunt, atque hi quidem et ceteros compriment et exercitui imperabunt.

MATTHAEUS. Quomodo vero imperabunt? Omnes omnibus eadem, an singuli quaedam universis, an diviso per partes imperio

MATTIAS. But even a kingdom is ruled by many in this sense, 5
each succeeding the other in order, for one king can't live forever.
But I'm asking you whether it is preferable that a ship have many
helmsmen and tillers at the same time or only one?

DOMENICO. But a ship could not even admit of a plurality of
helmsmen in that way.

MATTIAS. But what if it could?

DOMENICO. It would not be steered even reasonably well unless
they all were of the same mind and had the same experience.

MATTIAS. But how is that possible?

DOMENICO. It would be very difficult.

MATTIAS. One would need the consent and help of the other,
then.

DOMENICO. Indeed.

MATTIAS. Would a single helmsman need anyone else's help? 6

DOMENICO. No.

MATTIAS. Could he disagree with himself?

DOMENICO. Not if he were sane.

MATTIAS. A single man would then be more suitable and less
encumbered in controlling the ship than many would?

DOMENICO. It seems so.

MATTIAS. What about an army? Is it better commanded by a 7
several generals or by a single one?

DOMENICO. I think by several, if they are in agreement with
each other.

MATTIAS. But could they always be in agreement with each
other about everything?

DOMENICO. A majority if not all of them will be able to, and the
majority will subdue the rest and take command of the army.

MATTIAS. But how will they command it? Will all of them command all their soldiers to do the same thing, or will individuals
give certain commands for the whole body, or will the command

alii aliis, an, ut Terentius Varro et Paulus Aemilius ad Cannas fa-
ciebant, suis quisque statisque diebus universo exercitui praee-
runt?

DOMINICUS. Istud quidem nihil meo iudicio refert, modo inter
se, ut dixi, consentiant.

8 MATTHAEUS. Immo plurimum. Nam si omnes eadem sine discrimine omnibus imperabunt, primum, hoc erit obtundere milites,
non regere; deinde, cum alii eadem aliter imperent, milites, quod
optimum sit nescientes, in deteriora plerumque declinabunt. Cum
autem aequa imperatorum potestas sit, milites, cui potissimum parere oporteat ignari, aut nemini omnino parebunt aut secuti alii
alios, perniciosissimas in exercitu factiones excitabunt. Nam
consentire quidem duces inter se omnes in⁶ imperando, si modo
plures animos habebunt, non poterunt; sua enim unicuique imperandi ratio maxime placebit. Unusquisque praeterea principatum
affectabit et gratiosissimum se apud milites reddere semper studebit. Sed etiam si, id quod fieri nullo modo potest, omnes inter se
consentiant⁷ et omnia pariter et promiscue imperent, nihilo tamen
plus agent multi quam unus, siquidem universam singuli potestatem habebunt. Eadem autem utilitate proposita, imperia, sumptus
et pericula multiplicare supervacuum omnino et stultum est.

9 Quod si divisa potestate singuli quaedam omnibus imperabunt,
primum quidem idem eveniet, ut nihilo plus agant multi quam
unus; deinde magnae ex utraque parte discordiae orientur. Nam
duces quidem, si pares erunt, dignissima quisque munera affecta-
bunt, minora in alios reiicient; si erunt impares, ut alius alio maior
sit, qui maximus inter eos erit, is imperatoris locum obtinebit, ceteri omnes uni obsequentur. Milites vero, tam varium et multiplex

be divided into parts and different commanders command different soldiers, or, like Terentius Varro and Paulus Aemilius at Cannae,[1] will each general lead the whole army on fixed days?

DOMENICO. All that doesn't matter at all, in my judgment, so long as they agree among themselves, as I said.

MATTIAS. No, it matters a great deal. For suppose all will command all without distinction. This will be, first, to deafen the soldiers, not command them. Second, when different generals command the same things in different ways, the soldiers won't know which way is the best and will generally take the worse course. When there is equal power among generals, the soldiers won't know whom they should obey in particular, and so will either obey no one at all or different soldiers will follow different commanders, giving rise to destructive factions in the army. Leaders cannot all agree among themselves in commanding so long as they have more than one mind, for everybody likes his own way of commanding the best. Moreover, each one will aspire to be commander-in-chief and will always be striving to ingratiate himself with the troops. But even if all were to agree among themselves (which is impossible) and they gave all their commands indiscriminately on an equal basis, many commanders couldn't accomplish anything more than a single commander, since as individuals they were holding power as a whole. To multiply commands, costs and dangers for the same benefit is entirely superfluous and stupid.

But suppose power is divided and individual generals give certain commands to all soldiers. First, there would be the same result, that nothing would be gained by having many generals rather than one. Second, it would give rise to tremendous discord for both commanders and soldiers. For if commanders are equals, they will each try to get the most prestigious tasks and will push the lesser tasks on the rest. If they are unequal, so one is greater than another, the one who is greatest among them will take the place of the general, and all the rest will submit to that one man.

imperium fastidientes, dedignabuntur id a multis imperium accipere quod ab uno possint, neque quemquam ut legitimum imperatorem aut verebuntur aut amabunt. Postremo aliis alia imperantibus, unum aliquem omnium moderatorem ac ducem esse necesse erit, ad quem omnium quasi summa referatur, qui cetera omnia suo[8] iudicio atque imperio moderetur ac regat.

10    Si vero plures in partes exercitus distributus erit, ut suae quisque imperator parti praesit, non iam in uno exercitu plures imperatores erunt,[9] sed quot ipsi duces fuerint, totidem quoque exercitus efficientur, ita ut non singulis partibus, sed singulis exercitibus singuli imperatores praesint. Divisis porro exercitibus multiplicatisque imperatoribus quo pacto bellum geri possit aut quid evenire soleat, cum alii permulti saepe docuere, tum secundo bello Punico Q. Minutius, magister equitum Q. Fabii Maximi dictatoris, apertissime declaravit. Qui cum ab senatu dictatorem criminando impetrasset ut diviso illius exercitu partem ipse acciperet, pugnandi avidus, cum omni quem habebat exercitu in summum discrimen sua temeritate devenit, quod nisi Fabii diligentia et subsidio fuisset servatus, cum omni prorsus exercitu periisset. Non possunt igitur exercitus dividi ducibusque diversis committi sine summa tum ipsorum ducum tum vero militum calamitate atque ignominia.

11    Sin autem plures duces statis inter se diebus imperabunt, cum neque omnes eandem rei militaris peritiam habeant et sint inter se aemuli, neque poterit militaris disciplina in castris servari neque satis recte bellum geri. Dum enim unusquisque suo ductu bellum conficere et honorem aliis praeripere studebit, sine ulla ratione exercitum hosti obiiciet, temere omnia et inconsulto geret. Ita se

The soldiers will scorn such a motley command structure and will disdain to accept a command from many which they might accept from one, and they will neither fear nor love anyone as their legitimate general. Finally, with different people giving different commands, it will be necessary for there to be some one commander and director over all, to whom the substance of everything may be referred, who will direct and rule all other matters with his judgment and power.

But if the army is divided into many parts, and each general 10 commands his part, there will no longer be many generals in a single army, but there will be created as many armies as there are generals, so that the individual generals will not be leading separate parts, but separate armies. Further, while numerous individuals have often taught us this, the case of Quintus Minucius, master of horse to the dictator Quintus Fabius Maximus in the Second Punic War, illustrates with utter clarity how a war might be conducted and what the result would usually be when armies are divided and commanders multiplied.[2] When Minucius, by denouncing the dictator, had obtained from the Senate that Fabius's army should be divided and that he himself should receive command of a part, eager for battle, he ended up bringing his whole force into terrible danger through his rashness, and he would surely have perished with his whole army if he had not been saved by Fabius' careful help. Armies cannot therefore be divided and entrusted to different commanders without [risk of] the greatest calamity and ignominy to commanders and soldiers alike.

Suppose, however, there are many commanders who command 11 on different days, agreed upon between themselves. Since not all of them will have the same military experience and there will be rivalries between them, it will be impossible to keep military discipline in the camps and war will be waged in a less than satisfactory way. For so long as each commander strives to win the war under his own leadership and to snatch honor from the others, he will

atque alios brevi sua cum temeritate tum ambitione pessundabit, ut Varro ille Terentius ad Cannas fecit, qui dum Paulum collegam audire noluit, temere ad pugnam quo die ipse imperabat progressus, memorabilem illa populo Romano cladem attulit. Quo exemplo satis, ut arbitror, ostensum est illam imperandi vicissitudinem perniciosissimam esse. Sed etiam si saluberrima esse posset, ut aequam omnes peritiam haberent, aequis inter se animis alterne imperarent, quia unus tantum eodem tempore exercitui universo praeesset, unus imperator diceretur esse, non plures.

12 Quocunque igitur modo plures imperent, aut ad unum deveniant aut pessime imperent necesse est, proptereaque ab omnibus gentibus ad unicum bellum unicus semper imperator et olim constitutus est et hodie constituitur, neque ferme aliter umquam est factum quin ingens aliqua sit clades aut calamitas consecuta.

DOMINICUS. De imperatore quidem, quod ad rem nostram non pertinet, nolo contendere: vos istud videritis, qui bellicae disciplinae studiosi estis. Veniamus ad ea quae nostrae disputationi propinquiora sunt.

13 MATTHAEUS. Quid domus? Nonne humano consilio et conflatur et regitur?

DOMINICUS. Maxime.

MATTHAEUS. Quot eam patres familias administrant?

DOMINICUS. Singuli singulas.

MATTHAEUS. Quod censes si plures essent? Rectiusne singulas domos administrarent?

DOMINICUS. Nescio, sed opinor fieri posse, si maxime inter se concordes essent.

throw his army on the enemy without any plan and will do everything in a rash and thoughtless fashion. Thus in a short time he will ruin himself and others with his rashness and ambition, as Terentius Varro did at Cannae. Not wanting to heed his colleague Paulus Aemilius, he rashly set out for battle on the day he was in command, bringing on the Roman people that memorable disaster.[3] I think this example is sufficient to show that alternating command of an army is an utterly pernicious practice. But even if it were utterly beneficial, and all the generals had equal experience and commanded alternately among themselves with equal spirit and intelligence, since one person only was leading the whole army at a given time, he would be said to be one general, not many.

Hence, in whatever way a plurality commands, it necessarily    12 comes down to one person commanding or to several commanding in the worst possible way. And that is why all nations in the past and still today have always appointed a single commander for a single war, and have almost never done otherwise without it leading to some huge disaster or calamity.

DOMENICO. I certainly don't want to wrangle about generalship, which isn't relevant to our subject. You will see to that, as you are such devotees of the discipline of war. Let's come to matters which are closer to the subject of our debate.

MATTIAS. What about the household?[4] Isn't it formed and ruled    13 by human counsel?

DOMENICO. Absolutely.

MATTIAS. How many household heads administer it?

DOMENICO. One per household.

MATTIAS. What do you think about several heads? Would they administer their several households better?

DOMENICO. I don't know, but I think it could be possible, if they were in the greatest harmony with each other.

MATTHAEUS. Quo pacto? Ut alii pascuis, alii vineis, alii rei ur-
banae domesticaeque praeesset? Itane putas?

DOMINICUS. Cur non?

MATTHAEUS. Non iam isti patres familias, sed villici et procura-
tores erunt. Sed quis tandem ab illis annuam administratae provinciae rationem repetet, ne unusquisque sibi congerat ceterosque
defraudet, an eorum fidei standum erit?

DOMINICUS. Quidni? Publicam enim utilitatem, non suam
quisque curabit, si modo bonus pater familias esse volet.

14 MATTHAEUS. At quis eorum suam uxorem, suos liberos, suam
ceteram familiam esse atque ad se potissimum eorum omnium
educationem atque administrationem pertinere existimabit?
Eruntne et uxores et liberi, ut Plato volebat, communes? Vide ne
istud quidem hodie non expediat. An suam quisque uxorem, suos
liberos educabit ac reget?

DOMINICUS. Isto modo potius.

MATTHAEUS. Non plures ergo una familia patres, sed una domus familias plures habebit?

DOMINICUS. An non vidisti, rex, plures in una domo fratres
cum coniugibus et liberis defuncto patre diu simul communibus
impensis commorari?

15 MATTHAEUS. Tu vero non vidisti quantae inter eos non modo lites atque inimicitiae, verum etiam caedes ista de causa oriantur?
Dum enim suis quisque liberis parare aliquid et servare studet,
alienis subtrahat et societatem defraudet ac deserat necesse est.
Sed etiam si exactissime servari posset ista communio, plures tamen in una domo familiae, non unica, esse dicerentur. Vir enim et
uxor, si liberos aut servos habeant, familiam domumque confi-

MATTIAS. How would that work? Would someone be in charge of pasture-land, others of the vineyards, others business in town and domestic matters? Is that what you think?

DOMENICO. Why not?

MATTIAS. Well, already these aren't heads of household, but farm-overseers and agents. But who is going to get the annual report from these men on their responsibilities so that each one doesn't engross goods for himself and defraud the rest? Or will they rely on each other's loyalty?

DOMENICO. Why not? Each will be concerned for the public utility, not his own, so long as he wishes to be a good head of household.

MATTIAS. But who will reckon that his own wife, children and 14 other family members belong to them, and will think that their upbringing and governance is any special business of his? Will they have wives and children in common, as Plato wished?[5] Perhaps this wouldn't work out nowadays. Or will each educate and govern his own wife and children?

DOMENICO. The latter.

MATTIAS. So a single family will not have many fathers, but one household will have many families?

DOMENICO. Haven't you seen, king, after the death of a father, many brothers in a single household with their wives and children dwelling all together simultaneously and having their expenses in common?

MATTIAS. But haven't you seen how many lawsuits and hatreds 15 and even murders arise among them for this reason? So long as each is eager to keep and provide for his own children, he necessarily takes away from his brothers' children and cheats and lets down the fellowship between them. But even if their common interests could be adhered to with the utmost exactitude, many families would be said to be living in a single home, not a single family. A husband and wife, if they have children or servants, make up a

ciunt, neque capit haec societas plures dominos aut moderatores, nam illa in uxorem et liberos caritas nisi uni patri esse non potest. Proptereaque Lacedaemonius ille Lycurgus, cum a quodam interrogaretur cur Lacedaemone plurimorum principatum non faceret, 'Fac,' inquit, 'illum prius domi tuae,' satis hoc responso declarans domum nisi ex uno patre familias constare non posse.

16 DOMINICUS. Esto; constet. Quid tum postea?

MATTHAEUS. Nonne multae domus vicum faciunt?

DOMINICUS. Faciunt.

MATTHAEUS. Quis porro vico praeest?

DOMINICUS. Vicarius sive decurio sive tribunus: de nomine enim sollicitus non sum.

MATTHAEUS. Unusne iste est an plures?

DOMINICUS. Unus tantum.

MATTHAEUS. Nonne, ut multae domus vicum, ita multi vici civitatem faciunt?

DOMINICUS. Fateor.

17 MATTHAEUS. Quemadmodum igitur una domus ab uno patre familias, unus vicus ab uno vicario sive decurione optime gubernatur, cur non eodem modo civitas, quae multis domibus vicisque constat, ab uno etiam optime gubernetur?

DOMINICUS. Quia non eadem domus aut vici quae civitatis administratio est.

MATTHAEUS. Cur non?

DOMINICUS. Quia multo maior est civitas quam domus multoque eius administratio difficilior. Nam si exigua domus, quae octo aut decem hominum gubernationem continet, vix ab uno patre familias regi atque administrari potest, quam multis tandem rectoribus universa civitas, quae multa non hominum modo, sed domorum quoque milia continet indigere credenda est?

18 MATTHAEUS. At non obest magnitudo civitati quominus eam unus administrare possit, ut domui magnitudo non obstat quomi-

family and household, and this association does not admit of more than one master or director, for the love of a wife and children occurs only when there is a single father.[6] That is why the Spartan Lycurgus, when asked by a certain person why he had not made Sparta into a democracy, replied, "Make one first in your own household," a response that was enough to show that a household cannot exist except with a single head.[7]

DOMENICO. So be it—agreed. What then follows?　　　　16

MATTIAS. Don't many households make a neighborhood?[8]

DOMENICO. They do.

MATTIAS. Who then heads the neighborhood?

DOMENICO. A headman, a councilman, a chief—the name doesn't concern me.

MATTIAS. Is he one person or many?

DOMENICO. Only one.

MATTIAS. Is it not the case that, as many households make up a neighborhood, so many neighborhoods make up a city?[9]

DOMENICO. I admit it.

MATTIAS. Well then, just as one household is best governed by　17 one father, and one village by one headman or councillor, why in the same way wouldn't a city, which is made up of many households and villages, be best governed by a single person too?

DOMENICO. It wouldn't because the government of a city is not the same as that of a household or neighborhood.

MATTIAS. Why not?

DOMENICO. Because, as a city is much larger than a household, its government is correspondingly much more difficult. If a small household which embraces eight or ten men can scarcely be ruled and directed by a single head, how many rulers must we believe a city is going to need, which embraces not only many thousands of men, but thousands of households?[10]

MATTIAS. But the city's size doesn't get in the way of its being　18 ruled by one man, any more than the size of a household gets in

nus eam unus pater familias administret. Quid est enim aliud civitas quam magna domus aut rex princepsque civitatis quam magnus pater familias et, ut ait Plato, hominum subesse volentium pastor? Quemadmodum autem neque ulla est tam magna domus quae ab uno patre familias regi non possit, neque grex ullus tam numerosus cui pastor unus praeesse non queat, ita nullam puto esse civitatem, immo nullum imperium, tam amplum, tam longe lateque diffusum, quod unus princeps gubernare tuerique non possit. Horum enim omnium una atque eadem ratio est.

DOMINICUS. Mihi quidem videtur longe alia.

MATTHAEUS. Quare?

DOMINICUS. Rogas? Si eorum inter se curas et administrationem conferas, facile, ut spero, id aperteque perspicies.

MATTHAEUS. Age; confer.

19  DOMINICUS. Pater quidem familias, ubi domum commeatu semel communivit familiamque vestibus et ceteris rebus necessariis a frigore et calore tutam reddidit, de cetero quietem agit; pastor item, ubi gregi suo laeta pascua et salubres fontes adinvenit, curis omnibus solutus ac liber est; rex vero sive quisquis ille est unus cui civitatis aut imperii tutela commissa est, numquam otiosus esse, numquam agere quietem potest; immo maiores in dies gravioresque[10] curas habet. Nam ut omittam quam grave, quam laboriosum sit tot milia hominum regere, omnium causas negotiaque cognoscere, omnibus aequa iura distribuere, hinc bella insurgunt, hinc emergunt defectiones, inde caedes, rapinae seditionesque nuntiantur, quae quidem unus non modo non componere, sed ne cognoscere quidem aut audire satis potest. Iam vero civium inter se factiones, odia, furta innumerabilesque iniuriae quae quottidie in civitate eveniunt, quo pacto aut sedari ab uno aut cognosci queunt? Huc accedit annonae caritas, pestilentia, tempestates, ruinae, terrae motus, incendia et alia eius generis quam plurima, quae quidem tam gravia quam frequentia sunt, ita ut tam multis

the way of its being ruled by a single head. For what else is a city but a large household, or a king and city leader but a great head of household, and, as Plato says, a shepherd of those men willing to be subjects.[11] Just as there is no household so large that it can't be ruled by a single head of household, no flock so numerous that a single shepherd can't lead it, so, I think, there is no city, indeed no empire, of such ample extent that a single emperor could not govern and protect it. The principle behind all of these is one and the same.

DOMENICO. It seems to me far different.

MATTIAS. Why?

DOMENICO. Need you ask? If you compare their concerns and governance to each other, you'll easily spot the differences, I hope.

MATTIAS. Go ahead and compare them.

DOMENICO. The head of household, once he has supplied his household with provisions and protected his family from heat and cold with clothing and other necessities, is otherwise at peace. The shepherd too, when he has found pleasant pastures and clean water for his flock, is free of all care. But a king, or any single person entrusted with a city or an empire, never enjoys leisure or rest; indeed, his cares are larger and more burdensome each day. Let me pass over what a grave and laborious business it is to govern so many thousands of men, to take cognizance of all their legal cases and business, to distribute to all equally what is due to each. On this side wars break out, allies defect; on that side murder, plunder and sedition are reported, and one person cannot even understand or find out about all of these occurrences, let alone deal with them. Besides, factions and hatreds arise on a daily basis among citizens, thefts and innumerable acts of injustice, and how can a single person take cognizance of and settle all that? Add dearths, pestilence, storms, collapsing buildings, earthquakes, fires and other things of this kind which are as serious as they are common.

19

rebus simul unius quamvis prudentissimi animus vacare et in tam varias distrahi partes non possit.

20 MATTHAEUS. Multae quidem et graves regis sunt curae, neque ego hoc, qui quottidie in illis versor, negare umquam ausim. Sed, si diligenter adverteris, non sunt in suo genere pauciores ac[11] leviores illae quae patris familias pastorisque animum assidue vexant, atque haud scio an etiam plures gravioresque in suo genere dici possint. Nam, ut eas, quas tu de utroque commemorasti, missas faciam — quae non singulis annis, ut ipse existimas, sed singulis prope diebus instaurantur ac redeunt — patri quidem familias nunc uxoris, nunc liberorum vel mors vel valitudo affertur, nunc servorum furta, doli fugaeque nuntiantur, nunc aedificiorum ruinae aut incendia superveniunt, quae quidem et magna et celeri providentia indigent. Iam vero fames, pestilentia, morbi ceteraeque caeli ac terrae iniuriae quibus non homines modo, sed cetera quoque animalia obnoxia sunt, quantopere animum eius angunt, quantis eum[12] curis afficiunt? Quid liberorum ortus, educatio, institutio, collocatio? Quid nepotum cura sobolisque propagatio? Quid rei familiaris conservatio, amplificatio, distributio? Nonne etiam sapientissimi ac diligentissimi viri animum maiorem in modum sollicitant atque perturbant?

21 Pastoris vero administratio quot curis molestiisque referta est? Quot casibus obnoxia? Pecudes enim nunc morbis, nunc furtis rapinisque hominum, nunc bestiarum vi direptionibusque amittit, nunc errantes omnibus campis, silvis montibusque persequitur; iam vero aliae tussi, aliae scabie, aliae febri infestantur, quibus quottidie pascua, aquae[13] oviliaque mutanda, remedia omnis generis adhibenda. Quid quam frequenter lavandae tondendaeque sunt? Lactis praeterea expressio, confectio casei, foetuum educatio

The upshot is that one mind, however wise, cannot be free to deal with so many things at once without being utterly distracted.

MATTIAS. Many and grave indeed are the cares of a king, and as 20 someone with daily experience of such matters I should never dare deny that. But on closer examination the cares that constantly harass heads of household and shepherds are not fewer or lighter in their kind, and I daresay they could be said, in their kind, to be even more numerous and grave. Let me set aside the cares they have that you have already mentioned, which are taken up and return, not every year as you reckon, but nearly every day. A head of household has to deal now with the deaths and sicknesses of his wife and children, now with theft, cheating and running away on the part of the servants, now with collapsing buildings or fires, all of which require great forethought and timely oversight. Besides, there come famines, pestilence, disease and the other losses imposed by heaven and earth, to which not only men but all animals are subject. How much anxiety and care must these cost him? What about the fathering, upbringing, education and employment of children? What about his concern for his grandchildren and the propagation of his stock? What of the preservation, enlargement and distribution of family property? Won't these worry and agitate tremendously the mind of even the wisest and most careful man?

And how many cares and annoyances bedevil the shepherd's 21 management of his flocks? How many misfortunes is he subject to? He loses sheep now from disease, now from theft and plundering on the part of men, now from the violence and predation on the part of animals; now he pursues the wandering beasts through every field, wood and mountain. Besides, some become infected with coughing, some with scabies, others with fevers, thanks to which he has to change pastures, water sources and sheepfolds on a daily basis and apply cures of all kinds. What about how often they need to be washed and sheared? Moreover, there is the milk-

atque tutela et cetera eius generis innumerabilia, quam multas illi et quam graves curas afferunt, quanta eius animum sollicitudine molestiaque excruciant? Satisne tibi hae multae aut magnae tum patris familias tum pastoris curae videntur? Putasne eos per otium atque inertiam vitam agere, ut dicebas, posse?

22 DOMINICUS. At uterque servos habet qui ista curent permultos.

MATTHAEUS. Rex quoque, nonne servos ac[14] praefectos omnis generis innumerabiles habet?

DOMINICUS. At civitatis negotia longe maioris momenti sunt quam vel domus vel gregis. Bellum enim gerere, inire societates, pacem componere, ferre leges, iustitiam administrare, nonne multo maiora et graviora sunt quam vel alere puerum vel ovem curare? Immo si recte iudicare volumus, nulla ex parte sunt haec cum illis conferenda. Quae autem maius vel emolumentum si curentur vel si negligantur detrimentum afferunt, ea profecto et maiori studio et pluribus curatoribus videntur indigere.

23 MATTHAEUS. Scio haec cum illis non esse vel rerum pondere vel utilitatis magnitudine conferenda. Verum ego illorum curam, non utilitatem comparo. Quod si vel domus vel grex tam multis curis, tam assidua diligentia, tanta denique tutela in suo genere indiget quanta vel civitas vel provincia, et tamen unus illa rectissime administrat — immo non nisi unus administrare, ut docuimus, satis potest — quid est quod civitas quoque ab uno rectissime administrari non possit?

DOMINICUS. Ego ab uno recte posse non infitior et, quando tu ita vis, libenter concedo. Rectius autem ab uno quam a pluribus posse non censeo.

24 MATTHAEUS. At supervacuum est id a pluribus fieri quod ab uno recte possit. Quemadmodum autem, si quis vel unico currui duos aurigas vel unice navi duos gubernatores[15] velit praeficere,

ing, making of cheese, upbringing and protection of the young, and innumerable other things of this kind. How many grave cares will these things bring him, how much will they torture his mind with anxiety and worry? Do these cares of the head of household or the shepherd seem numerous and great enough for you? Do you think they can lead a life of leisure and ease, as you were saying?

DOMENICO. But both have many servants who take care of these things.   22

MATTIAS. Doesn't a king also have innumerable servants and officials of every kind?

DOMENICO. But the business of a city is of much greater importance than that of a household or a flock. Waging war, forming alliances, making peace, passing laws, administering justice: aren't these graver and greater concerns than either bringing up children or guarding sheep? Indeed, rightly considered, these two spheres of human activity are in no way comparable. The concerns that bring greater benefit when seen to or greater detriment when neglected are the concerns that seem to require more devoted support and more persons to take care of them.

MATTIAS. I recognize that the two spheres are not of compara-   23
ble magnitude either in terms of seriousness or utility, but I'm comparing their management, not their magnitude. If a household or a flock needs as much care, as much ceaseless diligence, as much protection in its kind as a city or province, and yet one person best governs the former — indeed, the former can't be adequately governed except by one person, as we've shown — why is it that a city too is not best governed by one man?

DOMENICO. I don't deny that it can be well governed by one man, and since you wish it so, I freely concede this. But I don't think it can be governed better by one man than by many.

MATTIAS. But there's a redundancy in the fact that what can be   24
well done by one can be well done by many. If someone wanted two charioteers to be in charge of a single chariot or two helms-

cum satis recte ab uno utrumque regi possit, ab omnibus ut nimis[16] cautus ac potius stultus irrideatur, ita cura et administratio
civitatis, quae uni recte convenit, si pluribus demandetur, superva-
cua et ridicula debet existimari.

DOMINICUS. Atqui non aeque recte ab uno atque a multis, ut
currus et navis, ita etiam civitas regitur.

MATTHAEUS. Quamobrem? Quid, obsecro, faciunt multi quod
unus facere vel, ut ego sentio, rectius vel saltem aeque recte non
possit?

25   DOMINICUS. Primum, omnia melius et intellegunt et diiudicant
multi quam unus. Quatuor enim, ut dicitur, oculi magis cernunt
quam duo et quatuor manus quam duae magis comprehendunt;
quatuor item homines plus virium habent quam duo, quae cum
omnibus in rebus ratio aeque valeat, civitatem quoque[17] a pluribus
meliusque quam ab uno regi manifestum est. Deinde, unus rex facilius ex optimo pessimus fit et, ut brevi dicam, in tyrannum com-
mutatur quam multi. Difficile enim est multos simul irasci, odisse,
amare, cupere et ceteris animi affectibus morbisque corrumpi;
unum autem facillimum est, quamquam tu paulo ante contra graviter copioseque disputasti.

26   Sed quod in ea re tibi concessi, in hac fortasse non concedam.
Praeterea, cum civitas ad commune omnium bonum et commodum instituta sit atque id quanto communius est tanto maius ac
divinius esse existimetur, multi ob hoc ipsum, quia multi sunt, ad
commune bonum curandum longe sunt quam unus aptiores. Nam
cum multi sint, etiam si pessime rempublicam regant et propriam
tantum utilitatem curent, paucorum utilitatem curare non possunt. Unus autem, si communem utilitatem deserat et sibi ipsi in-
dulgeat, unius tantum hominis commodum bonumque curabit,

men of a single ship when both could be governed by a single person, he would be laughed at by everyone as too cautious or rather stupid. So to turn over to many people the care and governance of a city, which rightly pertains to one person, ought to be regarded as superfluous and absurd.

DOMENICO. All the same, just like a chariot and a ship, so too a city is ruled with unequal ability by one and by many.

MATTIAS. Why? What can many do, I ask you, that one person can't do at least equally well or (as I think) better?

DOMENICO. First of all, many people understand and decide     25 better than one. As they say, four eyes see better than two and four hands grip better than two.[12] Likewise, four men have more strength than two, and since the same reasoning is equally valid in all circumstances, it's obvious that a city is better ruled by many than by one. Second, one king is more easily corrupted from best to worst and (not to put too fine a point on it) is changed into a tyrant than many are. It's difficult for many at the same time to become angry, to hate, to love, to desire and to be corrupted by the other passions and diseases of soul, but this is supremely easy for one person, although a little while ago you argued for the opposite view with great weight and at great length.[13]

But what I conceded to you in that context I should not per-     26 haps concede in this one. Especially since a city is founded for the common good and common convenience of all, and that which is more common is held to be in that degree greater and more divine,[14] the many, for the very reason that they are many, are far better suited to care for the common good than one person. For since they are many, even if they govern the republic in the worst possible way and only look out for their own utility, they cannot care for the utility of just a few people. But one person, if he abandons the common utility and favors himself, will be taking care of the convenience and good of just one person, than which nothing

quo quidem nihil esse potest vel humanae societati perniciosius vel
ab ipso reipublicae nomine alienius.

27    Huc accedit quod, cum in omni nostra actione tum vero in administratione reipublicae, consilium est vel maxime necessarium.
In omni enim re, ut ait Cicero, 'prius quam aggrediare, adhibenda
est praeparatio diligens.' Multorum autem praesertim liberorum,
hominum consilium et prudentius et tutius quam unius esse nemo
dubitat. Multi enim et maiorem omnium rerum experientiam ac
peritiam habent et decipi in communi salute minus possunt; unus
autem neque sane multarum rerum habere usum potest et in sua
causa plerumque decipitur. Quod si aut servorum aut mercenna-
riorum consilio utatur, id ingenuorum consilio neque fide neque
voluntate neque diligentia comparandum erit. Illi enim in re
aliena, spe praesertim laudis sublata, se levissime gerent. Quo fit
ut civitas quae plurium ingenuorum consilio regitur multo melius
quam quae unius regatur.

28    Postremo, stabilius multorum et diuturnius quam unius imperium est. Unus enim, etiam si optime regat, quia diu non vivit,
neque sane multa incohare neque perficere quae incohavit, neque
etiam quae perfecit servare aut stabilire satis potest; multi autem,
quia mori simul omnes non possunt, et incohant quae volunt et
quae incohavere perficiunt et, quae semel perfecere, perpetuo servant, ita ut eorum non modo stabile, sed continuum quoque et
diuturnum ac paene sempiternum imperium sit nullamque umquam aut intermissionem aut varietatem capiat, sed unum semper
atque idem permaneat. Quibus rationibus efficitur ut ego multos
uni, hoc est rempublicam regno, anteponam.

29    MATTHAEUS. Valide, mehercule, et efficaces sunt rationes istae,
Dominice,[18] et quibus responderi sine summa doctrina non possit,
quippe quae ex uberrimo illo disciplinarum omnium fonte, Aristo-
telis ingenio, proficiscantur. Tu enim, ut optimus imperator,
firmissimam aciem in postremis collocasti, quasi de summa impe-

can be more destructive to human society or more alien to the very name of commonwealth.

Moreover, counsel is necessary in all our activity, but most necessary of all in the governance of a commonwealth. Every matter, as Cicero says, requires careful preparation before addressing it.[15] No one doubts that the counsel of many men, especially free men, is wiser and safer than the counsel of one man. For many men have greater experience and knowledge of all things and are harder to deceive in matters concerning their common welfare; one person, however, cannot surely have much practice at many things and is generally deceived in his own cause.[16] If he makes use of the counsel of slaves and mercenaries, it will not be comparable to the counsel of free men either as regards its trustworthiness, its carefulness or its voluntary nature. The former conduct themselves unreliably in the affairs of others, being sustained by the hope of praise. Hence the city that is ruled by the counsel of many free men is much better off than the city ruled by one man's judgment.

Finally, power that belongs to many is more stable and long-lived than the power of one man. Even if one man rules extremely well, since he does not live for long, he cannot surely start many enterprises, nor finish those begun, nor even preserve and make stable the things he does finish. But many men, since they cannot all die simultaneously, both start what they want and finish what they've started and can preserve it once they have finished it. Hence their power is not only stable, but also continuous and lasting and almost eternal, and it never suffers any break or variation but remains always one and the same. That is why I prefer the many to one man, that is, a republic to a kingdom.

MATTIAS. Domenico, these are strong and effective arguments, by Hercules, and one may not respond to them without great learning, as they are derived from that richest source of all disciplines, the mind of Aristotle.[17] Like the best generals you have put your most solid battle line in the rear, as though you were going to

rii hoc ultimo proelio dimicaturus. Ego vero, cum quia rex sum, tum quia a philosophis omnibus imprimisque a divino illo Platone didici optimum omnium esse unius boni ac iusti regis principatum, quoad potero, meas partes defendam; tibi certe primo congressu non cedam, quod ne adversus Turcas quidem, cum dimicarem, facere consuevi.

30 Civitatem ais propterea melius a pluribus regi, quod plures omnia melius intellegant iudicentque quam unus, ut plus quatuor oculi cernant quam duo, et plus quatuor viri possint quam duo. Istud quidem tibi, si civitas corporis viribus administranda sit, quae multiplicatae plus ponderis ac laboris ferunt, facile concedam. Sin ingenii viribus et rationis imperio regenda sit, ut esse manifestum est, non concedam. Illa enim ingenii acies et vis rationis, cum[19] pura simplexque sit, omni prorsus inscitiae labe et mentis[20] perturbatione sublata, nihilo plus aliis coniuncta cernet quam sola. Ubi enim semel id, quod optimum est, per se satis abundeque viderit et ad ipsam recti metam sola pervenerit, etiam si comites illi innumerabiles addantur, quid illam iuvare, quid in ea re amplius videre aut quo illam ducere ulterius poterunt? Cedo: si tibi in circulo medium sive, ut Graeci vocant, *centrum* inveniendum sit, et tute[21] id invenire optime scias, indigebisne ad id inveniendum adiutore ac socio?

31 DOMINICUS. Minime.

MATTHAEUS. Poterisne id cum sociis melius an per te ipsum invenire?

DOMINICUS. Per me ipsum puto. Socii enim, aliquo forsitan errore aut imperitia ducti, me quoque in eundem errorem trahent facientque quod scio ut nesciam.

fight this last battle for supreme power. But I shall defend my side as best I can because I am a king and also because I have learned from all the philosophers, and principally from the divine Plato himself, that the best form of rule is that of a single good and just king.[18] I shall certainly not fall back at the first clash of arms, which I was not accustomed to do even when I fought against the Turks.

You say that a city is better ruled by the many because the 30 many know all things and judge of them better than one, as four eyes see better than two and four men are stronger than two. This I would readily concede to you if a city were to be ruled by bodily strength, which has more power and endurance when multiplied. But if it is to be ruled by strength of mind and the power of reason, as it manifestly is, I shall not concede this. For that mental penetration and force of reason, being something pure and simple, something that is destroyed by the weaknesses of ignorance and passion, discerns no better when conjoined with others' reason than it does when it is alone. Once a rational power by itself has seen in its fullness what is best and has reached on it own the very goal of the right and true, even if innumerable companions were conjoined to it, how could they help it, how much more intensely could they see into that matter, to what further insight could they lead it? Come now: If you had to find the middle, or what the Greeks call "the center," in a circle, and you knew perfectly well how to find it, should I allow that you will need a helper or associate to find it?

DOMENICO. Not at all. 31

MATTIAS. Could you find the center better with an associate or by yourself?

DOMENICO. By myself, I think. Associates might by influenced by error and ignorance and drag me too into the same error and cause me to forget what I know.

187

MATTHAEUS. Ubi vero id semel inveneris, poterisne ulterius in eo quaerendo progredi?

DOMINICUS. Nequaquam.

MATTHAEUS. Quid si tibi socii complures accedant? Poteritisne omnes aut melius quam tute id[22] reppereris aut aliud quam ipse reppereris medium invenire?

DOMINICUS. Qui fieri hoc potest, cum unicum in una re medium tantum sit?

32 MATTHAEUS. In qua potissimum re optima et sanctissima civitatis administratio continetur?

DOMINICUS. In cognitione et observatione iustitiae.

MATTHAEUS. Estne virtus iustitia?

DOMINICUS. Est et quidem maxima.

MATTHAEUS. In quo porro consistit summa virtus?

DOMINICUS. In mediocritate. Nam, ut ait Flaccus,

> virtus est medium vitiorum ‹et›[23] utrinque reductum.

MATTHAEUS. Si quis igitur unus hoc medium et optime invenire sciat et verissime invenerit, oportebitne eum ulterius quaerere?

DOMINICUS. Non si medium, hoc est virtutem, volet tenere; 'est' enim, ut idem Flaccus ait,

> modus in rebus, sunt certi denique fines
> quos ultra citraque nequit consistere rectum.

33 MATTHAEUS. Quid ergo illi ad rectum inveniendum socii vel innumerabiles conferre poterunt?

DOMINICUS. Nihil, si unus ipse optime sciat; sed pauci admodum qui sciant reperiuntur, proptereaque complures causis iudicandis praeficiuntur, ut inter eos vel plures vel saltem unus rectum discernat.

MATTHAEUS. Si unus id deprehendet, unus is verus et legitimus iudex erit; ceteri non erunt. Sin id plures perspicient, cum id

MATTIAS. And once you've found it, could you get any further by asking about it?

DOMENICO. By no means.

MATTIAS. What if many associates join you? Could all of those people find the center better than you yourself found it or find something other than you yourself found?

DOMENICO. How is that possible, since there is only one center in one circle?

MATTIAS. By what activity in particular is the best and most righteous civic governance constituted? 32

DOMENICO. By the recognition and observance of justice.

MATTIAS. Isn't justice a virtue?

DOMENICO. It is; in fact, the greatest one.[19]

MATTIAS. And in what does the best virtue consist?

DOMENICO. In the mean.[20] For as Horace says,

Virtue is a mean situated between vices on both sides.[21]

MATTIAS. Therefore if a single person knows best of all how to find this mean and has found it in very truth, shall he look for it any further?

DOMENICO. Not if he wishes to keep to the mean, that is, to virtue, for "there is," as Horace again says,

a due measure in things, there are in the end fixed limits,
and the right cannot stand beyond or below them.[22]

MATTIAS. What then can associates, even innumerable ones, contribute to helping him find what is right? 33

DOMENICO. Nothing, if the one man himself has perfect knowledge, but very few who know [perfectly] are to be found; hence a plurality of persons are put in charge of judging cases, so that, between them, either a plurality or at least one man may discern the right.

MATTIAS. If one man grasps it, he will be the one true and legitimate judge and the rest will not be. But if many perceive the

unum sit, unus quoque necessarius iudex erit, ceteri supervacui, quemadmodum, si quem currum unus ducere optime possit, plures administrare contendant.

34 DOMINICUS. Nonne quatuor oculi plus cernunt quam duo?

MATTHAEUS. Non si aeque acuti sint et in eodem loco constituantur habeantque eandem sibi subiectam ad videndum materiam.

DOMINICUS. Cur ergo, quod unus non videt, plures vident?

MATTHAEUS. Quia alii aliis acutiores sunt.

DOMINICUS. Idem etiam in reipublicae administratione accidit. Propterea enim plures regere melius existimantur, quia alii aliis ingeniosiores et perspicaciores sunt, et quod singuli per se videre fortasse non possent, vident universi.

MATTHAEUS. Quid si singuli optime omnia et perspicere et agere per se possent?

DOMINICUS. Fateor non fore plures necessarios.

MATTHAEUS. At poterunt, si erunt optimi.

35 DOMINICUS. Quotus vero quisque non dico in qualibet civitate, sed in qualibet etiam provincia optimus et, ut ipse vis, consummatissimus reperitur?

MATTHAEUS. Fateor admodum paucos, quia 'omnia praeclara rara,' sed tamen aliquos reperiri.

DOMINICUS. Ob istam ipsam causam plurium administrationem ego optimam esse dico, quia cum pauci optimi reperiantur, qui soli recte civitatem aut imperium administrare queant, multos simul ei rei praeficimus, ut quod virtuti deest, multitudine suppleatur.

MATTHAEUS. Non est igitur optima multorum administratio, sed, quia unum aliquem optimum reperiri posse diffiditis, necessario ad societatem retinendam inventa.

right, since the right is unitary, there will also be only one judge necessary and the rest will be superfluous, just as if many people were trying to drive a chariot that one person can drive perfectly well on his own.

DOMENICO. Don't four eyes see better than two?  34

MATTIAS. Not if they are equally acute and are standing in the same place and are looking at the same thing.

DOMENICO. Why then do many see what one person does not see?

MATTIAS. Because some have sharper eyes than others.

DOMENICO. The same also happens in the governance of a republic. The many are reckoned to rule better because some are more intelligent and perspicacious than others, and because everyone sees what individuals might perhaps not see on their own.

MATTIAS. What if an individual ruler could see and do all things excellently by himself?

DOMENICO. Then I admit that many rulers would not be necessary.

MATTIAS. But they will be able to, if they are going to be the best.

DOMENICO. But how many are there going to be in each region  35 who will count as the best and (as you yourself would have it) most perfect, to say nothing of each city?

MATTIAS. Very few, I confess, since "all things fine are rare,"[23] yet there are some to be found.

DOMENICO. It is for this very reason that I consider the government of the many to be the best. Since the best, who can govern a city or empire aright by themselves, are thin on the ground, we put the many in charge of government, so that what is lacking by way of virtue may be supplied by numbers.

MATTIAS. So the government of the many is not the best, but was invented of necessity to keep society together, since you doubt that a single excellent man may be found.

DOMINICUS. Sic est.

36 MATTHAEUS. Fateris ergo, si quis unus optimus reperiretur, non fore plurimorum statum necessarium; et posse aliquem reperiri non diffidis.

DOMINICUS. Ita est.

MATTHAEUS. At ego quid sit optimum, non ubi sit, disputo.

DOMINICUS. Fateor quidem non esse multos necessarios, si unus optimus reperiatur, sed si plures optimi reperiri queant, multo melius esse dico.

37 MATTHAEUS. Quid, obsecro, amplius facient multi quam unus?

DOMINICUS. Tutius rempublicam stabiliusque administrabunt, quod si quis labatur atque a recto declinet, ceteri eius errori occurrent et in officio permanebunt. Unus enim errare, labi, nescire, decipi, ut humana fragilitas est, facile posset; multi non possent.

MATTHAEUS. Quid si in diversas, ut fit, sententias distrahantur, neque unum aliquem habeant qui ceteros compescere ac moderari queat: nonne continuo civitas factionibus dividetur omnisque illa communio et concordia, quae respublicas omnes et facit et continet, e vestigio dissolvetur? Quid enim, obsecro, aliud in republica capitalia illa odia, quid perniciosas inter se civium contentiones, quid denique detestabilia ac nefaria bella civilia suscitat, nisi cum nemine aliquo reipublicae praesidente multi in ea excellere ac dominari volunt? Cum autem plures habere principes respublica, ut plura capita corpus, simul non valeat—aequalem enim et parem principatus ullus ferre non potest—multis locum illum occupare cupientibus, fit ut civitas partibus divisa in se ipsam armis consurgat brevique suis se viribus ipsa conficiat.

38 Quod quidem, cum in aliis permultis, tum in Romana vel maxime republica luce clarius licet intueri. Dum enim sub regibus

DOMENICO. That is so.

MATTIAS. You admit, then, that if a single excellent man were to 36
be found, the regime of the many would not be necessary, and you
do not doubt that someone could be found.

DOMENICO. That is so.

MATTIAS. All the same, I'm disputing what the best regime is,
not where it is.[24]

DOMENICO. I confess that many are not necessary if one best
man can be found, but if many best men could be found, I say
[the regime ruled by the latter] would be much better.

MATTIAS. What, I ask you, can many do beyond what a single 37
man can do?

DOMENICO. They can govern the commonwealth more safely
and more stably, because if someone becomes corrupt and goes
astray, the rest can check his error and continue in office. One
man could easily err, be corrupted, be ignorant or be deceived,
such being human fragility; many cannot.

MATTIAS. What if they become divided in their opinions and
lack someone to bridle and control the rest: won't the city be immediately divided into factions and all harmony and common interest — the things that create and maintain commonwealths — entirely disappear? For what else, I ask you, arouses in a republic
those blood feuds, those destructive rivalries among citizens, those
detestable and wicked civil wars, except many men who want to
achieve preëminence and dominate the republic in the absence of
someone to preside over it? A commonwealth cannot have many
leaders at once, like a body with many heads, for leadership cannot
brook an equal and peer. So when many people desire to take over
the leadership, the result is that the city splits into factions and
rises up in arms against itself and in a short time destroys itself
with its own forces.

This is a phenomenon which like many others may be best and 38
most clearly observed in the Roman commonwealth. For so long

fuit, summam inter se concordiam pacemque servavit; illis exactis numquam a seditionibus discordiisque cessavit, amissoque optimo illo et rectissimo regum principatu, tametsi pro uno rege duos dumtaxat consules et pro perpetuo annuos crearet, quasi nullum alium legitimum ac verum esse testaretur, nullum diutius ferre potuit, et nunc decem viros, nunc tribunos consulari potestate, nunc alterum e plebe consulem creando, numquam quievit donec, natura ipsa optimum illum unius principatum appetente, per ingentia bella civilia ad unum tandem rursus devenit. Quamdiu vero in unius optimi principis potestate permansit, civilium bellorum aut discordiarum nihil sensit; cum primum vero plures in ea excellere rursus voluerunt, ut Vitellii Severique temporibus, rursus ad civilia bella deventum est. Neque vero ab his malis hodiernae respublicae immunes sunt, testis est in vestra Etruria Senensis respublica, multis olim claris viris et optimarum artium studiis celebris, quae crebris civium seditionibus mutuisque tum caedibus tum exiliis eo, ut audio, redacta est, ut pristino illo splendore amisso, vix se a finitimis tueri possit. Vestra vero respublica, quam multis etiam seditionibus olim agitata sit, quam multos cives eiecerit, ipse optime scis, qui mecum ea de re saepenumero conquestus es, quod nisi optimum illum et praestantissimum civem Laurentium Medicem haberetis, qui sua virtute atque auctoritate civium animos moderatur ac regit, maximas nunc quoque, ut opinor, inter vos et perniciosissimas seditiones excitaretis.

39   DOMINICUS. Ita profecto est ut dicis, rex. Quicquid enim concordiae felicitatisque habemus, illi uni acceptum ferimus; est tamen ipse ita moderatus ac mitis, ut nihilo plus sibi[24] quam aequum sit vel potentiae vel auctoritatis arroget; immo, ex eo quod

as it was under the kings, it preserved the highest degree of peace and concord; once they were driven out and it lost that best and most upright leadership of the kings, although it created two consuls in the place of one king and an annual magistrate in the place of a perpetual king—as though to bear witness that there was no other true and legitimate [kind of] leadership [besides monarchy]—they were unable to endure this arrangement for long, and by creating now decemvirs, now tribunes with consular power, now another plebeian consul, they were never at peace, until by the action of Nature herself, who longed for that best leadership of one man, the commonwealth came at last again into the power of one man as a result of enormous civil wars. And for as long as it remained in the power of a single excellent prince, it experienced no civil wars or discords; but when a plurality of men first wished to enjoy preëminence in it, as in the times of Vitellius and Severus, it fell again into civil wars. Witness that modern republics are not immune from these maladies is the republic of Siena in your Tuscany, once celebrated for its many famous men and its zeal for the liberal arts. That city through incessant civil tumult, mutual slaughter and exile, as I hear, was reduced to a state where it lost its pristine splendor and could scarcely defend itself from its neighbors. You yourself, who have often complained of the fact to me, know very well how your own republic was formerly disturbed by many tumults and many banishings too. If you did not have that excellent and outstanding citizen, Lorenzo de'Medici, who controls and rules the spirits of your citizens with his virtue and authority, you would now be experiencing, in my opinion, the greatest and most destructive acts of sedition among yourselves.

DOMENICO. It is surely as you say, king. Whatever concord and 39 felicity we enjoy we have received from this one man; he is nevertheless so moderate and gentle that he arrogates to himself no more power or authority than is fair; indeed, he refuses much of what is rightly owed him, so that he seems to be not a single indi-

195

sibi iure debetur multum renuat, adeo ut non unus omnes moderari, sed unus omnibus parere ac subesse videatur.

MATTHAEUS. Ego quidem de homine tam multa audivi, ut eum incredibili amore studioque complectar; sed de Laurentio alias.

40 Perspicuum igitur est civitatem, quae a pluribus administretur, non posse diu a seditionibus et civilibus bellis tutam esse. Nam etiam si omnes a principio optimi sint, quia facile inter se, cum multi sint, dissentire possunt et factiones inter se et bella civilia excitare—quorum omnium nihil ab uno timeri potest—plures obesse reipublicae multum possunt, prodesse non possunt. Unde autem maius timeri detrimentum quam emolumentum sperari potest, illud profecto magis fugiendum atque evitandum est. Non sunt igitur multi, etiam si optimi sint, magis optandi quam unus, sed potius tamquam sine capite membra respuendi.

41 DOMINICUS. At multo facilius unus mutari et ex optimo pessimus effici potest quam plures.

MATTHAEUS. Qua ratione?

DOMINICUS. Quia unus, cum homo sit et perturbationibus obnoxius, amore, odio, ira, cupiditate et ceteris affectibus commoveri facile potest; multi simul non possunt.

MATTHAEUS. Cur non possunt? Nonne suus cuique animus est?

DOMINICUS. Quis istud neget?

MATTHAEUS. Nonne sua etiam unicuique voluntas est?

DOMINICUS. Hoc quoque negari non potest.

MATTHAEUS. Nonne suas quaeque voluntas cupiditates habet?

DOMINICUS. Habet quidem, sed boni viri malas noxiasque compescunt.

42 MATTHAEUS. Sunt tamen ipsi quoque homines, ut tu modo de uno dicebas, et affectibus animi omnes subiacent.

DOMINICUS. Sic est.

vidual controlling everyone, but a single individual obeying and serving everyone.

MATTIAS. I have heard so much about this man that I would embrace him with incredible love and eagerness, but let's speak of Lorenzo on another occasion.

It's clear then that a city governed by many men cannot long be 40 safe from tumults and civil wars. For even if all are excellent at the beginning, since owing to their numbers they can easily disagree and incite factions and civil wars among themselves—none of which is to be feared from one man—many [leaders] can do great harm to a commonwealth and cannot help it. Since one can fear injury more than one can hope for benefit [from shared power], one ought surely to flee from and avoid such a form of government. The rule of many is not more desirable than the rule of one, even if the many are excellent men; their rule is rather to be rejected, like limbs without a head.

DOMENICO. Yet one man can more easily be changed and be 41 made into the worst from the best ruler than many men can.

MATTIAS. In what way?

DOMENICO. Because one man, since he is a man and subject to emotions, can easily be affected by love, hatred, anger, lust and the other passions; the many cannot be so affected simultaneously.

MATTIAS. Why can't they? Doesn't each of them have a soul?

DOMENICO. Who would deny it?

MATTIAS. And doesn't each of them have a will too?

DOMENICO. This too is undeniable.

MATTIAS. Doesn't every will have its own desires?

DOMENICO. It does, but good men repress their evil and destructive ones.

MATTIAS. The many are nevertheless men too, as you were just 42 saying about one man, and they are all subject to passions.

DOMENICO. That is so.

MATTHAEUS. Dissentire igitur nonnumquam eos inter se et in varias diversasque opiniones incidere necesse est.

DOMINICUS. At veram ex illis disceptando sententiam eligunt.

MATTHAEUS. Quis inter pares iudex est?

DOMINICUS. Optimus quisque.

MATTHAEUS. Quo pacto alii uni cedunt qui se illi pares arbitrentur?

43 DOMINICUS. Tanta ipsius veri et recti vis est, ut illi etiam hostes cedant.

MATTHAEUS. Unum igitur aliquem ceterorum diiudicare sententias necesse est.

DOMINICUS. Est quidem, si omnes adeo inter se discrepent ut in unam convenire sententiam non queant; sed hoc perraro accidit.

MATTHAEUS. Quid? Unus potestne a se ipso dissentire?

DOMINICUS. Non si mentis compos sit.

44 MATTHAEUS. Hoc ergo unus minus mutabilis est quam plures, quod plures inter se dissentire possunt, unus non potest. Videamus autem utri tandem facilius corrumpi queant aut utri habeant maiores degenerandi causas, multi an unus. In utris, obsecro, tibi maior ambitio videtur esse: in uno, qui et ceteros omnes longe antecellit et quo iam progrediatur vix habet, an in multis, qui et pares inter se atque aemuli sunt et quo progrediantur habent plurimum?

DOMINICUS. Est quidem insatiabilis ambitio et quo altius evecta est, eo ascendere magis cupit; habet tamen, ut existimo, princeps unus maiores quiescendi causas quam multi.

MATTIAS. It is necessary then that they will sometimes disagree among themselves and fall into differences of opinion.

DOMENICO. But they choose the best of those opinions by debate.

MATTIAS. Who acts as judge between peers?

DOMENICO. The best of them.

MATTIAS. How is it that the others who think themselves his peers yield to this one?

DOMENICO. Such is the force of the true and the right that even his enemies yield to him.  43

MATTIAS. It is necessary then for some one person to choose among the views of the rest?

DOMENICO. It is indeed, if all so disagree among themselves that they can't agree on one opinion, but this happens very rarely.

MATTIAS. Can one man disagree with himself?

DOMENICO. Not if he is sane.

MATTIAS. Therefore in this respect one man is less mutable than many, because many can disagree among themselves but one cannot. But let's consider which regime in the end is more easily corruptible or which possesses greater causes of degeneration, the regime of the many or that of one man. In which regime, I ask you, does ambition seem to you greater: in that of one man, who far surpasses all the rest and has nowhere further to advance, or in that of the many, who are equal to each other and rivals and can further advance themselves?  44

DOMENICO. There does exist insatiable ambition which wants to rise higher the higher it is raised up, yet I do reckon that a single leader has more reasons to avoid conflict than many leaders will have.

45   MATTHAEUS. Pecuniae vero cupiditas in utris maiorem locum habet, in eone qui solus rerum potitur omnesque imperii opes possidet, an in illis qui neque rem familiarem amplam habent neque ex publico quicquam sine magno scelere possunt accipere?

DOMINICUS. Mihi quidem in his videtur, sed puto eos, propterea quod boni viri sint, ab omni tum ambitione tum avaritia vacuos esse.

MATTHAEUS. Atqui eos homines esse diximus. Quod si et plures ipsi et maiores degenerandi causas habent, facilius eos et saepius labi ac degenerare quis neget?

DOMINICUS. Non poterunt autem omnes simul irasci, amare, odisse, cupere et aliis perturbationibus affici.

46   MATTHAEUS. Eadem fortasse non omnes uno tempore afficientur, sed diversis et saepe etiam contrariis affici simul eos quid prohibet? Dum enim alius irascetur, alius fortasse cupiet, et quem hic maxime amabit, ille maxime oderit, ut quem hic servare potissimum cupiat, ille in primis affectet occidere. Quid quod unus unius affectus universo nonnumquam magistratui exitio est? Nonne enim propter unam Appii Claudii libidinem decemviri omnes sublati sunt? Non modo igitur omnes omnibus eodem tempore affectibus perturbari ac corrumpi, sed uno etiam unius affectu criminari et condemnari possunt. In uno vero principe haec evenire non queunt. Nam (ut omittamus id quod verissimum est, facilius unum quam multos posse ab omnibus affectibus liberum esse) contrariis certe tangi eodem tempore unus non potest. Quo enim pacto eundem amabit atque oderit? In eundem iram simul et misericordiam exercebit? Alieno vero scelere criminari princeps, cum

MATTIAS. In which regime does lust for money have larger 45
scope, in the regime of a man who alone controls everything and
possesses all the resources of empire, or in the regime of those who
do not possess ample family wealth and who cannot accept anything from public resources without villainy?

DOMENICO. It looks to me like it would be the latter, but I think
that they will be free from all ambition and avarice because they
are good men.

MATTIAS. Yet they *are* men, we said, and if they are many and
have more reasons to become debased, who will deny that they
will more easily and more often become corrupted and debased?

DOMENICO. They can't, however, all simultaneously become angry, love, hate, experience lust and be affected by other passions.

MATTIAS. They can't all perhaps be affected by the same passion 46
at the same time, but what prevents them from being affected by
different ones, often even contrary ones, at the same time? While
one will become angry, another will feel lust, and the man this one
loves most will be most hated by another, so that the man this one
wishes most particularly to serve, that one tries above all to kill.
What about the fact that a single passion of one man is sometimes
the destruction of an entire magistracy? Weren't all the decemvirs
removed simply on account of the lust of Appius Claudius?[25]
Therefore, not only can all of them be agitated and corrupted by
all the passions at the same time, they can also all be accused and
condemned because of one passion of one man; such things cannot happen in the case of one leader. Let's pass over an undeniable
point, that it's easier for one than for many to be *free* of all passions. It is surely the case that one man can't be affected by contrary passions at the same time. How is he going to love and hate
the same person at the same time? How will he show anger and
mercy simultaneously to the same person? But a prince, since he is
a single person [and not one member of a magistracy], cannot be

sit solus, non potest. Quae cum ita sint, multi uni in regendo praestare quomodo possint non video.

47 DOMINICUS. At etiam si in regendo non praestent, erunt civitati utiliores quam unus.

MATTHAEUS. Quo tandem pacto?

DOMINICUS. Quia cum civitas communis boni gratia instituta sit, ipsi, etiam si suum tantum commodum curent, quia multi sunt, multorum certe commodum et utilitatem curent necesse est. Unus non item. Nam si communem utilitatem negligat omniaque ad privatum commodum referat, quam longissime ab ipso civitatis fine, hoc est a communi utilitate, discedet. Quod si ad finem illum, cuius gratia civitas instituta est, quam proxime accedere, optime atque utilissime regere dicitur, multi profecto, qui ad eum propius accedunt, et melius et utilius regunt quam unus.

MATTHAEUS. Hic ego prudentiam tuam, Dominice, aliquantulum desidero.

DOMINICUS. Quamobrem, obsecro?

48 MATTHAEUS. Rogas? Si multi, boni cum sint, praestare uni non possunt, mali praestare qui poterunt? An tu publicam et communem ulla ex parte utilitatem curari aut ad finem civitatis, qui omnium bonum sine discrimine conficit, prope accedi putas, cum pauci rapiunt, pauci ditantur, pauci omnium bona per luxum libidinemque consumunt? Quod si multi lupi gregem invadant eumque omnibus modis vorent, diripiant, perdant quia suam ipsi ingluviem explebunt, num gregi utiles esse dicentur?

DOMINICUS. At non sunt eodem de grege lupi, ut de eadem civitate sunt cives.

MATTHAEUS. Neque ipsi sunt iam cives, cum alios opprimere ac vexare coeperunt.

DOMINICUS. Quid ergo sunt?

incriminated by another's crime. This being the case, I don't see how the many, as such, can excel a single person in ruling.

DOMENICO. But even if they don't excel him in ruling, they will  47
be more useful to the state than one man.

MATTIAS. How is that?

DOMENICO. Since the state was instituted for the sake of the common good, the many, even if they are only going to take care of their own interests, will necessarily be taking care of the interests of many people; one person does not do likewise. If he neglects common interests and does everything with reference to his private interests, he departs as far as it is possible to go from the purpose of the city, that is, from the common utility. But if to rule in the best and most beneficial way is equivalent to approaching as nearly as possible the purpose for which the state was founded, the many, since they come nearer to that end, surely rule better and more beneficially than one man.

MATTIAS. Here, Domenico, I would like to have a bit of your practical wisdom.

DOMENICO. Why is that, please?

MATTIAS. Need you ask? If the many can't excel one man [in  48
ruling] when they are good, can many evil men excel him? Do you think you can care for the public and common good in any degree or come nearer to the end of the city, which compasses the good of all without distinction, when a few people plunder [others' goods], a few enrich themselves, a few consume the goods of all out of luxury and lust? What if many wolves attack a flock and devour it, tear it limb from limb, destroy it: would they be said to be beneficial to the flock because they had filled their own gullets?

DOMENICO. But wolves don't belong to the same flock the way citizens belong to the same state.

MATTIAS. But they are no longer citizens when they start to oppress and harass the others.

DOMENICO. What then are they?

49 MATTHAEUS. Profecto tyranni; quod, si perniciosus atque intolerabilis in una civitate unicus tyrannus est, quid multi erunt? Sin
autem multi, qui omnium civium bona diripiunt, utiles tolerabi-
lesque putantur, unus profecto, qui multo minus absumit proptereaque minus diripit, hac ratione longe utilior et tolerabilior erit.
Sed cum unus ferri non possit, multi qui poterunt?

DOMINICUS. Ne me adeo, rex, dementem putes, ut tyrannos reipublice utiles aut tolerabiles esse dicam. Sed multos dico, propterea quod multi sint, etiam si suum dumtaxat bonum curent, non
posse bonum multorum non curare.

50 MATTHAEUS. At civitas publicum et commune bonum curari
vult, non privatum; isti multorum quidem, sed privatum bonum
curant. Quod si civitati conducere aliquo modo posset is qui ex
publico privatum commodum facit et sibi ea, quae communia omnibus sunt, usurpat, unus profecto, qui e publico, cum unus sit,
minus usurpat, maxime conduceret.

DOMINICUS. At ego non ut quisquam aliena usurpet, sed ut
omnes, quantum fieri potest, boni viri sint et publicae utilitati studeant volo. Sed hoc dixi ut intelligeres quanto existimarem multos
uno ad regendam civitatem accommodatiores esse.

MATTHAEUS. Ego vero, ut dixi, censeo multos, si mali sint, multum obesse; si boni sint, nihil prodesse.

51 DOMINICUS. Quid tu? Nonne consilium in rebus gerendis probas consultoque omnia melius quam temere provenire existimas?

MATTHAEUS. Immo omnibus in rebus consilium necessarium
esse puto, Sallustiique illud in mente atque adeo in ore semper habeo, 'priusquam incipias consulto et, ubi consulueris, mature facto
opus est.'

MATTIAS. Surely they are tyrants. If a single tyrant is pernicious 49
and intolerable in a state, what will be the effect of a multitude of
tyrants? But if the many who despoil the goods of all citizens are
thought tolerable and useful, surely the one ruler, who consumes
much less and therefore despoils less, will be by this reasoning
much more beneficial and more tolerable. If one tyrant is insup-
portable, how can many tyrants be endured?

DOMENICO. Don't think me so mad, king, that I would say tyrants are beneficial or tolerable in a republic. I am saying that
many men, because they are many men, even if they are only going
to care for their own good, cannot but care for the good of many
men.

MATTIAS. But the state wants the public and common good to 50
be cared for, not some private one; these men are caring for the
good of many, but it is a private good. However, if you can in
some way make profitable to the city a man who turns the public
interest into his private one and usurps what is common to all for
his own use, surely one man who (being just one man) takes less
from the public will be the most profitable to the city.

DOMENICO. All the same, I don't want some man usurping the
goods of others, but everyone to be a good man as far as possible
and to be zealous for the common benefit; I said this so you would
understand to what extent I reckoned that many were better
suited to rule the city than one.

MATTIAS. But as I said, I think many rulers are harmful if they
are bad and useless if they are good.

DOMENICO. Why? Don't you approve of taking counsel in man- 51
aging public affairs, don't you believe that everything prospers using good counsel rather than whim?

MATTIAS. In fact I think that counsel is necessary in all things
and I always have that saying of Sallust in my mind and on my
lips: "Take counsel before you begin, and when you have done so,
you must act in good time."[26]

DOMINICUS. Nonne igitur rempublicam a multis consilio iuvari censes, cum in ea, inconsulto senatu, nihil fiat?

52 MATTHAEUS. Censeo et quidem maxime, si prudentes et eius rei qua de agitur periti reipublicae consilium dent.

DOMINICUS. Nonne igitur hac in re multi uno potiores sunt? Multi enim iuvare suo consilio rempublicam possunt, unus non potest, nisi forte tu unius quam multorum consilium magis probas regique omnia suo consilio gerenda esse censes.

53 MATTHAEUS. Est quidem unius consilium nonnumquam melius quam multorum, praesertim si illi non plane prudentes ac periti sint. Multi enim, ut paulo ante dixi, inter se dissidere possunt; unus non potest. Multorum tamen quam unius consilium ego magis probo, regique sine aliorum consilio agendum esse nihil puto, verum non ob id multos uni antepono. Habet enim princeps unus non ex una civitate, sed ex universo suo regno delectum senatum, qui non nisi spectatae prudentiae, gravitatis, fidei omnisque virtutis viros contineat, qui, cum ex omnibus deligantur, optimi ac praestantissimi sint. Cum ad se rapere atque attrahere nihil queant agique tamen suam etiam rem intellegant, fideliter atque in commune consulant necesse est.

54 Respublicae vero, ut hodie quidem sunt, in senatum non nisi suos cives admittunt, nec eos quidem omnes, sed alios aliae. Delectum autem in ea re vel virtutis vel doctrinae vel rerum experientiae non habent. Sed Veneta quidem respublica, quae optimatum est, unius nobilitatis rationem habet: solis enim nobilibus, quos ipsi patricios vocant, senatum patefacit. Vestra vero, quae popularem statum retinet, concordiae magis omnium unionique in-

DOMENICO. Don't you think that the commonwealth is helped by counsel from many persons, and that nothing is accomplished when the Senate is not consulted?

MATTIAS. I do think so, and most of all, indeed, when prudent 52 men and experts on the relevant subject give their counsel to the commonwealth.

DOMENICO. In that case aren't many preferable to one? Many men can help the commonwealth with their counsel; one man can't—unless perhaps you prefer taking counsel from one person to taking it from many, and you believe that a king should conduct all business by his own counsel.

MATTIAS. Sometimes the counsel of one man is better than that 53 of many, especially if the latter are not really men of prudence and expertise. As I said a short while ago, many can disagree among themselves but one man cannot. Nevertheless, I prefer to take counsel from many rather than from one, and I think the king should do nothing without counsel from others, but I wouldn't prefer many [rulers] on that account. A single prince has a senate chosen, not from a single city, but from his whole realm, a senate that contains only men of conspicuous prudence, gravity, loyalty and every virtue. These men, since they are chosen from all men [in the kingdom], are the best and most outstanding figures, and since they cannot despoil or expropriate anything for themselves yet know how to conduct their own business, they necessarily give counsel faithfully and in the common interest.

Republics however, at least as they are today, admit only their 54 own citizens to the senate, and not all citizens at that. Different republics admit different [kinds of] citizens, and they don't make their choice on the basis of virtue, learning or experience of affairs. The Venetian republic, which has an aristocratic regime, takes only nobility into account and opens its senate only to the nobles whom they themselves call patricians. Your republic, however, which retains its popular constitution so as better to serve concord

serviens, nonnullos etiam de plebe admittit. Quoniam autem utraque mercaturae et quaestui tota dedita est, senatores civilis scientiae satis peritos habere meo iudicio non potest. Quid enim de republica aut dicere aut scire potest is qui in rationibus semper mercaturaque versatus, ex nummularia aut lanicia taberna in senatum rapiatur, neque de republica quicquam aut usu aut doctrina umquam didicerit? Quo fit ut multorum quidem consilium probem, vestrarum vero civitatum senatum non probem.

55 DOMINICUS. Si nostrarum civitatum senatum videres, aliter profecto sentires. Tanta enim est in viris illis gravitas, tanta prudentia, tantus usus, tanta facundia, tanta etiam doctrina ut, cum in senatu sunt, mercaturae numquam operam dedisse videantur, sed Romanam illam in dicendis sententiis et copiam et gravitatem referant. Quod quidem ex iis, qui ad te oratores saepenumero veniunt, te aliqua ex parte iudicare posse existimo.

MATTHAEUS. Sunt illi quidem magnae virtutis atque peritiae omnibus in rebus viri, sed paucos admodum inter vos tales esse eosque in hunc maxime usum ex omni numero deligi puto.

56 DOMINICUS. Immo optimum quemque domi ad consulendum retinemus; iuniores, qui et labores perferre queunt et videndi res novas cupidiores sunt, ad exteras nationes mittimus. Sed qualis sit senatus noster non quaerimus. Illud, quod tu plane fateris, quaerimus et iam, ut opinor, tenemus: multorum quam unius salubrius esse consilium.

MATTHAEUS. Fateor, ut dixi, multorum in omni re consilio utendum esse, sed ducem illis et moderatorem et quasi caput necessarium esse dico. Nam si pares sint, vel invidia vel aemulatione

and the unity of the whole, admits some men from the plebeian class. Since both republics are entirely given over to trade and profit-seeking, they cannot in my opinion have senators with sufficient expertise in politics. What can men know or have to say about public affairs who, having always been involved in trade and their accounts, are snatched from the counting house or the wool shop and put into the senate, never having learned anything about public business either in theory or practice? Hence I do approve getting counsel from many men, but I don't approve of the senates of your states.

DOMENICO. If you were to see the senates of our city-states, you 55 would surely think otherwise. For these men have such gravity, prudence, experience, eloquence, even learning, that they appear never to have devoted themselves to trade when they are in the senate, but remind you in their speech of the richness and gravity of the Romans. This is a characteristic, I reckon, you can judge in some measure for yourself from our ambassadors who often come to you.

MATTIAS. There are those among you of great virtue and experience in all things, but such persons are rather few in your city and I believe they are selected from the whole number mostly for this purpose [of impressing foreign rulers with their eloquence].

DOMENICO. In fact, we keep the best men at home to give coun- 56 sel; we send the younger ones abroad, who are able to endure the effort involved and are more eager to see new things. But our inquiry is not about the kind of senate we have. Our inquiry is about something you now admit and that we now, I think, hold: that the counsel of many persons is healthier than that of a single person.

MATTIAS. I do admit, as I said, that one should make use of the counsel of many men in all things. But I say that it is necessary for them to have a captain and moderator, a kind of head. If they are equals, envy, rivalry or cupidity of some sort can make them fight

vel cupiditate aliqua contendere inter se et dissidere poterunt; si principem habeant quem vereantur, non poterunt.

57 DOMINICUS. Atqui si pares sint, fidelius reipublicae et diligentius consulent, quippe qui se illius principes esse atque ad se ea, de quibus consultent, omnia pertinere intellegant, earumque rerum se laudem atque utilitatem omnem reportaturos sperent. Sin principi alicui subiaceant atque inserviant, tamquam de aliena re parum solliciti, omnia negligentius ac remissius agent, utpote qui nullam ad se eius rei vel utilitatem vel laudem putent perventuram, sed quasi mercenarii operam suam principi locent.

58 MATTHAEUS. Immo vero, qui principis concilio praesunt fidelissime omnia diligentissimeque consultant, neque minus eius rebus quam suis student atque invigilant atque haud scio an etiam magis. Nam in suis quidem rebus, si quid erratum est, a nullo poenas expectant; ipsi suum detrimentum aequo animo ferunt. Si quid autem in rebus principis praeter spem aut sententiam accidit, ipsi graves ab eo poenas metuunt. Emolumentum autem, si recte consulant, duplex consequuntur: alterum quod omnibus commune est, hoc est, suarum civitatum ac rerum sibi carissimarum conservationem, quo quidem fructu nullus bono viro gratior esse debet; alterum quod privatim unicuique pro meritis et dignitate tribuitur, hoc est, opes, honores, magistratus, praefecturas et quae inter homines maxima existimantur. Ad quae quidem generosissimus quisque maxime aspirat, laudem vero fidei atque integritatis a principe imprimis expectant. Mercenarii vero appellari, cum omnes non minus suae patriae quam principi consulant, nec volunt nec possunt. Quod si mercenarii et servi, tum spe praemii tum metu poenae, fidem dominis suis servant et operam illis iustam

and disagree among themselves; if they have a leader whom they fear and respect, they cannot.

DOMENICO. All the same, if they are equals, they will consult 57 the interests of the republic with greater fidelity and diligence, as men who understand that they are the leaders of the republic and that every matter on which they give advice is relevant to themselves. They will hope to win praise and benefits for themselves in these matters. If they were to serve and be subordinate to some prince, they would be relatively unconcerned about someone else's business and would act more negligently and with less energy in all things, being men who would think that the matter [under discussion] is irrelevant to their own future interests. They would be like mercenaries, renting their services to the prince.

MATTIAS. In fact, the men who preside over the prince's council 58 give all counsel in the most faithful and diligent manner, and show no less zeal and vigilance in his affairs than in their own, possibly even more. For if they make a mistake in managing their own affairs, they can expect no penalty and can bear their loss calmly; if something unexpected and unlooked-for happens in the prince's affairs, they have grave penalties to fear from him. But two kinds of emolument follow from giving good counsel. The first is the reward common to everyone: the preservation of their cities and of the things dearest to themselves, than which no fruit should be more welcome to a good man. The other is that, as a private individual, each man is rewarded in proportion to his merits and rank, i.e., he may look forward to wealth, honors, offices, governorships and the things men reckon the greatest rewards. All the noblest men aspire greatly to these things, but above all they look for their prince's praise for fidelity and integrity. They neither wish to be nor can be called mercenaries when they all consult their country's interests no less than their prince's. But if mercenaries and servants serve their masters and render them good service from hope of reward or fear of punishment, what value must we attach to the

reddunt, qua tandem fide atque integritate consulere existimandi
sunt ii qui et omnia summa a principe exspectant et suae patriae
salutem ac dignitatem suis consiliis contineri intellegunt et ad id
agendum non metu, sed amore adducti sunt?

59     At vestro[25] senatui quae potest esse fides, quae integritas, cum
omnes ad se rapere atque attrahere studeant, omnes excellere
atque eminere contendant, proptereaque mutuis odiis invidiaque
laborent, ex benefactis autem nemini se gratificari putent, a nemine praemium aut laudem, sed summam invidiam calumniasque
expectent, certatimque se odiis atque aemulationibus insectentur?
Quo fit ut multi, etiam si recte in commune consulere possint,
saepe abstineant, partim ut declinent invidiam, partim ne illis quibus nolunt inviti prosint, partim etiam quod cui gratificentur non
intellegunt. Nam, ut in proverbio est, qui omnibus servit, nulli
servit. Nemo enim privatim quicquam ei debere se putat qui, id
quod agat, ex publico officio agat. Quae cum ita sint, quo pacto
qui communia agunt, sua se agere possunt existimare? Aut quo
tandem affectu ac studio rebus illis incumbere putandi sunt?

60     Nostri vero, cum et censorem et remuneratorem habeant,
consultius omnia et circumspectius agunt certatimque suum officium principi probari student, scientes se ab eo et negligentiae
poenam et praemium industriae relaturos. Invidia in iis locum nullum habet; aemulatio laudis et virtutis habet. Omnes enim ingentia sibi praemia proposita esse sciunt, quae quidem non nisi per
summam fidem, diligentiam ac virtutem consequi possint,[26] neque
ea quisquam alteri nisi hac ratione possit eripere. Ita fit ut summo
inter se studio et concordia erga principis atque imperii dignitatem
salutemque contendant. Ille vero singulorum consilia senten-
tiasque expendit, cernit studia, moderatur affectus, omnes maxi-

loyalty and integrity of those who look to the prince for all the highest rewards and understand that the security and dignity of their own country is sustained by their own counsel, and who are led to give it, not by fear, but by love?

But what loyalty and integrity can your senate possess when everyone is eager to despoil and expropriate things for himself, when all are striving for preëminence and for this reason struggle with mutual hatred and envy, but think they can gratify no one with their good deeds and look for reward and praise from no one but only for extreme envy and calumny, and compete to harass each other with their hatreds and rivalries. Hence many men, even when they could give good counsel in the common interest, often abstain from so doing, partly to deflect envy, partly so as not to give involuntary assistance to those they don't want to assist, partly too because they don't understand whom they are going to oblige. For as the proverb has it, he who serves everyone serves no one. No one thinks he owes anything as a private person to someone who performs actions in his public capacity. This being the case, how can those who are acting in the common interest reckon they are acting in their own? With what passion and zeal are they going to apply themselves?

But our senators, since they have a moral censor and someone to reward them, act with greater prudence and circumspection. They compete in their zeal to have the prince approve their conduct, knowing they will receive from him punishment for negligence and reward for industry. Envy has no place among them, but rivalry in honor and virtue does. All know that they are being offered great prizes which they cannot win except by the greatest loyalty, diligence and virtue, and that no one can wrest these prizes from another except by showing these qualities. Hence they strive among themselves with the greatest zeal and harmony to enhance the honor and security of the prince and his power. He weighs the counsel and views of each one, he observes their zeal, he regulates

59

60

mis praemiis ornamentisque prosequitur, ita omnes sibi deditos atque obsequentes habet. His igitur rationibus multorum quidem consilium probo, sed principem illis et caput necessarium esse censeo.

61 DOMINICUS. De hoc quidem, quando tibi ita videtur, non repugno. Sed multorum certe stabilius imperium et diuturnius, proptereaque etiam melius, esse non negabis.

MATTHAEUS. Ego vero, nisi tu id mihi aliter probes, negabo utrumque.

DOMINICUS. Utrumque? An multorum quam unius diuturnius esse imperium mihi non concedes?

MATTHAEUS. Concedere tibi quidem facile non possum, sed si placet condonabo.

DOMINICUS. Cur, obsecro, non concedes?

MATTHAEUS. Cedo: quid tu diuturnum vocas?

DOMINICUS. Id nimirum quod sine mutatione ulla diu in eodem statu permanet.

MATTHAEUS. Quid regna? Nonne diu in eodem statu permanent?

DOMINICUS. Minime.

MATTHAEUS. Cur non?

62 DOMINICUS. Quia, cum singulorum regum vita non longa sit, regna ad alios atque alios reges transferantur necesse est; ea porro quae a tam multis diversae plerumque mentis hominibus administrantur, non possunt non mutari. Unusquisque enim, cum diversae ab aliis voluntatis sit, diversam quoque administrandi rationem habet.

MATTHAEUS. Tu igitur regna ob frequentem regum mutationem minus diuturna esse censes? Ubi, obsecro, frequentiores administrantium fiunt quam in republica mutationes, in qua non fere quisquam annum in magistratu excedit? Vos vero bimestres aut quadrimestres magistratus creatis: quid hoc brevius aut mutabilius dici potest? Quid, obsecro, potest tam brevi temporis spatio geri

their passions, he honors them all with the greatest rewards and distinctions, so that all of them show him deference and dedication. For these reasons I approve taking counsel from many men, but I hold that it is necessary for them to have a prince and a head.

DOMENICO. Since that is how it seems to you, I shall not carry 61 on the struggle. But you will surely not deny that the power of the many is more stable and enduring, and therefore better?

MATTIAS. But I do deny both [its greater stability and its greater longevity], unless you prove otherwise to me.

DOMENICO. Both? Won't you concede that the power of the many is more enduring than that of one?

MATTIAS. I can't easily concede it to you, but I shall make a present of it to you, if you like.

DOMENICO. Why, please, won't you concede it?

MATTIAS. All right, I give in. What do you call longevity?

DOMENICO. Obviously a state where everything remains the same and doesn't change.

MATTIAS. What about kingdoms? Don't they remain for a long time in the same state?

DOMENICO. Not at all.

MATTIAS. How not?

DOMENICO. Since the life of individual kings is not long, neces- 62 sarily kingdoms are transferred from one king to another. Furthermore, they are governed by so many men, usually with different intentions, that they cannot but change. Each one, since he has a will different from the others, has a different pattern of governance as well.

MATTIAS. Do you then hold that kingdoms are less enduring because there is a change of kings? Where, I ask you, are more frequent changes of governors made than in a republic, in which practically no magistrate lasts a full year in office? You choose magistrates for two or four months: what could be briefer and more mutable than this? What, I ask you, can be accomplished in

cum cives, antequam satis notum suum officium habeant, magistratu abire cogantur?

DOMINICUS. At eadem reipublicae administrandae forma permanet, successoribusque omnia suo ordine quasi per manus traduntur.

63  MATTHAEUS. Quid regna? Nonne eundem semper statum eandemque administrationis formam servant? Reges quoque, nonne omnia successoribus salva intactaque relinquunt et suo ordine liberis ac nepotibus per manus tradunt? Immo hoc quoque reges magistratibus ad diuturnitatem imperii potiores atque accommodatiores sunt, quod reges, etiam si diu non vivant, multo tamen diutius quam magistratus imperant. Nemo enim fere rex est qui non plures annos quam quisquam magistratus menses in[27] imperio expleat. Nam, ut de Augusto Caesare taceam, qui sex et quinquaginta annos imperium tenuit, Fredericus aetate nostra nonum et trigesimum annum in imperio agit; ego quidem, qui quinquagesimum aetatis non excessi, sextum et vigesimum iam annum regno praesum. Ad quod quidem tempus nullus umquam magistratus pervenit.

64      Huc accedit quod reges, cum se et toto suae vitae tempore imperio potituros sciant et diutissime se victuros putent, regnum tamquam suum omni cura conservant, omni studio augent, plurimis et optimis rebus muniunt atque adornant, summam inde tum a praesentibus[28] tum a posteris et gratiam et laudem petunt. Magistratus, cum breve admodum et statum imperii tempus habeant neque se ad id quandoque redituros sciant, imperium tamquam alienum nullo amore, nulla diligentia administrant, nullam inde vel a collegis vel a successoribus aut gratiam aut laudem expectant. Postremo reges, cum aut liberis aut hominibus sibi carissimis imperium relicturi sint, non minus de illorum quam de suo statu solliciti sunt et ut iis quam optimum et quam amplissimum imperium relinquant summo studio curaque conantur. Magistratus, cum aemulis aut etiam inimicis imperium sint tradituri, de succes-

so short a space of time when magistrates are compelled to leave office before they've fully mastered it?

DOMENICO. But the same constitutional arrangement remains in place and everything is handed off to successors in due order.

MATTIAS. And what about kingdoms? Don't they preserve al-  63
ways the same constitution and arrangement of offices? Don't kings too leave everything safe and intact to successors and hand them off in due order to their children and grandchildren? Indeed, in this respect too, with regard to longevity of power, kings are preferable and better fitted than [republican] magistrates, because kings, even if they don't live long, still hold power much longer than magistrates. There is almost no king who does not complete more years in power than a magistrate does months. To say nothing of Caesar Augustus, who held power for 56 years, [the emperor] Frederick [III] in our time has been in power for 39 years, and I, who am not yet fifty, have ruled now for 26 years in the kingdom. No magistrate is ever in office that long.

Moreover, kings, since they know they will be in power their  64
whole lives and think they are going to live a very long time, preserve the kingdom with all care as their own; they increase it with all zeal; they fortify and adorn it with many fine things; they seek the highest praise and gratitude for their actions from both the living and from posterity. Magistrates, since they have brief and fixed terms in power and know that they are never going to return to power, hold authority as though it were something alien to them, without devotion and without diligence; they expect no gratitude or praise for what they have done either from colleagues or successors. Finally, since kings are going to leave their power either to their children or to men whom they love, they are solicitous for their successor's estate no less than for their own, and they strive with the utmost zeal and concern to leave to them the best and most extensive empire. Magistrates, since they are going to hand over power to rivals and even enemies, take no thought at all for

sione omnino nihil cogitant; immo ea etiam quae incohare commode possent, ne laus illa ad alios transferatur, non incohant.

Multo igitur maior frequentiorque in rebuspublicis quam in regnis mutatio fit; quod si respublicas tu propterea diuturnas putas
quod diu eandem administrationis formam teneant, regna profecto
multo sunt quam ille diuturniora.

65   DOMINICUS. Non exprimo tibi satis fortasse quod volo. Non
enim respublicas ea de causa diuturnas puto quod ab aliis atque
aliis magistratibus non regantur, quod falsum imprimis atque
ineptum esset, neque eandem ab iis servari formam dico, quod
eosdem semper magistratus creent, ut consules, dictatores et alios
eius generis, sed quod numquam in ea magistratus ita cessent, ut
vidua quodammodo respublica atque omni regimine destituta re-
linquatur. Immo ita sibi invicem semper succedant continuen-
turque, ut nulla inter eos intervalla sint, atque ita sibi mutuo con-
iuncti annexique sint, ut numquam ordo ille perrumpi aut deficere
posse videatur. Quod quidem in regnis non accidit. Defunctis
enim regibus, regna omni prorsus rectore atque administratore
orba relinquuntur, imperiumque tam diu veluti sine gubernatore
navis fluctuat, donec rex aut princeps aliquis, qui gubernaculum
rerum suscipiat, quoquomodo inveniatur. Quo quidem interregni
tempore tantae plerumque seditiones et bella civilia exoriuntur, ut
maxima saepe et pulcherrima imperia evertantur. Omitto quam
multa superiorum regum aboleant, quam multa innovent, quam
multa commutent, ii qui novum aliquod regnum accipiunt. Qui
quidem motus et quam saepe accidant et quam perniciosi sint, tu
ipse, rex, optime nosti, qui, cum rex omnium consensu creatus es-
ses, hostes tamen et plurimos et gravissimos habuisti. De motibus
qui, antequam tu creareris, acciderant, nihil dico: salubres omnes
huic regno et utiles fuisse censeo, quando in te unum erant
finiendi. Sed accidunt saepenumero, ut diximus, illo interregni

what will happen afterwards; indeed, sometimes they don't make preparations they could easily make so that credit for it will not go to others.

Thus, much greater and more frequent changes occur in republics than in kingdoms. If you think that republics are more enduring because they keep the same form of governance for a long time, kingdoms surely are much more enduring than they are.

DOMENICO. Perhaps I did not express my meaning to you well 65 enough. I don't think republics are long-lived because they aren't ruled by successive magistrates, which is false, first of all, and not to the point, nor do I claim they keep the same regime because they always choose the same magistracies, like consuls, dictators and the like. My claim is that magistracies in a republic are perpetual, so that it is never left widowed, as it were, and bereft of any control. In fact, they always succeed and perpetuate each other so that there are no breaks between them, and they are linked together and joined in such a way that it looks like their pattern and sequence can never be disrupted or fail. This doesn't happen with kingdoms. When kings die, kingdoms are left orphaned of any guide and governor and their empire is tossed about like a ship without a steersman until some king or prince is somehow found to put his hand to the tiller. During these interregna so many coups and civil wars generally arise that the greatest and finest empires are often destroyed. I pass over how many achievements of earlier kings are wiped out, how many innovations are brought in, how many changes are made by those who take on some new kingdom. The tumults that occur, and how frequent and destructive they are, you yourself know, best of kings, for when you were chosen king by universal consent, you still had many formidable enemies. I say nothing of the unrest that occurred before your election; I believe it was all healthy and useful for this kingdom as it led eventually to your single rule. But they happen very often, as I said, these very serious and dangerous civil commotions during

tempore motus gravissimi ac periculosissimi et qui non sine magna civium clade et imperii diminutione sedentur. Qui quidem in republica, quae certam et quodammodo continuam magistratuum successionem habet, evenire non possunt; proptereaque eam regno diuturniorem iudico.

66 MATTHAEUS. Nollem equidem rerumpublicarum gratia te hanc partem attigisse, Dominice, qua respublicae fere omnes infames sunt. Ubi enim, obsecro, plures gravioresque seditiones, ubi frequentiora perniciosioraque bella civilia, ubi motus maiores quam in omni republica exoriuntur? Ubi saepius res ad interregnum redit? Ubi saepius omnium magistratuum genera et totius administrationis forma immutatur? Nam ne Atheniensium, Lacedemoniorum, Thebanorumque respublicas tibi commemorem, quae omnes quottidianis magistratuum mutationibus assiduisque seditionibus se ipsas everterunt, propone tibi, quaeso, ante oculos Romanam rempublicam, quae et maxima fuit et diutissime perduravit. Quot in ea, bone Deus, seditiones, quot intestinas discordias, quot bella civilia, quot magistratuum mutationes, quot interregna, quot denique omnis generis motus invenies! Ea tamen sic quoque ad quingentesimum annum libera non pervenit.

67 Omitto hodiernas respublicas, quae quam multis et quam gravibus quottidie seditionibus afflictentur, optime cernis. Una certe Senensis respublica nobis documento esse satis potest, quae quottidianis seditionibus mutationibusque agitata omnem paene splendorem amisit. De Genua, quae unius an plurium principatum servet in dubio est, nihil dico; factionibus certe et seditionibus ita dedita semper fuit, ut sine illis sustentari nullo modo posse videatur.

68 Quis vero unius principatus tantis umquam motibus obnoxius fuit? Quae seditiones regnorum, quae bella possunt aut cum Romanorum aut cum Genuensium motibus comparari? Nullum ad-

interregna, and they are not put down without great calamity for the citizens and loss of empire. Such commotions cannot occur in a republic, which has a regular and continuous succession of magistrates; and that is why I conclude that it is more durable than a kingdom.

MATTIAS. For the sake of republics, I should have preferred that 66 you not touch on this subject, Domenico, as nearly all republics have infamous reputations in this respect. For where, I ask you, is there more, and more serious, political violence, where are there more frequent and more destructive civil wars, where are there greater tumults than those that arise in a republic? Where do interregna more often occur in public affairs? Where are there more frequent alterations in the kinds of magistracies and in the whole constitution? I'll pass over the republics of the Athenians, Spartans and Thebans, which all destroyed themselves by changes of magistracy on a daily basis and by incessant political violence. Place before your eyes, please, the Roman republic, the greatest and most long-lived of them all. Good God! How much political violence it experienced! How numerous will you find to be the intestine discords, the civil wars, the instability of public offices, the periods of anarchy — in short, tumults of every kind! Yet it too did not arrive at its five hundredth year as a free republic.

I pass over modern republics; you can see very well how many 67 and grave are the acts of sedition that afflict them daily. The single example of the Sienese republic is enough proof, which has lost nearly all its glory from daily acts of sedition and revolution. I say nothing about Genoa; it's a matter of doubt whether it maintains a monarchical or republican constitution. Certainly it's so given over to factions and sedition that it seems it can't survive without them.

But what monarchy was ever subject to such great civil distur- 68 bances? Where are the coups and [civil] wars that can be compared to the uprisings of the Romans or the Genoese? As far as I

huc, quod ego quidem sciam, regnum ad reipublicae formam propter seditiones discordiasque devenit, respublicae vero se unius imperio ea de causa quam plurimae subiecere. Quod si diuturnior esset earum status, non multa per universum terrarum orbem regna, sed multae respublicae et quondam inventae essent et hodie invenirentur, quod contra esse clarissime cernis. Maxima enim orbis terrarum pars a regibus et olim administrata est et hodie administratur. At fiunt in regum creationibus nonnumquam motus; isti vero et perraro accidunt et salubres sunt; aliter enim aut eiici tyranni aut boni principes induci non possunt. Sed nulla tamen ob eam causam imperia eversa esse scio; nam quod de nostra creatione dixisti, utinam id vere possis dicere! Ego quidem, quantum potui, dedi operam ut me huic regno non inutilem exhiberem, neque hodie, quantum per valitudinem licet, ab hac mente desisto aut umquam dum vivam desistam; sed de me ipso alias.

69      Non evertuntur ergo regum mutationibus regna, sed instaurantur ac perpetuantur. Quid quod nonnullae familiae legitimo successionis ordine diutius quam ulla respublica regnant atque imperant? Gallorum quidem reges a Carolo, qui propter res gestas Magnus est cognominatus, oriundi, septingentos fere iam annos imperio sibi per manus tradito regnant, atque ita regnant ut nullum videatur ea familia imperii sui finem habitura. Quod si respublicae seditionibus et motibus intestinis saepenumero evertuntur, regna vero, sive delectu novi principis sive legitima eiusdem generis successione, in eodem diutissime statu permanent. Utrum tandem diuturnius imperium sit, tuum sit iudicium. Sed esto; concedamus tibi diuturniores esse respublicas. Censen tu iccirco meliores esse? DOMINICUS. Ego quidem censeo.

MATTHAEUS. Cur ita iudicas? Omniane quae diutissime durant optima esse putas?

know, no kingdom has ever devolved into a republic owing to sedition and strife, but many republics have subjected themselves to monarchical power for that reason. But if their constitutions were more durable, there wouldn't be so many kingdoms around the world, but you'd find many republics in the past and many today. But you see with the utmost clarity that the contrary is the case. The greatest part of the world, in former times as today, has been governed by kings. All the same, there is sometimes instability when kings are chosen, but this happens very rarely and is a healthy thing, for otherwise tyrants could not be expelled and good princes brought in. I know of no empires that have fallen for this cause; indeed, would that you could say truly what you have said about my own election! I have labored as far as I could to make myself useful to this kingdom, nor have I abandoned this intention today, as far as my health allows; nor shall I ever abandon it while I live. But let us speak of me on another occasion.

Kingdoms are not therefore destroyed by changing their kings, 69 but are renewed and perpetuated. And what of the fact that some families reign and hold power in legitimate succession longer than any republic? The kings of the French, beginning with Charles, called the Great on account of his deeds, have reigned now for almost seven hundred years by passing down their power to each other from hand to hand, and they reign in such a way that it seems that family will see no end to its power.[27] If republics are often destroyed by coups and uprisings, kingdoms preserve their constitutions for a very long time, whether by electing a new prince or by legitimate succession in the same line. You can come to your own conclusions about which form of power in the end is more enduring. But let that go; suppose we grant you that republics are more enduring. Do you hold that they are better on that account?

DOMENICO. I do hold that.

MATTIAS. Why do you come to that conclusion? Do you think that whatever lasts longest is best?

DOMINICUS. Puto.

70 MATTHAEUS. Optima igitur erit diutissima pestilentia, diutissima fames, diutissimum bellum et, ut ad ea quae nostrae disputationi propinquiora sunt veniam, diutissima tyrannis, diutissimus paucorum potentium aut etiam ipsius populi status optimus erit existimandus.

DOMINICUS. At ista omnia, per se mala cum sint, temporis diuturnitate bona effici non possunt. Tempus enim omnia in utramque partem perficit: si mala accepit, reddit peiora; si bona, multo meliora. Quod si bona sit a principio respublica bonisque legibus instituta, quo diuturnior erit, eo meliorem effectum iri puto.

71 MATTHAEUS. Vide, quaeso, ne tempus omnia potius corrumpat ac destruat. An non illud tibi Nasonis venit in mentem:

tempus edax rerum tuque, invidiosa vetustas,
omnia destruitis vitiataque dentibus aevi
paulatim lenta consumitis omnia morte,

et illud:

Labitur occulte fallitque volatilis aetas.

Nec bona tam sequitur quam bona prima fuit?

Quod quidem, si recte consideraveris, verissimum esse deprehendes. Quid enim est, per immortalem Deum, quod non longinquitas temporis labefactet ac solvat? Propone tibi ante oculos quicquid vel arte conficitur vel natura generatur: nihil omnino in suo statu permanere invenies. Quod enim est tam solidum ac tam firmum aedificium quod non vetustate dissolvatur et corruat? Quis fructus vel a terra vel ab arbore tam pulcher ac tam bonus producitur, qui non intra paucos annos deformis insipidusque reddatur? Iam vero nullum est tam generosum animal quod non brevi

DOMENICO. I do.

MATTIAS. So the longest plague will be the best, the longest    70
famine, the longest war? To come nearer the subject of our debate,
must we think that the longest tyranny, the longest oligarchy and
the longest-lived democracy is the best?

DOMENICO. But all these regimes, being intrinsically bad,[28] cannot become good through the passage of time. Time perfects everything on both sides: if regimes acquire evil traits they get
worse; if they are good, they become much better. But if a good
republic is founded from the beginning with good laws, it gets
better the longer it endures, I think.

MATTIAS. But perhaps time rather corrupts all things and de-    71
stroys them? Doesn't that verse of Ovid's come to mind:

> Devouring Time, and you, envious Age, consume all things,
> and slowly gnawing them with your teeth, reduce them all
> little by little to lingering death![29]

and this one:

> Flying time slips away in secret and deceives us.[30]

> Nor is the age that follows good like the age before.[31]

If you consider this aright you will find it to be most true. For
what is there, by the immortal God, that longevity does not corrupt and dissolve? Place before your eyes whatever art has made or
nature brought forth: you will find that nothing at all remains in
its fixed condition. What building is so solid and strong that it is
not ruined by age and decay? What fruit of earth or tree is so
beautiful and good that within a few years it is not misshapen and
tasteless? Furthermore, there is no animal so noble that it does not

et forma corporis et animi vigore degeneret. Neque vero terra ipsa in suo semper statu permanet, nam neque eandem nobis rerum omnium copiam quam maioribus nostris praebebat neque eandem etiam bonitatem praebet. Ipsa quoque rerum natura degenerare in nobis et deficere quodammodo videtur: non enim homines ea vel corporis proceritate vel animi magnitudine procreat qua olim dicitur procreasse:

Nam genus hoc vivo iam decrescebat Homero.

72  Quod si non solum ea quae humana industria fiunt, verum etiam quae a[29] natura ipsa producuntur atque ipsi etiam homines temporis diuturnitate corrumpuntur atque degenerant, rempublicam, ab hominibus institutam diversosque hominum animos et ingenia continentem, meliorem in dies effici aut etiam in eodem statu diu permanere posse existimamus? Videmus generosissima equorum boumque armenta, nisi quotannis delectu habito restituantur atque instaurentur, brevi maiorem in modum degenerare atque deficere. An aliam credimus hominum quam ceterorum animalium esse naturam? Quid aliud esse civitatem quam ingentem hominum gregem existimamus? Quod si nulli animalium greges possunt sine assiduo delectu et reparatione servari, civitatem credimus, etiam si ab initio optima fuerit, diu sine mutatione aut reformatione posse permanere? Diuturnitas igitur illi ad bonitatem meo iudicio nihil prodest; immo potius, nisi reformetur saepius et quasi renovetur, obest plurimum. Cives enim, a legum observatione et bonis moribus paulatim deficientes, nisi quottidie emendentur et tamquam agri excolantur, ingentem vitiorum squalorem et situm contrahunt.

73  Regna vero, regum sive negligentia sive perversitate, aliqua ex parte collapsa principum mutatione resurgunt et quasi renovantur. Quamobrem utilissimam illam principum mutationem regnis esse

quickly lose its bodily beauty and mental vigor. Not even the earth itself remains always in a fixed condition, for it does not provide us with the same abundance of all things that it provided to our ancestors, nor even things of the same quality. Nature herself seems to degenerate in use and in a certain sense to fall short, for it does not create men of the same bodily height or mental capacity as formerly it was said to have made:

This race began to get smaller when Homer was still alive.[32]

If not only things made by human effort but also things made by Nature herself, even mankind, are corrupted and become worse with the passage of time, shall we reckon that a republic, which is founded by men and holds within it various human spirits and minds, can become better in time or even remain in the same fixed condition? We see that the best-bred herds of horses and cattle, unless they are kept up and renewed every year by selection, rapidly degenerate and die out. Do we think that human nature is different from that of the other animals? What do we reckon a city is except a large herd of men? But if herds of animals cannot be preserved without careful breeding and maintenance, do we believe a city, even if it was excellent in the beginning, can survive long without change and reform? Longevity therefore in my opinion is of no advantage to a city with respect to goodness; indeed, if it is not instead reformed frequently and renewed, as it were, it is a great disadvantage to it. Citizens who fail little by little in their observance of the law and in good morals contract the squalor and rot of the vices if they are not corrected on a daily basis and placed under cultivation like fields.

Kingdoms, however, that have become ruined in some part through the negligence or perversity of kings rise again and are renewed by a change of leadership. On this account I believe such a

72

73

censeo. Dum enim novi reges initio imperium optime administrare et subditorum benivolentiam sibi bonis artibus comparare student, omnia in meliorem statum redigunt et, quantum in se est, reparant atque instaurant. Multorum igitur imperium neque diuturnius, ut cernis, est quam unius, neque, etiam si esset, ob id melius esse ullo pacto[30] posset. Itane tibi adhuc videtur, an nondum etiam?

DOMINICUS. Ita plane mihi nunc videtur. Nescio enim quo pacto, cum ego aliquid dico, meas maxime rationes probo easque verissimas esse iudico; cum contra te audio graviter copioseque disserentem, puerilia quaedam et ridicula dixisse videor, ita tu omnes rationes meas pervertis, mentem omnem immutas et mihi quaecunque vis e vestigio tua eloquentia persuades.

MATTHAEUS. Istud quidem non mea eloquentia, sed partim optima tua mens, partim ipsius veri vis facit, quae quidem tanta est ut etiam invitos se cognoscere et fateri compellat. Sed habesne aliud quod pro hac re velis dicere?

DOMINICUS. Nihil omnino: ita meas rationes omnes disiecisti pervertistique.

MATTHAEUS. At ego quid te interrogem habeo.

DOMINICUS. Dic, obsecro, aliquid quo facilius adhuc in tuam sententiam et libentius veniam; videor enim tuis magis rationibus coactus quam mea sponte venire.

MATTHAEUS. Cedo. Quid tu civitatem esse aut qua de causa institutam putas?

DOMINICUS. Coetum hominum virtutis studio in unum congregatorum ad bene vivendum institutum esse puto.

MATTHAEUS. Quid porro appellas 'bene vivere'?

DOMINICUS. Utique secundum virtutem vivere.

change of leadership to be extremely useful to kingdoms. For so long as new kings are eager in the beginning to govern their empire well and to acquire the good will of their subjects through good behavior, they restore everything to a better state and repair and renew everything as much as they can. Thus the power of the many is no more enduring, you see, than that of one man, and even if it were, it would not on this account be in any way better. Do you agree so far, or are you still unconvinced?

DOMENICO. It now seems clear to me. I'm not sure why, but when I say something, my reasons seem highly plausible and I accept them as most true; but when I hear you discussing the contrary view with gravity and at length, I feel I've said something childish and silly — so much do you turn around all my arguments and change my whole mind and instantly persuade me of whatever you wish through your eloquence.

MATTIAS. It's not my eloquence. Partly it's your excellent mind    74
that does it, partly the force of the truth itself, which indeed is so great that it compels even those who are unwilling to understand and acknowledge it. But do you have some other relevant point you wish to make?

DOMENICO. Nothing at all. You've dashed my arguments and turned them all on their heads.

MATTIAS. Well, I have something to ask you.

DOMENICO. Say something, please, to let me come round to your opinion more easily and willingly. I seem to come round to it more when forced by your arguments than by my own free will.

MATTIAS. I'll do that. What do you think a city is, or for what reason is it founded?

DOMENICO. I think it is a society of man who have gathered together in the pursuit of virtue, established to achieve the good life.[33]

MATTIAS. And what do you mean by "the good life."

DOMENICO. Living according to virtue, no doubt.

75 MATTHAEUS. Quo tandem pacto eam te et facilius et melius consequi posse existimas: si quem habeas a quo institui, quem imitari possis, an si per te ipsum eam tibi comparare studeas?

DOMINICUS. Nimirum si praeceptorem atque exemplar habeam.

MATTHAEUS. Unumne an plures discendi atque imitandi gratia magis probes?

DOMINICUS. Unum profecto, si quem unum et optimum et doctissimum queam reperire; plures enim neque in doctrina concordes neque in imitatione atque exemplo similes esse possunt.

76 MATTHAEUS. Si quis igitur in omni virtute optimus atque absolutissimus reperiatur, is unus tamquam omnium speculum atque exemplar civibus instituendis praefici potius debet quam plures.

DOMINICUS. Ita mihi quoque videtur.

MATTHAEUS. Quid tu, concordiamne esse censes in civitate utilem?

DOMINICUS. Immo ita necessariam ut sine ea consistere omnino civitas non possit; ea enim una sublata, civitatis omnino nomen tollitur.

MATTHAEUS. Recte sentis: hic enim est unicus civitatis finis. Nam quemadmodum medicus aegri sanitatem, gubernator navis portum, imperator victoriam, ita qui civitatem instituit pacem, concordiam et unionem sibi propositam semper habet, ad eamque tum consequendam tum servandam suas actiones omnes, sua studia et consilia dirigit. Age vero, uter[31] lucem terris melius potest et praebere et servare: solne qui eam ex se emittit neque potest, etiam si velit, esse non clarus, an luna quae lumen et ab illo accipit et amittere facile potest?

DOMINICUS. Sol sine dubio melius.

77 MATTHAEUS. Calorem vero utrum, obsecro, et maiorem praestat et diutius retinet, ignisne qui a natura ipsa illum accepit, an ea quae ab igne calefacta sunt?

MATTIAS. How can you better and more easily achieve this life, 75
do you reckon: by having a person by whom you can be taught
and whom you can imitate, or by trying to achieve it on your own?
DOMENICO. It's undoubtedly better if you have a teacher and example.
MATTIAS. Do you think it's better to have one person or many
to teach and to set an example?
DOMENICO. Surely one person, provided I could find someone
who is both excellent and learned. Many people cannot agree on
one teaching and cannot provide similar examples for imitation.
MATTIAS. If then someone of perfected excellence in every virtue 76
may be found, this one person ought to be set before the citizens
who are to be educated as a mirror and exemplar for everyone,
rather than many persons.
DOMENICO. This is my view as well.
MATTIAS. What about harmony in a state — do you think that is
something useful?
DOMENICO. Indeed it's so necessary that the state can't exist at
all without it; take it away and you take away the state's raison
d'être entirely.
MATTIAS. You're right; for harmony is the unique end of the
state. Just as a doctor has as his purpose healing the sick, or a
helmsman finding port, or a general winning a victory, so the man
who establishes a state has peace, concord and unity as his purpose and directs all his actions, efforts and counsels to achieving
and preserving those things. Now then, what can better provide
and maintain light for the earth: the sun, which emits light of itself and cannot not be bright, even if it wanted to, or the moon,
which takes light from another source and can easily lose it?
DOMENICO. Doubtless the sun.
MATTIAS. Which offers more heat and keeps it longer, [the ele- 77
ment of] fire, that receives it from Nature herself, or something
that is heated by fire?

DOMINICUS. Ignis profecto, a quo calor omnis in cetera proficiscitur.

MATTHAEUS. Utrum autem et melius et celerius madefacit, ipsane aqua, an ea quae humida et aquosa sunt?

DOMINICUS. Quis dubitat aquam, quae humoris omnis parens et ministra sit, omnia uberius et citius humectare?

MATTHAEUS. Concordiam quoque et unionem utrum, obsecro, et parere civibus et tueri melius potest, idne quod natura simplex atque unum et sui simile semper est, an id quod multiplex, varium et mutabile esse cernitur?

DOMINICUS. Nimirum id quod per se unum est.

78 MATTHAEUS. Quid autem per se magis unum et sui simile potest inveniri quam unus ipse, qui neque potest esse non unus neque a se ipso umquam dissentire?

DOMINICUS. Sic est.

MATTHAEUS. Unus igitur qui concordiam atque unionem civibus praestare melius potest quam plures, melius profecto et salubrius quam plures civitatem reget.

DOMINICUS. Ita videtur.

MATTHAEUS. Visne hoc etiam clarius cernere?

DOMINICUS. Quo pacto?

MATTHAEUS. Si multi civitatem administrarent, nonne eam tum demum optime administrare dicerentur, cum maxime concordes inter se atque uniti essent, denique cum unius mentis, unius voluntatis, unius affectus et quasi vir unus efficerentur?

DOMINICUS. Ita est.

79 MATTHAEUS. Si multi igitur, nisi maxime uniantur, recte administrare non possunt et tum demum rectissime administrant, cum ita concordes sunt ut vir unus esse videantur, nonne is qui semper unus est, neque potest a se ipso dissidere, multo omnia rectius administrabit?

DOMINICUS. Administrabit profecto.

DOMENICO. Surely fire, from which comes all heat present in other things.

MATTIAS. What makes things wet better and more rapidly, [the element of] water itself, or things that are wet and watery?

DOMENICO. Who can doubt that water, the parent and agent of all wetness, makes everything more swiftly and abundantly wet?

MATTIAS. What can better create and protect concord and unity among citizens, something which by nature is seen to be simple, one and always like itself, or something which is multiple, diverse and mutable?

DOMENICO. Doubtless that which is one by its own nature.

MATTIAS. What more unified in its own nature and like itself    78
can be found than that one man who cannot not be one and who cannot ever disagree with himself?

DOMENICO. That is so.

MATTIAS. The one man who can better offer harmony and unity to citizens than many can surely rule the city better and more wholesomely than many men can.

DOMENICO. It seems so.

MATTIAS. Do you want to see the matter more clearly still?

DOMENICO. How?

MATTIAS. If many govern the city, wouldn't they be said to be governing best at the point when they are most harmonious and united, in short when they become of one mind, of one will, of one feeling, when they almost become one man?

DOMENICO. That is so.

MATTIAS. If then many men cannot correctly govern unless they    79
are completely unified and they only govern in the most correct way when they are so harmonious that they seem like one man, won't the one who is always one and cannot disagree with himself govern all things much more correctly?

DOMENICO. Surely he will.

MATTHAEUS. Quid quod vis omnis separata ac dispersa minus valida ac firma est quam si uno in loco adunata et coniuncta esset? Difficilius enim navem aut molem aliquam impellunt multi quam si unus idem posset efficere. Neque etiam quamvis multi possent impellere, nisi vim omnem in unum quodammodo contraherent atque unirent; immo quicquid possunt, ob id ipsum possunt, quod uniti sunt. Quod si eadem in uno coacta et cumulata vis esset, nonne multo id facilius meliusque ab ipso efficeretur?

DOMINICUS. Procul dubio.

80  MATTHAEUS. Eodem modo, si universa civilis potentia et summa reipublicae in unum coeat atque ad unum quempiam deferatur, nonne multo validior ac stabilior erit existimanda quam si in multis dispersa et dissipata sit? Ille quoque, nonne aptius rempublicam et facilius geret quam si aliis multis obnoxius atque obligatus sit?

DOMINICUS. Ita puto.

MATTHAEUS. Vis afferam tibi huius rei maximum et clarissimum argumentum?

DOMINICUS. Cupio.

81  MATTHAEUS. Romani, qui libertatis et reipublicae nomen prae ceteris gentibus coluere, cum gravius aliquid et periculosius immineret, dictatorem creabant, penes quem unum summa rerum omnium potestas esset, ne in re subita senatum cogere et sparsam reipublicae potentiam contrahere — quod difficile admodum et periculosum erat — saepius oporteret, satis hoc uno testimonio declarantes vim unitam quam dispersam aptiorem esse, hoc est, unum potiorem esse quam plures.

DOMINICUS. Profecto sic est.

MATTHAEUS. Clarius adhuc et apertius idem ut intuearis volo.

DOMINICUS. Quo pacto possum?

MATTIAS. What about the fact that all force is less strong and stable when separated and dispersed than it is when united and joined in one place? Many men move a ship or any mass with greater difficulty than if one person could do the same, nor could many men move anything unless they in some way pull together and unify their power into one; indeed, whatever they do, they do by virtue of being united. But isn't it much better and easier if the same power is accumulated and concentrated in a single person?

DOMENICO. No doubt.

MATTIAS. In the same way, if the highest and fullest civil power 80 of a commonwealth is united and invested in a single man, must it not be reckoned much stronger and more stable than if it were dispersed and dissipated in many? Would not that one man carry out public business more fittingly and easily than if he were subject to and bound by many others?

DOMENICO. I think so.

MATTIAS. Would you like me to advance the best and clearest proof of this?

DOMENICO. I would.

MATTIAS. The Romans, who cultivated a reputation for liberty 81 and disinterested government beyond that of other nations, when faced with some grave peril, used to create a dictator, a single person with supreme and universal power, so that in emergencies they would not be obliged too often to convene the Senate, and bring together the dispersed political power of the commonwealth, something that was difficult and dangerous to do. By this one proof they announced that united power was more effective than dispersed power, i.e., that one ruler was preferable to many.

DOMENICO. That is surely the case.

MATTIAS. I want you to visualize the same point even more clearly and manifestly.

DOMENICO. How can I do that?

MATTHAEUS. Cedo: quid est in rerum natura quod alteri maxime repugnet atque adversetur?

DOMINICUS. Album nigro, bono malum, optimo pessimum[32] et cetera quae inter se 'contraria' nominantur.

MATTHAEUS. Recte iudicas. Quis igitur est pessimus omnium principatus?

82 DOMINICUS. Si pessimum scirem, optimum quoque eadem ratione scirem. Contrariorum enim, ut a philosophis nonnumquam audivi et natura etiam ipsa deprehendere videor, eadem est disciplina, cognitoque altero alterum facile intellegitur.

MATTHAEUS. Faciam ergo utrumque ut scias. Quid, obsecro, imprimis curare debet qui recte civitatem administrat?

DOMINICUS. Bonum commune ac publicum.

MATTHAEUS. Quisnam ab eo longissime abest?

DOMINICUS. Qui privatum et suum tantum curat.

MATTHAEUS. Quis porro is est?

DOMINICUS. Mihi quidem tyrannus videtur, qui unius dumtaxat hominis, hoc est suum,[33] bonum curat.

MATTHAEUS. Recte sentis; si igitur tyrannus est pessimus, quis, obsecro, erit optimus?

DOMINICUS. Nimirum rex ipse.

83 MATTHAEUS. Quid, rides fili?

IOANNES. Quod Dominicus contra se dicere et quod hactenus negavit affirmare et fateri suo ore coactus est.

DOMINICUS. An non audivisti, Ioannes, tria esse in rerum natura validissima: vinum, regem, verum? Ego cum a duobus, hoc est a rege et a vero, oppugner, resistere qui possum? Sed perge, obsecro, rex; si quid aliud superest, explicare. Nihil enim mihi gra-

MATTIAS. Well now, what exists in nature that is most at odds with and contrary to something else?

DOMENICO. Black and white, good and evil, best and worst, and the rest of the things that are called "opposites."

MATTIAS. You're right. What then is the worst of all forms of rule?

DOMENICO. If I knew the worst, I should also know the best by the same reasoning. Teaching about contraries is the same teaching, as I have sometimes heard from philosophers and as I seem to grasp too from Nature herself: once you know one contrary, you can easily understand the other. 82

MATTIAS. So I'll see to it that you know both. What ought to be the first concern of someone who rightly governs a state?

DOMENICO. The common and public good.

MATTIAS. And who is farthest from that good?

DOMENICO. The man whose concern is only for his own private interest.

MATTIAS. And who is that?

DOMENICO. The tyrant, I think, who is concerned only for the good of one man, namely his own.

MATTIAS. You're right. If then the tyrant is the worst ruler, who will be the best?

DOMENICO. The king, naturally.

MATTIAS. Why are you laughing, my son? 83

JANOS. Because Domenico has been forced to contradict himself and to affirm and admit with his own mouth what he has hitherto denied.

DOMENICO. Haven't you heard, János, that the three strongest things in nature are wine, a king and the truth? Since I've been attacked by two of them, by a king and by the truth, how can I resist? But go on, king, and if there's anything left, please explain it. There is nothing that can be more welcome to me than to learn

tius esse potest quam ut et haec quae utilissima sunt et abs te potissimum doctissimo viro et rege sapientissimo discam.

84 MATTHAEUS. Fateris igitur id, quod a principio negabas, optimum esse regis principatum?

DOMINICUS. Fateor istud quidem tuis rationibus adductus; sed unicus adhuc mihi restat scrupulus qui me male habet.

MATTHAEUS. Quis iste est?

DOMINICUS. Si optimus erat regum principatus, cur sunt institutae respublicae?

85 MATTHAEUS. Dicam. Omnia quae quatuor illis sive elementis sive seminibus composita et compacta sunt, quia contrariis qualitatibus constant et in eodem diu permanere statu non possunt, a summo illo et perfectissimo gradu paulatim declinent atque degenerent et ita ad interitum perveniant necesse est. Quod quidem cum ceteris rebus tum vel maxime hominibus accidit, qui supremum ac dignissimum inter animantia omnia gradum sunt sortiti. Nam cum ab initio singuli viri optimi ac moderatissimi singulis civitatibus aut provinciis regendis praeficerentur atque ob id regium nomen esset inventum, invalescente paulatim libidine, ambitione, avaritia ceterisque nefariis cupiditatibus, alii atque alii, seu nominis specie capti sive imperandi cupiditate adducti, locum illum aut vi aut dolo aut pessimis artibus occupavere, neque se melius in retinendo gerebant quam gesserant in adipiscendo. Ubi enim eum locum semel invaserant, effusis omnium flagitiorum habenis, subditos adulteriis, stupris, rapinis, caedibus et omni libidinis et crudelitatis genere affligebant. Quae cum illi diutius ferre non possent, caesis tyrannis aliam principatus speciem instituerunt. Nam cum se singulos bonos viros et virtute praestantes a quibus regerentur reperire posse diffiderent, unius loco plures, quos ipsi optimos iudicaverant, sibi praeesse voluere, ut quod unus non faceret,

these most useful teachings, especially from you, who are a most learned man and a most wise king.

MATTIAS. So you admit what you denied at the beginning, that 84 the best form of rule is that of a king?

DOMENICO. I admit that I have been led to this view by your arguments, but I have one misgiving left that troubles me.

MATTIAS. And what is that?

DOMENICO. If the best form of rule was that of kings, why are republics founded at all?

MATTIAS. Let me tell you. All things that are composed of the 85 four elements or seeds, since they are made up of contrary qualities and cannot remain in the same state for long, gradually fall away and degenerate from that highest and most perfect degree, and so necessarily come to destruction. This happens to other things but most of all to human beings, who have been allotted the highest and most worthy rank among the animals. While in the beginning the best and most self-controlled individuals were put in charge of ruling [regere] individual states and provinces — and it was on this account that the name "king" [rex] was invented — with the gradual spread of lust, ambition, avarice and other wicked desires, more and more rulers were captivated by the attraction of the name "king," or perhaps by lust for rule, to take over the king's place either by violence, fraud or the worst behavior, and they did not conduct themselves any better in retaining power than they had in acquiring it. Once they had laid their hands on that post, the reins holding back every crime were loosened, and they inflicted upon their subjects adulteries, rapes, seizures, murders and every sort of lust and cruelty. When the subjects could bear it no longer, they slaughtered their tyrants and instituted another species of government. Since they had no confidence that they could find to rule them individual good men, outstanding for virtue, they decided to put many men whom they considered excellent in charge in place of one man, so that what

multi facerent et, ut tu paulo ante dixisti, quod unius virtuti dees-
set, multorum diligentia suppleretur. Atque hanc quidem principatus speciem, quoniam ex optimo quoque constaret, nostri 'optimatum gubernationem,' Graeci *aristocratiam* appellavere.

86     Hi quoque, cum ceteros spoliare atque opprimere, omnia sibi
usurpare ac rapere, omnia ad suum commodum referre coepissent,
in eum paulatim statum declinavere qui a nostris 'paucorum potentia', a Graecis *oligarchia* dictus est, et ex optimis brevi pessimi
sunt effecti. Hos quoque populus diu non ferens, eam principatus
formam, quae a Graecis *politice*, a nostris 'respublica' proprie dicitur, ex omnibus aeque constantem instituit, ut omnes vicissim omnibus et praeesse et subesse possent. Haec quoque diu incolumis
atque incorrupta non mansit; plebs enim, ex dominatione in superbiam insolentiamque elata, nobilitatem vexare atque opprimere
omnibus modis coepit, donec in eum tandem statum deventum
est, qui a nostris 'plebeius principatus', a Graecis *democratia* nomi-
natur, quo quidem abiectior ac detestabilior esse nullus potest;
neque enim locus iam ullus degenerandi aut collabendi relictus est.
Regius igitur, ut diximus, principatus est optimus, sed tyranno-
rum metu in alium atque alium commutatus.

DOMINICUS. Intellego.

MATTHAEUS. Vis hoc ipsum clarissime atque apertissime cernere?

DOMINICUS. Volo.

87 MATTHAEUS. Intuere igitur naturam ipsam, quam nos ut optimam bene vivendi magistram ac ducem omnibus in rebus sequi
imitarique debemus, quo pacto omnia quae alieno imperio et gu-
bernatione indigebant, unius arbitrio et potestati subiecerit. Nam

one might not do, many might do, and (as you said just now) so that the vigilance of many might take the place of one man's virtue. This kind of rulership, since it too consisted of all the best men [*ex optimo*], we [Latins] call "government of the optimates" and the Greeks "aristocracy."

But these men too, when they had begun to despoil and oppress the rest, to seize and expropriate everything for themselves and to judge everything by reference to their own interest, gradually declined into the condition that we call "the power of the few" and the Greeks "oligarchy," and the best were quickly turned into the worst. The people could not put up with these men too for long, and established that form of rule which is properly called "polity" by the Greeks and "republic" by us [Latin-speakers], consisting of all the people equally, so that everyone takes turns ruling and being ruled. This form of rule also did not remain sound and uncorrupted for long, for the common people, roused to pride and insolence by their supremacy, began to harass and oppress the nobility by every means, until at last there arrived the condition that we call "rule by the plebs" and the Greeks call "democracy" — than which no form of government is more ignoble and detestable — for there was now no room left for further degeneration and corruption. Royal government, therefore, as we said, is the best, but changes into one form of government after another through fear of tyranny.[34]

DOMENICO. I understand.

MATTIAS. Would you like to see this illustrated in the clearest and most manifest way?

DOMENICO. I would.

MATTIAS. Cast your gaze then upon Nature herself, whom we ought to follow and imitate as the best mistress of living well and as our captain in all things. See how she subjects to the decision and power of one all things that need another's command and governance. To begin with the smallest things, the bees, which at na-

ut a minimis ordiamur, apes, quae natura duce coetum et societatem colunt mirumque inter se ordinem servant, uni regi obtempe-
rant, quem non ipsae de turba temere delegerunt, sed ab ipsa natura insignem forma et diademate praeditum acceperunt. Grues
quoque, cum gregatim volent iter facturae, unam ex suis cui pa-
reant, quam sequantur itineris ducem deligunt.

88     Venio ad nos ipsos. Cum corpus hoc nostrum membris plurimis compositum sit, quorum alia alios motus aliaque offitia sint
sortita, unum caput cetero corpori dominatur et, tamquam in ex-
celsa quadam arce constitutum, et intellectum et sensus omnes intra se continet, ceterorumque membrorum officia pro arbitrio moderatur. Ab uno quoque corde, quod omnis motus fons et origo
est, cetera membra suos privatim motus accipiunt. Corpori vero
universo regendo servandoque unus animus praepositus est, qui
contrarias illas elementorum qualitates ita inter se connectit et
continet, ut summus philosophorum Aristoteles dicere non dubi-
taverit, magis ab animo corpus quam a corpore animum contineri.
Animi quoque partes ratio una gubernat et cohibet; virtutes etiam
ipsas prudentia sola moderatur. In numeris vero ipsis, nonne
unum excellentissimum est, ita ut ab uno ceteri, non a ceteris
unum exoriatur? A quo quidem et Plato et Pythagoras et alii
quam plurimi omnia profecta esse voluere. Denique omnia quae
apud nos natura instituit, ad unum aliquid referuntur.

89     Quid superiora? Nonne hoc etiam modo composita et constituta sunt? Sol enim unus ceteris non modo planetis, verum etiam
stellis ita antecedit ac praestat, ut eum unum multi ex veteribus
tum deum tum animam mundi esse existimaverint. Cetera porro
caelestia corpora, quae motum aliquem vel ipsa habent vel aliis
quoquomodo infundunt atque immittunt, a primo illo et excellen-
tissimo auctore atque impulsore motum omnem accipiunt. Quid

ture's command practice common life and society and observe a marvelous order among themselves, obey a single king, whom they do not choose rashly from the mob; they take from Nature herself one who is remarkable in form and supplied with a diadem.[35] Cranes too, when they want to make a journey in a flock, choose one of their own to obey whom they follow as the leader on their journey.[36]

I come now to ourselves. Although this body of ours is composed of many members, and the various members are allotted different motions and functions, one head commands the rest of the body, and as though placed in a high citadel, holding within it the intellect and all the senses, it controls the functions of the other members in accordance with its judgment. Also, from a single heart, the source and origin of all motion, the rest of the members receive their individual motions. One soul is put in charge of ruling and preserving the whole body, which links and limits those contrary qualities of the elements within it in such a way that Aristotle, the supreme philosopher, did not hesitate to say that the body is contained in the soul more than the soul is in the body.[37] The soul's reason alone governs and restrains its parts;[38] prudence alone regulates the virtues themselves too. In the case of the numbers, is not the number one the most excellent, so that the rest of the numbers take their beginning from it, not it from them? Plato and Pythagoras and many others indeed held that all things proceed from the One.[39] In short, all things that Nature has established in our sphere are related to unity.

What of things above? Aren't they composed and constituted this way too? The single sun goes before and ranks ahead not only of the other planets, but even of the stars, so that many of the ancients believed this one thing was God or the World-Soul.[40] And the rest of the celestial bodies, which either themselves have some motion or in some way instill or direct that motion in others, receive all motion from that first and most excellent originator and

88

89

multa? Nonne unus in rerum natura Deus est? Qui si omnia regi
a pluribus melius cognovisset, mundum, quem optime regi cupie-
bat, neque solus produxisset neque solus tot iam saeculis adminis-
traret ac regeret. Quod si Deus ipse et mundum optime solus administrat et universam rerum naturam ita instituit, ut omnia quae
aliquo pacto administranda sunt ad unius imperium atque arbitrium referantur, nonne mens humana, quae quoddam ipsius Dei
simulacrum est, illum in suis artibus atque actionibus, quoad potest, debet imitari et, ut adeo in rerum natura factum videt, ita
suos coetus et societates constituere, ut omnes unius imperio subiaceant, ad unius arbitrium gubernentur? Nos vero, nonne illum
optimum debemus principatum existimare, quem a[34] Deo et in se
ipso servari et in universa rerum natura constitutum esse videamus?

DOMINICUS. Ita est profecto ut dicis, rex, neque istis rationibus
obsisti potest.

90  MATTHAEUS. Hoc quidem nobis ratio faciendum suadet, neque
vero umquam fere aliter factum invenies. Repete animo nationes
omnes; omnia saecula in memoriam redige: universum terrarum
orbem a regibus semper administratum fuisse, respublicas autem
et paucas admodum extitisse et brevi interiisse comperies. Nam,
ut primos illos homines omittamus, de quibus sacro Hebraeorum
volumini tantum credimus (quos tamen sub unius principatu
vixisse invenimus), Aegyptii, qui de hominum principio cum Scythis maioribus nostris contendunt, Osirim, Amasum, Vesorem
atque alios innumerabiles reges semper habuisse traduntur; brevi
admodum tempore, cum Romanis[35] subiecti essent, ut ceterae nationes, non reges habuere, sed sub imperatoribus principibusque
vixere; hodie quoque, extincto Romanorum imperio, reges creant,
quos ipsi soldanos appellant. Assyrii quoque, qui nunc Aegyptiis
regibus parent, semper aut reges ipsi habuere aut aliarum gentium

efficient cause. In short, is there not one God in Nature? If He had known that all things were better ruled by many, He would not have created the world (which he wanted to be excellently ruled) by Himself, and He would not have governed and ruled it by Himself for so many ages. And if God himself rules the world best by Himself and has set up Nature so that all things which are in some way subject to government should be related to the power and judgment of one, should not the human mind, a kind of image of God Himself, imitate Him in its behavior and actions as far as possible and, just as it sees done in Nature, thus should it establish its associations and societies, so that they may be subject to the power of one and governed according to the judgment of one? Shouldn't we reckon that to be the best form of government which we see God has preserved in Himself and established in all of Nature?

DOMENICO. It is surely as you say, king; your arguments are irresistible.

MATTIAS. Reason indeed persuades us that this [establishing 90 one-man government] must be done, and you will almost never find it done otherwise. Recall to mind all the nations, go back through all the ages, and you will discover that the world was always governed by kings and that only a few republics have existed which rapidly perished. Let's set aside the earliest men, concerning whom we rely a great deal on the sacred books of the Hebrews — whom, nevertheless, we find to have lived under the government of one man. The Egyptians, who rival our ancestors, the Scythians, as the first humans, are said always to have had Osiris, Amasus, Vesor and innumerable other kings. For a rather brief time, when like other nations they were conquered by the Romans, they didn't have kings but lived under Roman generals and emperors.[41] Today too, the Roman empire having died out, they elect kings whom they call Sultans.[42] The Assyrians too, who today obey the Egyptian kings, always either themselves had kings

regibus paruere; eorum enim regnum, quod a Nino et Semiramide incohasse traditur, primo ad Medos, mox ad Persas, inde ad Graecos, tum ad Romanos, postremo ad Aegyptios translatum est. Persae, qui antea Medis subiacebant, a Cyro incohantes, diu suae gentis reges habuere, a Magno deinde Alexandro subacti, partim Macedonum, partim Romanorum imperio perlato, ad suos tandem principes rediere. Graeci quoque, ab initio Phoroneum, Inachum, Acrisium, Danaum, Agamemnonem, Cecropem, Aegeum, Cadmum atque alios reges quam plurimos, sed in aliis atque aliis civitatibus habuere, ita ut singulae paene civitates suos privatim reges constituerent; mutato deinde saepe statu, sub Romanorum tandem potestatem pervenere. Eo porro imperio Constantinopolim translato, diu aliis atque aliis tum Romanis tum suis principibus paruere, nunc Turcarum regibus subiecti sunt. Vestra etiam Italia, Dominice, ante urbem conditam ab aliis atque aliis regibus semper administrata est. Romani vero, ut scis, et a regibus incepere et in principes sive imperatores desiere. Quid dicam de Hispania, Gallia, Germania ceterisque occidentis provinciis? Nonne et a regibus olim obtentae sunt et hodie a regibus obtinentur? Nos certe, qui ab Scythis oriundi sumus, et illic semper sub regibus viximus et hic reges semper instituimus.

91    Quid multa? Omnes denique, ut vides, nationes regium hoc imperium et semper expetivere et hodie maiorem in modum expetunt. Respublicae autem et paucae admodum omni aevo fuisse memorantur, et illae quae fuerunt, brevi aut extinctae sunt aut ad unius principatum redactae. Athenienses enim et Lacedaemonii, qui reipublicae formam quandoque servavere, non sane diu eo statu contenti, omne principatus genus experti sunt, donec in Macedonum primo, deinde in Romanorum ditionem pervenere. Carthaginenses a regibus e Phoenicia in Africam traducti, cum se ad

or obeyed the kings of other peoples; indeed their kingdom, which
is reported to have begun with Ninus and Semiramis, passed first
to the Medes, then to the Persians, from there to the Greeks, then
to the Romans, and finally to the Egyptians. The Persians, who
had earlier been subject to the Medes, beginning with Cyrus, for
long had kings of their own people, before being subdued by Alexander the Great. Having passed partly under Macedonian, partly
under Roman power, they at last returned to their own princes.
The Greeks too initially had Phoroneus, Inachus, Acrisius,
Danaus, Agamemnon, Cecrops, Aegeus, Cadmus and numerous
other kings, but in this or that city, so that nearly every city established its own individual kings. Then, after rapid changes of constitution, they came in the end under Roman power; when the
empire was transferred to Constantinople, they obeyed various of
their own[43] or Roman emperors, and are now subject to the Turkish kings. Your Italy, Domenico, was always ruled by this or that
king before the foundation of Rome. The Romans, as you know,
started with kings and ended up with emperors. Why mention
Spain, France, Germany and the other western provinces? Weren't
these places occupied by kings long ago; don't they remain kingdoms today? Certainly we [Hungarians], who trace our origins to
the Scythians, always lived there [in Scythia] under kings, and always established kings here [in Hungary].

In short, all nations, as you see, have always sought out this 91
royal power and seek it even more today. However, in all of recorded history there have been only a few republics, and those
quickly either died out or changed into one-man governments.
The Athenians and the Spartans, who at various times had republican constitutions, weren't happy very long in that state and went
through every kind of government before coming under the sway,
first of the Macedonians, then of the Romans. The Carthaginians
were led by their kings from Phoenicia to Africa, but when they

reipublicae statum convertissent, brevi a Romanis subacti atque ad internecionem deleti sunt.

92     Romani, qui omnium maximam ac diutissimam rempublicam habuisse referuntur, sub regibus ab initio ducentis amplius annis vixere. Illis porro exactis, cum reipublicae formam et libertatis nomen retinere vellent neque possent aliquo principe et duce carere, pro unico rege duos consules divisa potestate creaverunt.[36] Ne quis autem diuturnitate imperii res novas moliri et sibi asserere imperium posset, pro perpetuo rege consules annuos instituere. In subitis tamen et trepidis rebus, ne quid respublica detrimenti caperet, unum, ut diximus, dictatorem penes quem universum imperium esset creabant. Hoc quoque statu sic etiam non diu retento, ad unius tandem principatum rediere. Qui quidem, tametsi principis nomen mutavere, ut pro imperatore pontificem maximum habeant, unius tamen hodie quoque principatum retinent.

93     Veneti quoque, quorum nostra aetate respublica maxima et potentissima est, tametsi concilia, magistratus et omnia publica munera per optimates obeunt et in plerisque rebus optimatum, ut diximus, principatum servant, regiae tamen dignitatis speciem quandam et imaginem retinentes, ducem seu principem senatus creant, cui summam dignitatem atque imperium communi consensu ultro deferunt, hoc testimonio aperte declarantes et optimum esse unius principatum et illo[37] se carere non posse.

94     Postremo vos ipsi, qui reipublicae in omnibus formam retinetis, nonne totius senatus et reipublicae principem sorte ducitis, quem usitato vocabulo, ut ex civibus vestris audivi, Iustitiae Vexilliferum appellatis? Quid, obsecro, sibi vult aliud vel dignitas illa vel nomen, nisi ut et in republica unum aliquem ducem ac principem necessarium esse ostendatis, et illum praecipuum legum iusti-

exchanged their constitution for a republican one, they were swiftly subdued by the Romans and entirely wiped out.[44]

The Romans, who are recorded as having had the greatest and most long-lived republic of all, in the beginning lived under kings for more than two hundred years; after these were driven out, since they wished to keep the constitution of a commonwealth and the name of liberty and could not be without some leader and captain, in place of a single king they elected two consuls with power divided between them. But to prevent anyone claiming power for himself or plotting revolution owing to the long duration of his power, they laid it down that consuls should have annual terms in place of a king in perpetuity. In emergencies and parlous situations, however, to prevent any harm coming to the state, they chose a single dictator (as we said) with universal powers. This constitution too they did not keep for very long, returning finally to government by one man. They have kept one-man government down to this day, though they changed the name of their prince and now have a supreme pontiff in place of a king. 92

The Venetians too, who have the greatest and most powerful republic of our age, although their councils, magistracies and all public offices are performed by aristocrats and in most matters they follow an aristocratic form of government, as we said, nevertheless retain a kind of appearance or image of the royal dignity and elect a doge or leader of the senate, to whom they willingly entrust the highest rank and power by common consent. They openly announce thereby that one-man government is the best and that they cannot do without it. 93

Finally, there are you yourselves, who have kept the republican form in everything: don't you select by lot a leader of the whole senate and republic whom you call by the familiar name of Standard-Bearer of Justice? What else does this title of honor intend to show but that, even in a republic, it is necessary to have a single captain or leader and that he ought to be the leading guardian and 94

tiaeque custodem et cultorem esse oportere significetis? Nonne
igitur vos quoque huius de qua loquimur regiae dignitatis non mediocrem effigiem atque imaginem retinetis? Nonne vos ipsi, vestro
iudicio ac testimonio, hunc esse optimum principatum fatemini?

95      Sed quidnam tibi mortalium vel acta vel instituta commemoro?
Ille unicus humani generis auctor et parens, Deus, cum salutis
nostrae gratia ad nos e[38] caelo descendere et ut homo inter homines versari vellet, nobis, quid faciendum esset, apertissimo non
modo testimonio, verum etiam exemplo declaravit. Nam et eo potissimum tempore nasci voluit quo universum terrarum orbem
princeps unus Augustus Caesar obtinebat et, dum inter nos vive-
ret, unicum sibi regium nomen assumpsit et, cum a nobis in caelum rediret, uni Petro Christianum nomen et rempublicam com-
mendavit, uni fundandam regendamque tradidit, uni denique ius
omne in animas arbitriumque permisit. Nonne hoc exemplo nobis
satis abundeque Christus, quis esset optimus principatus, ostendit? Quid, obsecro, amplius desideramus? Nonne omnis eius actio
nobis ad eruditionem atque imitationem est proposita?

96      Quod si ita faciendum esse et ratio docet et natura ostendit, si
homines hoc omnibus saeculis observarunt, si Christus denique
hoc, non solum ipso nascendi tempore comprobavit, sed et apud
nos manens ita fecit, et a nobis discedens ita suis faciendum instituit, possumusne an sit optimus unius principatus dubitare? Est
igitur, mihi credite, hic unus principatus multo ceteris omnibus
anteponendus, si modo ille, sive rex sive princeps, optimus atque
integerrimus sit, subditosque omnes non ad suum, sed ad illorum
commodum iuste moderateque et tueatur et regat.

97      Sed quia virtus in nobis ita imminuta est, ita defecit, ut bonum
principem reperire homines se posse diffidant, ambitio vero ita in-
valuit ut omnes praeesse ac dominari velint, ad multorum principatum deventum est. Quod si intellegerent homines quam grave,

keeper of the laws and justice? Don't you also, therefore, preserve no insignificant symbol and image of the royal office of which we speak? Aren't you yourselves admitting by your own judgment and testimony that this is the best government?

But why should I be reminding you of the deeds and institu-    95
tions of mortal men? That one author and parent of the human race, God, when He wished to come down to us from heaven and live as a man among men, showed us what must be done not only by the most manifest testimony, but even by His example. For He chose to be born at that particular moment when Caesar Augustus, a single emperor, ruled the world, and while he lived among us He took that unique royal name upon himself[45] and, when He left us and returned to heaven, entrusted the Christian name and commonwealth to Peter alone, handing it over to him alone to found and rule, and allowing him alone all justice and judgment over souls. Did not Christ by this example show us well enough, and abundantly so, which was the best form of government? What more do we want, I ask you? Is not all of His activity set out for our instruction and imitation?

But if reason teaches and nature shows that we must do this, if    96
men throughout the ages have followed this, if Christ, finally, demonstrated this not only by the epoch of His birth but by enacting it whilst among us and ordering His followers to practice it upon leaving us, can we doubt that one-man government is the best? Believe me, this one form of government is much preferable to all the rest, so long as the king, prince or emperor is an excellent man of the utmost integrity and rules and protects all his subjects justly and moderately in accordance with their interest, not his own.

But since virtue is so diminished among us and has so far failed    97
that men lack confidence they can find themselves a good prince, while ambition has so gained force that everyone wants to be preëminent and to dominate, we have descended to the govern-

quam laboriosum, quam difficile sit ceteros recte gubernare ac regere, profecto id onus subire nemo cuperet. Verum quia non quid in ea re laboris ac molestiae sit, sed quid inesse possit voluptatis cogitamus, principatus ipsos non ad alienam iniuriam ac necessitatem propulsandam, sed ad libidinem atque avaritiam nostram explendam expetimus, decipimur profecto, decipimur illa specie honoris ac nominis. Nam, si recte atque accurate regia dignitas consideretur, multo plus habet molestiae, laboris atque oneris quam voluptatis aut commodi et, ut breviter Aquinatis verbis exprimam,

plus aloes quam mellis habet.

98    Rex enim ante omnia disciplinae militaris atque imperatoriae facultatis peritissimus sit necesse est, ita ut eam rem non domi tantum atque in otio voluminibus legendis didicerit, sed in castris quoque et apud hostes pugnando exercendoque perceperit. Ad eam porro, nisi et auctoritas nominis et felicitas quaedam, egregiis suis virtutibus et rebus gestis comparata, accesserit, nihil eum iuvabit militaris scientia.

99    Ille vero non modo imperatoriae, castrenses ac bellicae, sed togatae quoque domesticaeque virtutes — humanitas, facilitas, liberalitas, comitas — principi sunt in omni vita maxime necessariae. Domi autem legum imprimis latio et iurisdictio ad eius munus atque officium pertinet, in eoque regia et civilis facultas constituta est, ut leges defendat, tutos omnes ab iniuriis praestet, fidem omnibus aeque servet, unicuique ius suum sine discrimine tribuat, gratum se et beneficum in omnes pro cuiusque meritis et dignitate ostendat, totum regni corpus ita tueatur ac foveat, ut nullum eius membrum desertum ab se aut neglectum esse patiatur. Bella vero ita gerat, ut nihil ex illis nisi pacem quaesisse videatur; regnum non modo ad praesens, sed in posterum quoque ab hostibus tutum ac pacatum reddat. Modestia vero et continentia, cum omni-

ment of the many. If people knew how burdensome, laborious and difficult it was to rule and govern other men rightly, no one, surely, would want to bear this burden. But since we do not consider the effort and vexations of rule but the pleasure we may find in it, and seek out leadership positions, not to defend others against injustice or need, but to satisfy our lust and avarice, we are surely deceived — deceived by that semblance of honor and reputation. If we considered the royal office correctly and carefully, it includes much more vexation, labor and pressure than it does advantage, and (to express myself succinctly in Juvenal's words),

it has more bitter aloe than honey.[46]

A king above all must be extremely experienced in the discipline of war and in the ability to command, in such a way that he learns these things, not only by reading books at home and at leisure, but in the camps too and by training and fighting in the presence of the enemy. And unless he adds to this a reputation also for authority and success derived from his outstanding virtues and deeds, military science won't help him at all. 98

Not only must he have the virtues associated with command, the camp and war, but also the virtues of home and the forum — kindness, accessibility, liberality, friendliness — are highly necessary for him throughout his life. At home, an ability to legislate and judge are first of all pertinent to his role and office, and in it the royal and civil power is constituted to defend the laws, to protect everyone from injustice, to keep equal faith with all, to show good will towards everyone in proportion to the merits and rank of each, to protect and foster the whole body of the kingdom in such a way that it allows no member of it to be left behind or neglected. The king should wage his wars in such a way that he appears to seek nothing from them but peace. He pacifies his kingdom and makes it safe from enemies, not only for the present, but also for the future. All men should have modesty and temperance, but 99

bus hominibus tum regibus qui exemplo aliis futuri sunt, est vel
maxime necessaria.[39]

100      Quid dicam de prudentia, omnium regula ac moderatrice virtutum? Cum nulla vel mediocris hominis actio carere illa debeat,
qualis tandem et quanta in regibus, qui in maximis semper et gravissimis rebus versantur, est futura? Neque vero qui tam multis
hominum milibus imperaturus est, tam multis responsurus, tam
multis et variis de rebus disceptaturus doctrina atque eloquentia
carere ullo modo potest. Rex enim illiteratus, ut vulgo rectissime
dicitur, est asinus coronatus. Quo enim pacto leges condet, feret
sententias, iura distribuet, regnum administrabit si, non dico aliquam aut mediocrem, sed maximam quoque et absolutissimam iuris scientiam non habeat? Contiones vero aut in civitate aut in castris habere, in concilio sententiam dicere, legatis atque aliis ad se
venientibus respondere sine summa dicendi copia et facultate non
poterit. Omitto mathematicas disciplinas, quae illi ad bella gerenda et imperatorium munus obeundum necessariae sunt.

101      Quid illa, quae sibi ut proprium virtutis nomen assumpsit, for-
titudo? Quantopere est regibus non adversus hostes modo in bellis, sed domi quoque adversus omnes fortunae impetus, adversus
omnes animi et corporis aegritudines expetenda? Quid in rebus
gerendis et in omni principis actione, quantopere est illa celsitudo
animi et rerum humanarum despicientia necessaria? Pietas autem
et religio ita debet regio animo insidere atque infixa esse, ut ne mi-
nimam quidem rem sibi sine divina ope incohandam putet; immo
nihil omnino existimet sibi sine divinae beneficentiae auxilio posse
succedere.

102      A regio autem animo omnis crudelitas, omnis ambitio, omnis
avaritia, omnis libido, omnia foeda ac nefaria flagitia, omnes denique cupiditates ac perturbationes animi abesse longissime de-

they are of the utmost necessity to a king, who is going to set an example for others.

What should I say of practical wisdom, the measure and mod- 100 erator of all the virtues? Although the actions of not even the average man should lack this virtue, how much practical wisdom, and of what quality, will kings have to have, who are always involved in the most important and most serious affairs? Nor can a man lack in any way learning and eloquence who is going to command so many thousands of men, who is going to give legal rulings to so many, who is going to debate so many different subjects. For, as the popular saying very truly runs, an unlettered king is an ass with a crown.[47] How will he establish laws, pass sentences, allot rights and govern a kingdom, if he does not have, not some, not an average, but the greatest and most perfect grasp of the law? He can't hold assemblies either in the city or the camp, he can't give his opinion in council, he can't respond to ambassadors who visit him without great ability and resourcefulness of speech. I leave out the mathematical disciplines, which are necessary to him in order to wage wars and carry out the tasks of command.

What about the virtue that has assumed for itself the proper 101 name of virtue: fortitude?[48] How much should kings desire to have it, not only in wartime against enemies, but at home too, against all the blows of fortune, against all diseases of mind and body? How necessary is that elevation of mind and contempt for all human things in the conduct of affairs and in all the activity of the prince? Piety and religion ought so to implant themselves within the royal mind that he believes he cannot undertake even the smallest matter without divine aid. Rather, he should reckon that nothing at all can be successful for him without the help of divine beneficence.

All cruelty, all ambition, all avarice, all lust, all foul and wicked 102 crimes, all desires and passions, in short, should be utterly absent from the royal mind. Let the prince we seek be pious and suppli-

bent. Sit ille quem quaerimus princeps in Deum pius ac supplex, in patriam officiosus, in subditos iustus, clemens in supplices, severus in contumaces, in hostes aequus, in delinquentes acer, in suos beneficus, in omnes mansuetus. Sit denique in omni vita atque actione talis qualem nequeo monstrare et sentio tantum, cui quidem persimilem et Plato et Xenophon Socraticus descripsere. Regnum vero non sibi solum, sed successoribus quoque et posteris optime constituendum et conservandum putet. Ac suarum quidem virtutum et rerum gestarum laborumque omnium, universae denique bene actae vitae praemium, non laudem ab hominibus et gloriam futilem atque inanem quaerat, sed omni spe et cogitatione maius atque augustius a summo illo ac beneficentissimo parente praemium, beatitudinem atque immortalitatem, expectet speretque fore ut sibi amplior et solidior ab illo gloria et merces referatur. Hic igitur est ille quem desideramus princeps; hic est ille quem unum pluribus anteponere non veremur. Quod si quis huic similis regnum aliquod administret, num in eius, obsecro, regno, an in quavis republica malitis esse dubitabitis?

103 IOANNES. Ego quidem minime dubitabo. Immo vero, pater, hac disputatione edoctus, etiam mediocre regnum quamvis optimae reipublicae anteponam.

DOMINICUS. Neque ego, rex, si talem reperire principem queam, patriam dubitem mihi carissimam derelinquere et in eius me regnum conferre, ita sum hac tridui disputatione immutatus atque in optimi regis cupiditatem adductus.

104 MATTHAEUS. Placet utrumque vestrum in meam sententiam esse adductum, neque mediocrem ex hac disputatione fructum mihi videor esse consecutus, quod et filium a nobis quasi deficientem receperim et praestantissimae reipublicae civem, non in postremis habitum, ad regii principatus cupiditatem traduxerim.

105 Tu, itaque, fili, quem mihi successurum et opto et spero, cuius gratia haec omnis disputatio suscepta est, da operam ut eum quem

ant before God, dutiful towards his country, just to his subjects, clement to suppliants, severe to those who defy him, fair to enemies, strict with the delinquent, beneficent towards his own, gentle towards all. Let him, finally, be in all his life and activity the kind of man whose greatness I am unable to show but only perceive, similar to the man Plato and Xenophon the Socratic described;[49] but he will believe that a kingdom is best established and preserved not for himself alone, but for his successors too and for posterity. And as the reward of all his virtues and deeds and labors, of the whole of his well-conducted life in short, he will not seek the praise of mankind and futile, empty glory, but will look for a reward greater and more august than all hope or expectation from that highest and most beneficent Parent, [namely] blessedness and immortality, and he will hope that God will grant him a more ample and more solid glory and reward. He therefore is the prince we desire; he is the one man whom we are not afraid to prefer to the many. If someone like him governs some kingdom, would you have any doubts about being in his kingdom, or would you prefer to be in some republic or other?

JANOS. For my part I have no doubts at at all; indeed, father, I have learned from this debate and would prefer even an average kingdom to a republic, no matter how good it was.

DOMENICO. Nor would I, king, if I could find such a prince, hesitate to leave behind my dearest country and betake myself to that kingdom, so much have I been changed by this three-day-long debate and led to desire an excellent king.

MATTIAS. I'm glad that both of you have come over to my view. It seems to me I've had no small profit from this debate, since I have received back my son who was almost lost to me and I have led a by no means disreputable citizen of a famous republic to desire royal government.

So you, my son—whom I hope and choose to succeed me, for whose sake this whole debate was undertaken—work hard to copy

103

104

105

breviter descripsimus principem, quantum potes, exprimas atque effingas, neque quid alii faciant, sed quid tibi faciendum sit cures, speraque fore ut, si haec servaveris, omnium optimum, si contempseris, omnium pessimum principatum efficias.

106    Tu vero, Dominice, tametsi semper optimum esse unius principatum tibi persuadere debes, tamen quia et magna nunc optimorum principum inopia est et vestra respublica optimis legibus atque institutis gubernatur habetque aliquam etiam illius regii principatus imaginem, patriam tuam prae ceteris defende ac cole, daque operam ut eius leges ac mores et tuearis et serves, tibique persuade, si in ea optime ac rectissime vixeris, te non deteriorem regio nactum esse principatum.

Sed iam advesperascit. Surgamus; satis enim disputatum est.[40]

and imitate as far as you can the prince we have briefly described, and take care to do, not what others do, but what you should do. You should expect that if you observe these precepts you will bring into being the best form of government; if you despise them, the worst.

And you, Domenico, although you should persuade yourself 106 that one-man government is always the best, nevertheless, since there is a great lack now of excellent princes and your republic is governed by excellent laws and institutions and possesses a kind of image of that royal government, defend and respect your country, and persuade yourself, if you shall live in it with the utmost goodness and rectitude, that you will have met with a form of government not worse than a kingdom.[50]

But sundown is approaching. Let us rise; we have debated enough.

## Appendix

Raphael Brandolinus Iunior Lippus Ioanni Medici diacono cardinalis s. Mariae in Navi nuncupato S. D.

Cum nullum maius atque praeclarius defunctorum memoriae conferri beneficium possit quam si quid assumitur quod eorum laudi sempiternae consulat et per eos posteritatem maxime ad virtutem accendat, statui Lippi germani lucubrationes in unum redactas in lucem proferre, ut ex hac eius industria exactaque diligentia, in summa praesertim rei familiaris angustia et miserabili, quae mihi cum illo communis est, caecitate — et quam ipsa rerum ac temporum varia conflictatio reddit miserabiliorem — illi quidem nomen et gloria quam meretur, mihi saltem huius lucis aliquid comparetur, quippe quorum ille non in fortunis quas ad usus etiam vitae necessarios non multum cupivit, vel in corporis venustate, cuius caruit eminentissimo sensu, sed in virtute ac honestate et divinarum rerum contemplatione felicitatem omnem esse ponendam existimavit.

Ego, etsi eius in hoc genere laudis assequendi spem mihi effulgere non videam, imitandi tamen eiusque vestigiis inhaerendi studio semper incumbo. Quare, cum tris eius libros de comparatione popularis et regii status in republica, quos Pannoniae inceptos, Florentiae per dialogum absolverat, nuper evolvissem, tuo nomini

# Appendix

## Raffaele Brandolini's Dedication to Cardinal Giovanni de' Medici

This second dedication to Cardinal Giovanni de' Medici, the future Pope Leo X, is preserved only in L (see Note on the Text). It must have been written between 1503 and 1511, but its most likely date is 1505–1506, when Raffaele repackaged a number of his uncle's works and dedicated them to prominent figures in the papal curia. (See Mayer, 50; Mitchell, 18, note 6; and Lenzuni, 101).

Raffaele Lippi Brandolini the Younger to Giovanni de' Medici, Cardinal Deacon of Santa Maria in Nave, greetings.

Since no greater and more excellent benefit can be conferred on the memory of the dead than if a task is taken on to serve the interests of their eternal praise, and through them to inflame posterity to embrace virtue most of all, I decided to publish the collected studies of my uncle Lippi, so that from his effort and exacting application he might win the reputation and glory he deserves, and I at least some reflected splendor — especially amidst the collapse of our family fortunes and in the wretched state of blindness that I share with him, and that the convulsions of the times and of affairs have rendered more wretched still. He indeed was a man who reckoned all felicity to lie, not in the goods of fortune, for which he had no great desire — not even for those goods necessary to life — nor in attractiveness of body, whose most eminent sense organ he lacked, but in virtue, honor and the contemplation of things divine.

Although I see no gleam of hope that I might achieve this kind of reputation, I have always longed to imitate him and follow in his footsteps. Hence when I recently read through his three books comparing the popular and the royal constitution of a commonwealth that he began in Hungary and finished in Florence in dialogue form, I decided they should be dedicated in your name for

dicandos multis de causis mihi proposui, tum quod eos ille interveniente Matthiae Corvini optimi ac sapientissimi Pannoniarum
regis obitu, cuius maxime hortatu opus aggressus fuerat, Laurentio
Medici, parenti tuo, unico saeculi nostri virtutum ac litterarum
omnium praesidio summoque non Florentinae modo reipublicae
totiusque regionis Etruscae, sed universae etiam Italiae ornamento
censuerat offerendos, ut qui iustissimo ac munificentissimo
nostrae tempestatis rege amisso eum civem deligendum videbat,
cui tam praeclarum opus merito debebatur, cuiusque vel iudicii
gravitati vel ingenii acumini vel rerum peritiae posset maxime
confidere; tum quod ipse verissimam prudentiae, pietatis, munificentiae, fortitudinis, innocentiae, ceterarum parentis virtutum
imaginem referens dignissimus procul dubio videris, qui [su]per
ius quoque hereditarium paternae laudi immortalitatique succedas. Quandoquidem eam tute tibi ab ineunte aetate vitae formulam praescripsisti ut sive publice seu privatim in summo rerum
discrimine versareris, peropportunum et prope divinum consilium
captares, quo fratres atque propinquos omnis difficillimis temporibus sublevasti, quique sic sitam in te pietatem semper habuisti, ut
omnibus praeditus virtutibus non immerito iudicareris. Quibus ea
inopes beneficentia es complexus, ut qui tuae rei familiaris angustiam metiretur, te parentem quoque Laurentium in eo virtutis genere facile crederet superasse; qui autem ignoraret, illum in te revixisse arbitraretur. At domesticas per exilium calamitates, quae
multiplices ac prope infinitae fuere, acerrimos quoque invidorum
morsus qua animi celsitudine ac innocentia pertulisti! Ea nempe
qua unus ex fortissimis innocentissimisque nostrorum temporum
viris posses iure optimo iudicari.

Accipe igitur, pater humanissime, parentis prius lucubratum,
deinde tuo nomini recognitum opus, quod uni tibi et gratissimo

many reasons. First because it was his view that, after the death of Mattias Corvinus, the best and wisest king of Hungary, at whose urging he started the work, the books should be offered to your father Lorenzo de' Medici, the unique bulwark of virtue and literature in our age and the highest ornament, not only of the Florentine republic and the whole region of Tuscany, but even of all Italy. With the loss of that most just and generous king of our time, he thought that he should choose the citizen who most deserved so excellent a work and whose serious judgment, sharp intelligence and worldly experience he could trust the most. Then there is the fact that you yourself appear beyond doubt to be the worthiest of men, an image of your father's practical wisdom, piety, generosity, courage, innocence and other virtues, and you have succeeded, also, by hereditary right to your father's immortal renown. Since you have on your own from earliest youth prescribed for yourself a pattern of life, such that you have involved yourself in decisions of high responsibility in both public and private life, you have sought after the most advantageous and almost divine counsel. The result is that you have rendered full assistance to your brothers and those near to you in the most difficult of times, and you have always had piety so implanted within you that you are rightly regarded as a man gifted with every virtue. With these virtues you embrace in your benevolence those without resources, so that the man who took into account your family's [present] limitations would believe you had surpassed even your father Lorenzo in that kind of virtue, and [even] the man who was ignorant of the true situation would think Lorenzo lived again in you. With what high-mindedness and blamelessness have you borne the multifarious and nearly infinite domestic calamities of exile and the bitter attacks of the envious! Surely this establishes, with perfect justice, your reputation as one of the bravest and most blameless men of our times.

Accept then, kindest father, this work, earlier composed by my uncle and then certified in your name, a work that belongs by right

filio et unico familiae Medicum fulcimento et viro optimo et pien-
tissimo cardinali et denique paternae laudis heredi merito debebatur. Accipe, inquam, ac una mecum existima hanc tibi dedicatio-
nem optimum revisendae patriae omen ac certissimum esse: quod
si tibi tandem aliquando, ut ego quidem et optimus quisque civis
maxime sperat, contigerit, et illa per te pristinum decus ac veterem
dignitatem ‹recuperabit› et tu per illam incredibilem gloriam sem-
piternamque ad posteros memoriam propagabis. Vale.

to you alone, the most gracious son and unique support of the Medici family, an excellent man and a most pious cardinal, and finally the heir of your father's high esteem. Accept it, I say, and join me in thinking that this dedication to you is an excellent and most certain omen of your seeing your country again. If this at some time shall at last happen to you, as I and every good citizen strongly hopes, she will through you recover her pristine glory and former rank, and through her you will perpetuate your incredible glory and the eternal remembrance of posterity. Farewell.

# Note on the Text and Translation

As noted in the Introduction, the text of Aurelio Lippo Brandolini's *De comparatione reipublicae et regni* survives in only two manuscripts. The earlier, *R*, is the dedication copy to Lorenzo de' Medici, written sometime between Brandolini's return to Florence (April 1490) and Lorenzo's death in April 1492.[1]

R    Florence, Biblioteca Riccardiana, MS Ricc. 672

The other, *L*, is a presentation copy to Cardinal Giovanni de'Medici (later Pope Leo X), written probably between 27 December 1503 and 1 October 1511.[2]

L    Florence, Biblioteca Medicea Laurenziana, MS Plut. LXXVII, 11

To judge from the omissions in *R*, both MSS must be independent witnesses to the archetype, presumably the author's copy. It is not impossible that Brandolini retouched certain passages between the time *R* was copied and his death in October 1497. *L* in any case sometimes offers better readings than *R* and has occasionally been corrected by a second, contemporary hand (*L²*). It seems less likely that the slight improvements in *L* were made either by the scribe or by Aurelio's younger brother, Raffaele, who presented the work to Cardinal Giovanni (see Appendix).

The spelling in both manuscripts is idiosyncratic (even for the period) as well as inconsistent, and there is no evidence that it represents Aurelio Brandolini's own orthographic preferences. The spelling has thus been modernized in accordance with the preference of the I Tatti series, as has punctuation and capitalization.

The text has been edited twice. The first edition, by the Hungarian scholar Jenö Ábel, was published in 1890 as part of an anthology of texts illustrating the reign of King Mattias Corvinus

of Hungary. Ábel based his text on *L* and seems to have been unaware of the existence of *R*. Ábel's edition is extremely rare (only five copies are known worldwide according to the records of OCLC). The text was edited again as a *tesi di laurea*, completed under the direction of the late Mario Martelli at the University of Florence, by dott.ssa Lorenza Biagini.[3] The thesis was never published. I was able to consult it at the Biblioteca Nazionale Centrale in Florence and found it useful in identifying sources.

Brandolini's *Comparison* presents a challenge to theorists of translation who believe that technical terminology always can and should be translated using consistent referents in the target language. This view ignores the fact that sometimes technical terms have several meanings that reflect different stages in the historical evolution of a term. A case in point is the word *respublica*, which in ancient Latin means "the state," "public affairs" or "disinterested government," i.e., a good constitution serving the public interest, whether monarchical, aristocratic or popular. Its lexical opposite is "tyranny." In antiquity it does not mean, as it does today, "non-monarchical government" or "a government that represents the popular will." The word only began to assume that sense in Italy in the later fifteenth century, a new meaning that is reflected in Brandolini's title and throughout the work.[4] When used in this sense the word is here translated by the English word "republic." However, in the *Comparison* the word sometimes retains its ancient and medieval meaning, especially when King Mattias is speaking, and in these contexts is translated "commonwealth." *Princeps* is another context-dependent word: it can refer to the leading citizen or citizens of a popular or aristocratic regime; it can stand for a "prince" in the Renaissance sense (i.e., it can be a generic term for any individual with sovereign power, as in Machiavelli's *Il Principe*); and it can refer to the Roman emperor. *Principatus*, which by the time of Lipsius, if not before, comes to mean "one-man rule," for

Brandolini (as well as the scholastics and early Renaissance humanists generally) has the more generic meaning of "political leadership" or "government" or "governance," depending on the context. *Imperator* can mean either "general" or "Roman emperor." *Civitas* can mean simply "city" or it can carry its Roman-law meaning of "sovereign city-state," contrasted with *urbs*, which refers to any city whether sovereign or not. *Status* is particularly chameleonic as in the early Renaissance it normally means "the power, resources, prestige and authority of an individual or collectivity" but in Brandolini's text sometimes comes close to its later Renaissance meaning of "state."

The work, as the author himself implies in his preface, was dedicated to Lorenzo in an unpolished state and is occasionally marred by unclear and incomplete thoughts. Where it seemed helpful, Brandolini's sentences have been completed or clarified by words or phrases added by the translator, indicated by square brackets.

## NOTES

1. For a description of both MSS, see Lenzuni, 100–103.

2. See G. B. Picotti, *La giovinezza di Leo X* (Milan: Hoepli, 1928), 610. Picotti points out that Giovanni is described as *unicum familiae Medicum fulcimentum*, which implies that Piero de'Medici, Lorenzo's son, is now dead, providing a *post quem*; the *ante quem* is the election to the papacy of Giovanni, here styled Cardinal.

3. For the editions of Ábel and Biagini, see Bibliography. (Copies of Biagini's *tesi*, as of all Italian *tesi di laurea*, are on deposit at the *biblioteche nazionali centrali* of Italy.)

4. See my article, "Exclusivist Republicanism and the Non-Monarchical Republic," forthcoming in *Political Theory*; in the *Comparison* see 3.86.

# Notes to the Text

༈

1. LIPPI BRANDOLINI IN LIBROS DE COMPARATIONE REIPUBLICAE ET REGNI AD PRESTANTISSIMUM VIRUM LAURENTIUM MEDICEM FLORENTINE REIPUBLICE PRINCIPEM PROHEMIUM *LR*

2. a *R*

3. ut *after* petatur *cancelled in R*

4. principatus *L*

5. fueram accitus *transp. L*

6. dicerentur *before correction by* $L^2$

7. e *L*

8. utrumque *L before correction*

9. modo regem *transp. L*

10. is qui *L*

## BOOK I

1. LIPPI BRANDOLINI DE COMPARATIONE REIPUBLICAE ET REGNI AD PRESTANTISSIMUM VIRUM [VIRUM *omitted in R*] LAURENTIUM MEDICEM FLORENTINE REIPUBLICAE PRINCIPEM LIBER PRIMUS, IN QUO MATTHIAS PANNONIORUM REX, IOANNES FILIUS ET DOMINICUS IUNIUS EQUES FLORENTINUS LOQUENTES INTRODUCUNTUR *R*: IN QUO . . . INTRODUCUNTUR *omitted in L*

2. *omitted in L*

3. laxandis *before correction in L*

4. quid *before* mihi *in L*

5. nitidissimum *L* (*compare* Quintilian 10.1.13).

6. etiam *L*

7. ipsos *R*

8. *Corrected:* sciphum *LR*

9. instituere *L*

10. hac (*or possibly* hic) *before* unum *L*

11. diss(a)eptum *L*

12. Illis *R*

13. *om. L*

14. *added s.s.* *L*²

15. audeo repugnare *transp. L*

16. Neque . . . adversari *omitted in R*

17. maxime me *transp. L*

18. Si praemia poenasque . . . floreant *omitted in R*

19. tamen *L*

20. excutiamus *L* (*cf. 1.56*)

21. rerum nobis *transp. R*

22. *omitted in L*

23. Sed . . . id] Sed quando id me *L*

24. *omitted in R*

25. *Emended:* Eliguntur *LR*

26. aut *L*

27. *omitted in L*

28. quid *R*

29. effectibus *L*

30. hi *L*

31. *added by L*²

32. *omitted in L*

33. enim *R*

34. evitandi *L*

35. *omitted in* L

36. sentit R

37. *omitted in* L

### BOOK II

1. LIPPI BRANDOLINI DE COMPARATIONE REIPUBLICAE ET REGNI AD PRESTANTISSISUM VIRUM LAURENTIUM MEDICEM FLORENTINAE REIPUBLICAE PRINCIPEM LIBER SECUNDUS *LR*

2. custodiet *Juvenal*

3. alterutrum R

4. lege ipsa L

5. Atqui lex . . . non eget *omitted in* R

6. -que *added by* L²

7. perit et prurigine] cadit et porrigine *Juvenal*

8. quando R

9. -que *omitted in* L

10. esse nullam *transp.* L

11. qui terram ita constituisset *omitted in* R

12. *omitted in* R

13. reputamus L

14. *omitted in* L

15. exercentur R, L *before correction*

16. *added s.s.* L²

17. *omitted in* R

18. *added s.s.* L²

19. rege Macedonum *transp.* L

20. omnibus *after* ita R

21. Si praemia . . . floreant *om.* R

22. *sc.* socerioni

23. huic . . . favere] huic magis quam illi favere *L*

24. nos ipsos *L*

## BOOK III

1. LIPPI BRANDOLINI DE COMPARATIONE REIPUBLICAE ET REGNI AD PRESTANTISSIMUM VIRUM LAURENTIUM MEDICEM FLORENTINE REIPUBLICAE PRINCIPEM LIBER TERTIUS *LR*

2. ignosces *before* nimiae *transp. R*

3. a *omitted in R*

4. Quod *R*

5. *omitted in R*

6. *omitted in R*

7. consenserint *L*

8. *omitted in R*

9. erant *R*

10. -que *omitted in R*

11. aut *L*

12. *omitted in R*

13. *omitted in L*

14. et *L*

15. si quis . . . duos gubernatores] vel unicae navi duos gubernatores, si quis vel unico currui duos aurigas *L*

16. minus *R*

17. *omitted in L*

18. Dominicae *L*

19. si *R*

20. omni . . . mentis *omitted in R*

21. tu te *L*

22. id *added ed.*

23. *omitted by LR; supplied from Horace.*
24. *added s.s.* $L^2$
25. vero *R*
26. possunt *L*
27. in *omitted in L*
28. principibus *R*
29. *omitted in L*
30. modo *L*
31. utrum *L*
32. optimum pessimo *R*
33. ipsius *after* suum *R*
34. ab *L*
35. Romani *R*
36. creavere *R*
37. eo *R*
38. et *R*
39. *scil.* sunt . . . necessariae.
40. Valete *added at end in L*

# Notes to the Translation

་ཤི༈

## PREFACE

1. "Earlier" (*superius*) could also be translated "higher."

2. See Plato, *Republic* 9.576d-e, *Statesman* 302e and Aristotle, *Politics* 3.13.1284b.

3. Most flourishing (*florentissima*): a well-worn trope indicating the city of Florence.

4. Hungarians: lit. Pannonians. The Hungarians were originally a people of central Asia who in the tenth century occupied the region of the ancient Roman province of Pannonia. Hence the humanists referred to them in classicizing fashion as Pannonians. Sometimes in less complimentary style they were referred to as the Huns, owing to the mistaken identification of them with the barbarian nation that invaded the Roman empire in the fifth century CE. Another mistaken identification (embraced by King Mattias at 3.90) is with the Scythians, in antiquity a semi-nomadic people dwelling to the north and east of the Roman empire, along an arc extending from the Danube to the Caucasus, and known for their uncivilized but unspoiled mores.

5. On Socratic dialogue, see the Introduction.

6. On Domenico Giugni, see the Introduction.

## BOOK I

1. Saturnalia: A Roman feast in honor of the god Saturnus, held on 17 December. While a number of its features were taken over by the Christian holiday of Christmas, in its merriment and ritualized acts of social disorder it resembled more the week leading up to Mardi Gras before Lent. Lent is a period of forty day's penitence before Easter.

2. Juvenal 8.140–41. Brandolini refers to Juvenal throughout the work as "Aquinas," from the Roman satirist's place of birth, the town of Aquino in ancient Campania.

3. Vergil, *Aeneid* 1.646.

4. Either there or anywhere else: i.e., either in its original Mediterranean lands or in other places like Germany where it was subsequently revived. It should be noted that Mattias Corvinus spent much of his career at war with the Holy Roman Emperor, Frederick III.

5. Orosius 1.14 and 2.7 (see also Justinus 1.8), probably via Dante, *De monarchia* 2.8.5–6. Brandolini mistakenly refers to the Thamyris as Tanaus and calls her a king rather than a queen; he mistakenly calls Vesoges "Vesor" (see also 3.90 below); his source may be the *Epitome* of Trogus 1.1.

6. Livy 1.16; Plutarch, *Life of Romulus* 28.1–2.

7. Livy 5.46 (the Senones are the Galli Senones); Plutarch, *Life of Camillus* 5.23.

8. Plutarch, *Life of Fabius Maximus* 23.1.

9. Livy 2.48–50.

10. Wiped out future wars: i.e., by utterly destroying the city. The two Scipios, respectively, are Publius Cornelius Scipio Africanus (236–183 BCE), who defeated Hannibal at the battle of Zama, and his grandson by adoption, Publius Cornelius Scipio Aemilianus (185–129 BCE), who conquered Carthage and razed it to the ground in 146 BCE.

11. In Rome it was the custom for a general who had conquered a province to add the name of the province to his own name as an *agnomen* (not *cognomen*, as Brandolini incorrectly states). The numerous generals who belonged to the Caecilii Metelli clan had many such *agnomina*, including *Macedonicus*, *Dalmaticus*, *Creticus* and *Balearicus*.

12. On the invented filiation of the Hunyadi kings with the Roman *gens Valeria*, see *Matthias Corvinus, the King*, 143.

13. Marcus Valerius Messalla Corvinus (64 BCE–8 CE), Roman general and orator; as a statesmen he at first followed republican principles but eventually came over to Octavian and the principate.

14. I.e., Lucius Septimius Severus (145–211 CE), Roman general and emperor from 193 to 211.

15. Mucius Scaevola: see Livy 2.12; Valerius Maximus 3.3.1.

16. Livy 2.10; Valerius Maximus 3.2.1.

17. Livy 7.6.1–6; Valerius Maximus 5.6.2; Pliny the Elder, *Natural History* 15.78; Varro, *De lingua latina* 5.31.148.

18. Marcus Valerius Messalla Corvinus: see note 13, above. For the story, see Livy 7.26.12; Valerius Maximus 8.15.5.

19. Livy 2.5.8; Valerius Maximus 5.8.1.

20. Valerius Maximus 5.8.3; Cicero, *De finibus* 1.7.24.

21. Servius, *In Aeneidem* 1.637, 1.726.

22. *Epitome of Livy* 13; Eutropius 2.12; compare Valerius Maximus 4.3.5 and Cicero, *De senectute* 16.55, where the same story is told of Manius Curius and the Samnites.

23. Valerius Maximus 4.3.5.

24. Livy 1.58 (on the rape of Lucretia by Sextus Tarquinius, son of Tarquin the Proud); also Valerius Maximus 6.1.1; Ovid, *Fasti* 2.685–856.

25. Livy 3.44–54; Eutropius 1.18; Aurelius Victor, *De viris illustribus* 21.

26. Compare Augustine, *De civitate Dei* 1.1.

27. János Hunyadi (c. 1387–1456), Mattias's father, who enjoyed brilliant successes against the Turk in the early 1440s before being defeated in the disastrous Crusade of Varna (1444) and in the second Battle of Kosovo (1448).

28. Aesop's fables in the collection of Phaedrus, 1.6. In Phaedrus' version it is the frogs who complain to Jove, not the Earth.

29. Plato, *Republic* 5, 473c-d; *Laws* 712a, 713d; but intermediate sources are entirely possible as the dictum was among the most common Platonic quotations of the Renaissance.

30. This paragraph is a kind of formal *divisio*, summarizing the argument for the superiority of republics and outlining the debate that follows in Book I and the remaining two books.

31. Compare Cicero, *Paradoxes of the Stoics* 5.34. See also Francesco Patrizi, *De institutione reipublicae* (written in the 1460s), 1.4: "Nihil enim magis cupit popularis multitudo quam potestatem vivendi habere ut velit: quam quidem libertatem Cicero esse affirmat. Florentinus autem iureconsultus libertatem esse dixit naturalem facultatem eius quod cuique facere libet, nisi quod vi aut iure prohibetur." (The citizen body of a people desires nothing so much as the power of living as it wishes, which Cicero affirms to be liberty. A Florentine jurisconsult said that liberty was the natural capacity to do as each person wishes, unless violence or legality prohibits it).

32. Florentines of the fifteenth century effectively had no citizen rights if they did not pay any taxes or duties or if they were in debt to the commune.

33. Although the Medicean Council of Seventy established in 1480 was sometimes referred to in the documentation as a *senatus*, Brandolini here seems to mean the Signoria, formally the sovereign body of Florence, consisting of eight priors of the guilds chosen from the four quarters of the city, along with the Standard-Bearer of Justice. See also 1.56–58, 3.94, below.

34. On the Florentine "scrutiny" which determined eligibility for office, see Rubinstein, *Government*, Part I, chapter 3.

35. The Latin words for "the passions," *animi perturbatio*, are of Stoic provenance, used by Cicero to translate the Greek term *pathos*; see Cicero, *De finibus* 4.11.

36. Domenico follows the view of Aristotle, *Politics* 3.15.1286a.

37. On the grounds for the *divieto*, or being excluded from office, see Rubinstein, *Government*, 5.

38. It may be noted that it was for Aristotle a sign of oligarchy, a corrupt form of government, when property qualifications were too high for the poor to hold offices. See *Politics* 6.6.1320b.

39. I.e., the Signoria, the same body whom Brandolini elsewhere refers to as the Senate. See 1.46 above and note.

40. I.e., words that require other words to complete their meaning, that are meaningless by themselves.

41. The Otto di Practica, a magistracy founded in 1480 under Lorenzo de'Medici. The magistracy was held for six months and dealt with matters of foreign policy and the rule of the Florentine state in Tuscany. By 1494, when it was disbanded, it had largely eclipsed the Signoria in public power. See Rubinstein, *Government*, 229.

42. The advisory colleges of the Signoria were the Twelve Good Men (*Dodici Buonuomini*) and the Sixteen Standard-Bearers (*Sedici Gonfalonieri*). See Rubinstein, *Government*, 6.

43. I.e., customary law, specific to Florence.

44. Optimates: A term from Roman history, meaning persons of high birth and social standing, contrasted with *populares* or commoners.

45. The popular classes were prohibited in Venice from holding the more elevated magistracies, which were reserved for a legally-defined class of patricians.

46. A monarchical version of the principle of Roman law concerning corporate bodies, *quod omnes tangit debet ab omnibus approbari*, "what touches all ought to be approved by all," adapted by canon lawyers from Justinian's *Code* 5.59.5.2, but frequently cited as a principle of republican government in Italy.

47. A satirical version of a favorite dictum attributed by Plutarch to Cineas, the envoy of the King Pyrrhus (*Life of Pyrrhus* 19.5), who said that the Roman Senate appeared to him like a council of kings. See also Justin 18.2.10.

## BOOK II

1. Compare Cicero, *Tusculan Disputations* 2.67.

2. Livy 3.31–33.

3. Livy 1.19; Plutarch, *Life of Numa Pompilius* 6–19.

4. Jurisconsults whose works are excerpted in *Corpus iuris civilis*, the code of civil law compiled for the Emperor Justinian (AD 529–534) and used as

a law textbook in all European universities with law faculties after the twelfth century.

5. Plato, *Laws* 1.630d, 1.632d.

6. Plato, *Statesman* 294a.

7. Juvenal 6.221.

8. Compare Aristotle, *Nicomachean Ethics* 8.10.1160b.

9. Juvenal 6.365 (Ox 31–32).

10. See Cicero, *De officiis* 2.23. For the need of a 'kingly man' to oversee the application of the laws to particular cases, see Plato, *Statesman* 294a-300c.

11. This is Aristotle's position; see *Politics* 3.11.1282b; 3.16.1287b. The subject was frequently debated in scholastic literature on politics; see James M. Blythe, *Ideal Government and the Mixed Constitution in the Middle Ages* (Princeton, 1991), 42–45, 54–58, 62–70, 92–98 and passim. That the king should be above the law to correct its inequities and imprecisions is the usual position of Plato as well as medieval authors such as Thomas Aquinas and Giles of Rome.

12. Craftsman *(artifex)*: the word Cicero uses (*Timaeus* 6) to translate Plato's *demiurgos*.

13. See Aristotle, *Politics* 3.15.1286a for a similar argument.

14. Compare Romans 2:14.

15. Aesop's fables in the collection of Phaedrus 1.2. Compare Plato, *Laws* 9.874e-875d.

16. Plato, *Laws* 10.898a-b.

17. Juvenal 2.79–81.

18. Plato, *Laws* 3.704b-705c, 4.704–705. Brandolini seems to rely directly on Plato rather than on the parallel passages in Aristotle, *Politics* 7.6.1327a-b and Leonardo Bruni, *Laudatio Florentine urbis*, ed. Viti, p. 388.

19. Plato, *Laws* 5.741e-743d.

20. Compare Plato, *Laws* 8.847c-e.

21. Brandolini, through the mouth of Mattias, here probably means to indicate Venice, a traditional enemy of the Hunyadi dynasty and a city often accused of trading with the Ottoman enemy.

22. Terence, *Adria* 427: *Omnes sibi malle melius esse quam alteri.*

23. Plutarch, *Life of Lycurgus* 8.

24. Juvenal 2.63.

25. Gemoniae: rock steps cut into the Capitoline Hill near the prison, on which the naked bodies of certain criminals were thrown after their execution for public exposure and disgrace. See L. Richardson, Jr., *A New Topographical Dictionary of Ancient Rome* (Baltimore, 1994), p. 345. "The Gemoniae" here is perhaps intended to stand for the Stinche, the Florentine prison.

26. Juvenal 2.45–46.

27. Plutarch, *Life of Solon* 5.2, where the statement is made by Anacharsis to Solon; Valerius Maximus 7.2.ext.14, where the statement is attributed to Anacharsis.

28. Augustine, *City of God* 4.4.

29. Vergil, *Georgics* 4.564–55, though in the original it is Vergil, not Naples, that "flourishes in studies." Parthenope is an alternative classical name for Naples.

30. Pavia was under the rule of Duke Gian Galeazzo Sforza, whose sister, Bianca Maria, was engaged to János from 1487 to 1494. The two never married, despite what seems to be implied here.

31. Mattias's third wife, Beatrice of Aragon (1457–1508), was the daughter of Ferdinand I, King of Naples.

32. Joshua 10:12–14.

### BOOK III

1. A famous Roman defeat, described in Livy 22.34–52.

2. Livy 22.12–14, 27–30, where the master of horse in question is Marcus Minutius Rufus.

3. Livy 22.42–50.

4. The household (*familia*): Not just family in the modern sense but, for wealthier families, an economic entity comprising family, servants, and workers and their property. "Heads of household" translates *pater familias*, the father of the family, who in Roman law had absolute authority over the rest of the household.

5. Plato, *Republic* 5.449a-466a. For the hostility and embarrassment this doctrine aroused among Quattrocento Italian humanists, see J. Hankins, *Plato in the Italian Renaissance*, 2 vols. (Leiden, 1990), 1: 65–66, 131–34, 150–53, 240–41.

6. Aristotle, *Politics* 2.4.1262a-b.

7. Plutarch, *Life of Lycurgus* 19.3.

8. Aristotle, *Politics* 1.2.1252b. A *vicus* can be either a rural settlement or an urban neighborhood.

9. Ibid.

10. Domenico's criticism of Mattias mirrors Aristotle's of Plato in *Politics* 1.1.1252a; Aristotle is thinking of Plato, *Statesman* 259b, where Plato states there is no difference between ruling a large household and a small city.

11. Plato, *Laws* 4.713d; see also Aristotle, *Ethics* 8.11.1161a.

12. Aristotle, *Politics* 3.16.1287b.

13. See above, 2.10–11, 2.16–17.

14. A common scholastic tag based on Aristotle, *Ethics* 1.2.1094b.

15. Cicero, *De officiis* 1.21.73.

16. Aristotle, *Politics* 3.9.1280a, 3.11.1281b.

17. Especially the so-called "treatise on kingship," *Politics* 3.14–18, if not via an intermediate source such as Giles of Rome's *De regimine principum*, book 3.

18. Plato, *Statesman* 302e, *Republic* 8.543c-d; pseudo-Aristotle, *Secretum secretorum* (believed in the Renaissance to be by Aristotle) and Aristotle, *Politics* 3.17.1288a; a modern example might have been Giles of Rome, *De regimine principum*, book 3 (an authoritative source for the common scholastic view that Aristotle held monarchy to have been the best constitution).

19. Aristotle, *Nicomachean Ethics* 5.1.1129b.

20. Ibid. 2.6.1106a-b.

21. Horace, *Epistles* 1.18.9

22. Horace, *Sermones* 1.1.106–107.

23. Cicero, *De amicitia* 21.79.

24. "What the best regime is, not where it is": i.e., he is discussing what the best regime is in the abstract, not whether it is or has historically been possible in Florence.

25. Livy 3.44–54, and see above, 1.11.

26. Sallust, *Bellum Catilinae* 1.

27. The French monarchy was descended from Charlemagne (AD 747–814, King of the Franks from 768) and his Carolingian heirs; it had resided in the Capetian family and the related house of Valois from 987 to the date of composition of Brandolini's dialogue, some five hundred years.

28. Brandolini is following the Aristotelian analysis of constitutional types, where tyranny, oligarchy and democracy (corrupt popular power) are considered bad, and kingship, aristocracy and "polity" (the virtuous rule of the many) are held to be good.

29. Ovid, *Metamorphoses* 15.234–236.

30. Ibid., 10.519.

31. Ovid, *Ars amatoria* 3.66.

32. Juvenal 15.69; compare Homer, *Iliad* 1.271–272, 12.447–449 and 20.285–287.

33. Compare Aristotle, *Politics* 1.2.1253b, 3.6.1278b; Cicero, *De republica* 6.13: "a society of men linked by a system of laws."

34. Of the various accounts of constitutional degeneration found in ancient political theory (principally Plato's *Republic*, book 8, Aristotle's *Politics*, book 5, and *Nicomachean Ethics* 8.10), Brandolini's account follows most closely that in Polybius 6.2–9. Books 1–5 of Polybius's Roman history had been known in the Latin West since the 1420s, but the relevant parts of Book 6 were not available in print until 1529. It is known, how-

ever, that manuscripts of the work were available in Florence from at least 1504, and book 6 had certainly been read by Machiavelli by the second decade of the sixteenth century. Brandolini could not have known the account of constitutional degeneration in Cicero, *De republica*, book 1, which was only recovered in the nineteenth century.

35. Pliny the Elder, *Natural History* 11.16–17; compare Seneca, *De clementia* 1.19.2.

36. Pliny the Elder, *Natural History* 10.23.30.

37. That the body is in the soul and not vice versa is, rather, a famous dictum of Plato in the *Timaeus* 36d9-e3.

38. The model of reason controlling the other parts of the soul, i.e., the appetites and passions, is widely diffused in Greek philosophy, especially in Plato and Aristotle.

39. The doctrine is found in Plato's *Parmenides* as well as in Plotinus and the Neoplatonists generally.

40. See Marsilio Ficino, *De sole*, especially caps. 2 and 4, in his *Opera omnia* (Basel, 1576; repr. Turin 1983), 1: 966–967.

41. Egypt was conquered by Octavian Caesar in 30 BCE although it had been in the Roman sphere of influence from the mid-second century BCE onwards.

42. The Egyptians were ruled by the Mamluk sultans between the thirteenth and the early sixteenth centuries, when they were conquered by the Ottoman empire.

43. Their own emperors: Western writers often refer to the Byzantine empire after Charlemagne as "the empire of the Greeks," distinguishing it from the Carolingian, Ottonian and other continuators of the Roman Empire in the West.

44. Brandolini here follows Polybius 6.51.

45. On Christ's cross Pilate and the Roman executioners hung the mocking label: "Jesus of Nazareth, King of the Jews" (*Jesus Nazarenus rex Iudaeorum*); see John 19:19.

46. Juvenal 6.181.

47. John of Salisbury, *Policraticus* 4.6.

48. See Bruni, *Isagogicon moralis disciplinae*, ed. Viti, p. 220.

49. Probably Plato's *Republic* and *Statesman* as well as Xenophon's *Cyropaedia* are meant.

50. Because the just behavior of rulers, whether singular or plural, is the ultimate criterion of good government, as is stated by Scipio in Cicero's *De republica*, quoted in Augustine, *City of God* 2.21.

# Bibliography

ॐ‌ॐ‌ॐ

## TEXTS

Ábel, Jenö. *Olaszországi XV századbeli íróknak Mátyás Királyt dicsöítö müvei.* (Magyar Tudomanyos akadémia. Irodalomtörténeti emlékek, köt 2.) Budapest: Kiadja A. M. T. Akadémia Irodalomtörténeti Zizottsága, 1890. Contains the *Comparison* on pp. 77–183.

Biagini, Lorenza. "Edizione critica del *De comparatione rei publicae et regni* di Aurelio Lippo Brandolini." Tesi di laurea, Università degli Studi di Firenze, 1995.

## STUDIES

*All'ombra del lauro: Documenti librari della cultura in età laurenziana. Firenze, Biblioteca Medicea Laurenziana, 4 maggio—30 giugno 1992.* Edited by Anna Lenzuni et al. Exhibit catalog. Cinisello Balsamo: Silvana, 1992.

Di Pierro, Giuliana. "Una inedita controversia di Lippo Brandolini sul primato fra le lettere e le armi alla corte di Ferrante d'Aragona." *Annali della Facoltà di Lettere e Filosofia dell' Università di Bari,* 24 (1981): 401–19.

Hankins, James. "Humanism and the Origins of Modern Political Thought." In *The Cambridge Companion to Renaisance Humanism,* edited by Jill Kraye, 118–141. Cambridge: Cambridge University Press, 1996.

———. "Exclusivist Republicanism and the Non-Monarchical Republic." Forthcoming in *Political Theory.*

Klaniczay, Tibor. *Mattia Corvino e l'Umanesimo italiano.* Rome: Accademia Nazionale dei Lincei, 1974.

Mayer, Elisabetta. *Un umanista italiano della corte di Mattia Corvino: Aurelio Brandolini Lippo.* (Biblioteca dell' Accademia d'Ungheria di Roma, 14.) Rome: P. Russo, 1938.

*Matthias Corvinus, the King: Tradition and Renewal in the Hungarian Royal Court, 1458–1490.* Edited by Péter Farbaky et al. Exhibition catalogue. Budapest: Budapest History Museum, 2008.

Mitchell, Shayne Mary. "The *De comparatione rei publicae et regni* (1490) of Aurelio Lippi Brandolini." M.Phil. thesis, University of London, 1985.

Najemy, John. *A History of Florence, 1200–1575.* Malden, Massachusetts: Blackwell, 2006.

Puskás, István. "Monumento al Principe: Il dialogo di Aurelio Lippo Brandolini intitolato *De comparatione rei pubblicae* [sic] *et regni.*" *Nuova Corvina: Rivista di Italianistica* 20 (2008): 187–193.

Rotondò, Antonio. "Brandolini, Aurelio Lippo." In *Dizionario biografico degli italiani.* 14: 26–28. Rome: Istituto della Enciclopedia italiana, 1960-

Rubinstein, Nicolai. "Italian Political Thought, 1450–1530." In *The Cambridge History of Political Thought, 1450–1700,* ed. J. H. Burns with Mark Goldie, 30–65. Cambridge: Cambridge University Press, 1991.

———. *The Government of Florence under the Medici (1434 to 1494).* Second edition. Oxford: Clarendon Press, 1997.

Thorndike, Lynn. "Lippus Brandolinus: *De comparatione rei publicae et regni.* A Treatise in Comparative Political Science." In *Science and Thought in the Fifteenth Century. Studies in the History of Medicine and Surgery, Natural and Mathematical Science, Philosophy and Politics,* 233–260. New York: Columbia University Press, 1929.

# Index

Lowercase roman or arabic numerals refer to pages in the introduction and appendix, respectively. Two-part arabic numbers (e.g., 3.90) refer to book and paragraph of the English translation; notes to the translation are indexed by the book and note number to which they refer (e.g., 1n28). References to Brandolini's Preface are by "Pref." and paragraph number (e.g., Pref.3) or note number (e.g., Pref.n3).

*Publication of this volume has been made possible by*

The Myron and Sheila Gilmore Publication Fund at I Tatti
The Robert Lehman Endowment Fund
The Jean-François Malle Scholarly Programs and Publications Fund
The Andrew W. Mellon Scholarly Publications Fund
The Craig and Barbara Smyth Fund
for Scholarly Programs and Publications
The Lila Wallace–Reader's Digest Endowment Fund
The Malcolm Wiener Fund for Scholarly Programs and Publications